PENGUIN TRAVEL LIBRARY

SLOWLY DOWN THE GANGES

Born in London in 1919 and educated at St. Paul's School, Eric Newby worked briefly in advertising before sailing to Australia and back as an apprentice in a Finnish four-masted barque in 1938–39, a voyage he described in *The Last Grain Race* (Penguin, 1986).

In 1942, while serving with the Special Boat Section, he was captured after an attack on a German airfield in Sicily. *Love and War in the Apennines* describes his escape with the aid of the girl he subsequently married. For nine years or so he worked in the wholesale fashion business, "tottering up the backstairs of stores with armfuls of stock" (of which he wrote in *Something Wholesale*), and in a Mayfair Couture house, leaving it in 1956 to make the expedition hilariously chronicled in *A Short Walk in the Hindu Kush* (Penguin, 1981). His journey down the Ganges was made in 1963–64 after some years as fashion buyer to a chain of department stores. From 1964 to 1973 he was Travel Editor of *The Observer*.

Other books by Eric Newby include *The World Atlas of Exploration*, *Great Ascents*, and *The Big Red Train Ride* (Penguin, 1985), an account of a trip on the Trans-Siberian Railway. His latest book, *A Book of Travellers' Tales*, was published by Viking in 1986.

Eric Newby

Slowly Down The Ganges

PENGUIN BOOKS

PENGUIN BOOKS

Published by the Penguin Group

Viking Penguin Inc., 40 West 23rd Street,
New York, New York, 10010, U.S.A.
Penguin Books Ltd, 27 Wrights Lane,
London W8 5TZ England
Penguin Books Australia Ltd, Ringwood,
Victoria, Australia
Penguin Books Canada Ltd, 2801 John Street,
Markham, Ontario, Canada L3R 1B4
Penguin Books (N.Z.) Ltd, 182–190 Wairau Road,
Auckland 10, New Zealand

Penguin Books Ltd, Registered Offices:
Harmondsworth, Middlesex, England

First published in Great Britain by
Hodder and Stoughton Ltd 1966
First published in the United States of America by
Charles Scribner's Sons 1967
Published in Penguin Books 1986

3 5 7 9 10 8 6 4

LIBRARY OF CONGRESS CATALOGING IN PUBLICATION DATA
Newby, Eric.
Slowly down the Ganges.
(Penguin travel library)
Reprint. Previously published: London : Pan Books
in association with Collins, 1966.
1. Ganges River (India and Bangladesh)—Description
and travel. 2. Newby, Eric—Journeys—Ganges River
(India and Bangladesh) I. Title. II. Series.
DS485.G25N4 1986 915.4'10452 86-12371
ISBN 0 14 00.9572 1

Printed in the United States of America by
R. R. Donnelley & Sons Company, Harrisonburg, Virginia
Set in Garamond

To Wanda — my fellow boatwoman

"The Ganga has been a symbol of India's age-long culture and civilisation, ever-changing, ever-flowing, and yet ever the same Ganga. She reminds me of the Himalayas, snow-covered peaks and the deep valleys which I have loved so much, and of the rich and vast plains below where my life and work have been cast."

Jawaharlal Nehru

"Here I asked repeatedly, and received a different account . . . Perhaps these particulars vary in different instances. At all events it is a proof how hard it is to gain, in this country, accurate information as to facts which seem most obvious to the senses."

Narrative of a Journey through the Upper Provinces of India
Reginald Heber, D.D., Lord Bishop of Calcutta

Contents

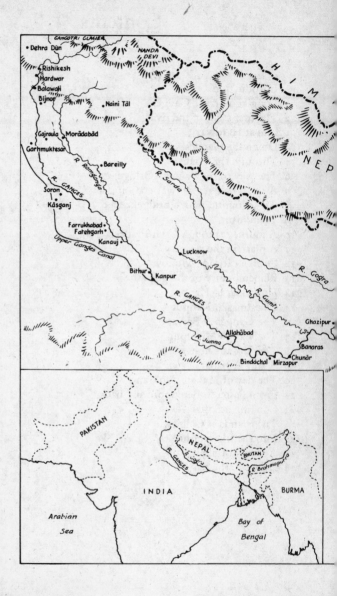

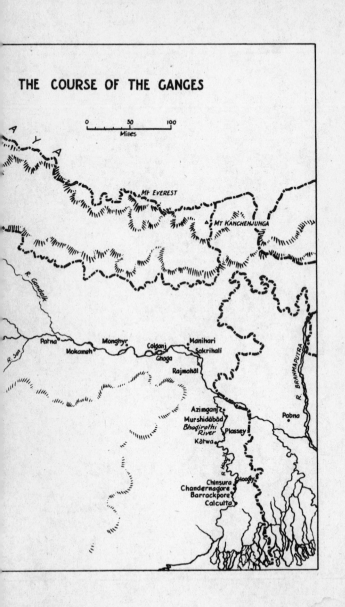

THE COURSE OF THE GANGES

0   50   100
Miles

A
Y
A

Mt EVEREST

Mt KANCHENJUNGA

R. Gandak

R. Son

Patna

Mokameh   Monghyr   Colgan   Manihari
                       Ghoga   Sakrihali

                    Rajmahal

R. BRANHAPUTRA

                    Azimganj
                    Murshidābād   Pabna
                    Bhagirathi
                    River   Plassey
                    Kātwa

                    Chinsura   Hoogly
                Chandernagore
                    Barrackpore
                    Calcutta

Introduction

This is the story of a twelve-hundred-mile journey down the Ganges from the place where it enters the Plains of India to the Sandheads, forty miles offshore in the Bay of Bengal, made by two Europeans in the winter of 1963–4. It is not an heroic story such as that of Franklin and his companions chewing leather on the banks of the Coppermine River but having got there (it is difficult to envy Franklin); of Ives seeing for the first time the great canyon of the Colorado; of Garnier reaching the headwaters of the Yangtze; or of Bailey and Morshead travelling sixteen hundred miles on foot through the gorges of the Tsangpo. We were born too late for such feats, even if we had had the courage and determination to perform them. We were even prevented from emulating the painter James Fraser's long journey to the sources of the Bhagirathi Ganges – one which is made by numerous pilgrims – by the coming of the snow and our own meagre resources. It is not a book about India today; neither is it concerned with politics or economics. It is certainly not erudite, as must be obvious to anyone who has the patience to read it. It is about the river as we found it.

In most standard works of reference the Ganges does not even rate an entry in the tables which list the great rivers of the world, for it is only 1,500 miles long from its source in the Himalayas to the Bay of Bengal. The Nile, the Amazon, the Mississippi/Missouri are all more than two and a half times as long as the Ganges. The Irtysh and the Yangtze are both twice as long. The Congo, the Yellow River, the Mackenzie, the Niger, the Danube, the Euphrates, the Brahmaputra and the Indus, to name only a few, are all longer. But, all the same, it is a great river.

It is great because, to millions of Hindus, it is the most sacred, most venerated river on earth. For them it is *Ganga Ma* – Mother Ganges. To bathe in it is to wash away guilt. To drink the water, having bathed in it, and to carry it away in bottles for those who have not had the good fortune to make the pilgrimage to it is meritorious. To be cremated on its banks, having died there, and to have one's ashes cast on its waters, is the wish of every Hindu. Even to ejaculate *"Ganga,*

Ganga", at the distance of 100 leagues from the river may atone for the sins committed during three previous lives.

In almost any bazaar in India one can buy a little, oblong paperback book. It is rather like a book of tickets for some Eastern tram service. It contains two works, bound up together. They are the *Gangastottara-sata-namavali* and the *Ganga-sahasra-nama-stotra*. They enumerate the 108 and the 1,000 names of the Ganges, all printed metrically and in columns so that they can be chanted devotionally; but unless one is an expert in Sanskrit, as was Colonel Pickering in *Pygmalion*, it is impossible to understand them. She is The Pure, The Eternal, The Light Amid the Darkness, The Cow Which Gives Much Milk, The Liberator, The Destroyer Of Poverty And Sorrow, The Creator of Happiness, to give only a few of her names.*

The Ganges was not always so highly regarded. When the Aryan invaders first entered India they were more impressed by the Indus. It was only later that they gave *Ganga* the highest position, as *Sursari*, River Of The Gods – perhaps because they had found out what European scientists discovered later: that its water has remarkable properties. Bottled, it will keep for at least a year. At its confluence with the River Jumna which, particularly at the time of the great fair which takes place there every January, contains dangerous numbers of *coli*, the Ganges itself is said to be free of them. At Banaras thousands drink the water every day at bathing places which are close to the outfalls of appalling open drains. They appear to survive. The presence of large numbers of decomposing corpses seems to have no adverse effect on it. (Before setting off we were advised that when we wanted to make tea sedimentation could be accelerated by stirring it with a stick of alum; but we never did this.) Taken on board sailing ships in the Hooghly at Calcutta it is said to have outlasted all other waters. In spite of this many Hindus have reservations about how far down-river they are prepared to drink it. Some say as far as Dhulian, near the place where the Ganges under the name of the Bhagirathi and later the Hooghly, takes off for Calcutta. The inhabitants of Soron, on the Upper Ganges far north of cities like Allahabad and Banaras, believe that this is the last point at which the water is really good because, they say, no sewage has yet entered it. (At Soron there is a large tank, reputed to be fed by the Ganges, the waters of which have the peculiar property of dissolving the bones of the dead within three days of their being deposited in it.)

It is certainly responsible for more good than evil. Even cholera,

---

* The 108 Names of the Ganges are enumerated at the end of the introduction.

one of the great killers, does not go down the river. It is born in the stagnant waters of the Delta in Bengal and ascends it carried by pilgrims who visit the sacred places in hundreds of thousands every year. The great nineteenth-century epidemics started in Bengal, spread to Hardwar, one of the holiest places of all on the Upper Ganges; then north-west into the Punjab and from there overland into Afghanistan, Persia, Russia and finally into Western Europe. Even today the seasonal rise in the incidence of cholera coincides with the great religious fairs which take place on the banks of the river.

The Ganges first sees the light of day when it emerges from an ice cave above Gangotri, 13,800 feet up in the Garhwal Himalayas. Hindus believe that it was from this cave that *Ganga*, the daughter of King Himavat and the nymph, Mena, was persuaded to come down to earth by Bhagiratha, a descendant of King Sagar, in order to redeem from hell the souls of the sixty thousand sons of the king who had been reduced to ashes by a holy man whom they had slighted.

There is some dispute between the devotees of Siva and Vishnu, the two principal sects of Hindus, as to which god assisted at the birth of *Ganga*. Vishnuvites believe that she rose from the big toe of Vishnu's left foot, Sivites say that to break her fall on earth Siva allowed her to flow through his hair, which can still be seen hanging in the form of icicles from the roof of the cave.

At Hardwar, with twelve hundred miles of its course still to run to its nearest outlet to the sea it has already fallen 12,800 feet and here, only 1,000 feet above the sea, it begins to irrigate the land with the aid of wells and canals, and to give electric power. On its way to the sea it passes through three states: Uttar Pradesh, Bihar and West Bengal. In them live 150,000,000 people, almost a third of the entire population of India. Of these nearly half live in Uttar Pradesh. There are 69,000 villages in Uttar Pradesh with populations of less than 500 and in this state more than eighty per cent of the cultivated holdings are of less than five acres (some are as little as half an acre). For much of its course the Ganges is not a navigable river in the real sense of the word, although, in spite of the fact that millions of cubic feet of water are drawn off from it, its strength is constantly renewed by the rivers that flow into it. It is in the 600-mile stretch between Allahabad and Rajmahal that it really gathers strength. At Rajmahal, in full flood, it goes down at 1,000,800 cubic feet a second which is greater than the maximum discharge of the Mississippi (the Thames at Staines discharges at 6,600 feet a second in full flood). Fortunately it brings down with it vast quantities of silt which it deposits free of charge for a season before sweeping it further downstream. A Victorian engineer,

Sir Charles Lyell, estimated that 335,000,000 tons of silt were discharged each year at Ghazipur on the Middle Ganges. "Nearly the weight of sixty replicas of the Great Pyramid." A useless comparison. "It is scarcely possible," he goes on, "to present any picture to the mind which will convey an adequate conception to the mind of the mighty scale of this operation, so tranquilly and almost insensibly carried out by the Ganges." Whether some smallholder in Bihar, watching his half-acre slipping noisily into the water and his family being swept downstream on top of a haystack would regard the operation as being either tranquil or insensible is open to question. No one knows for certain the depth of the alluvial silt in the Delta.

Like the black sheep of the family sent to Australia, the Ganges is always trying to straighten itself out. It sets its current strongly against one bank, undercutting it and leaving sluggish water on the other shore on which new deposits are made, until it finally breaks through and begins the whole process afresh. The Gangetic Plain is riddled with old, dead watercourses that the Ganges has forgotten about. At Kasimbazar in Bengal, where one of the first British trading stations was established in 1658, there is a flight of steps from which it is said that Warren Hastings used to come ashore. Only the river has gone, leaving a few pools choked with water hyacinth. The once-illustrious city of Kanauj on the Upper Ganges is now so far from the actual stream that, passing it in a boat in the dry season, one does not realise that it is there at all. Rajmahal, once the capital of Bengal was left high and dry, three miles from it, in 1863. Later, in the seventies, it was seven miles from it. Now the Ganges has returned. Too late, the city is moribund. The Bhagirathi, the short, eighty-mile stretch which connects it with the Hooghly is more or less dry for eight months of the year. Power-vessels bound for Calcutta have to make a 400-mile detour through East Pakistan to reach the port which is itself always in danger of suffering the same fate as Rajmahal. Four hundred miles out in the Bay of Bengal the sea is discoloured by the silt brought down by it. The Ganges justifies the one hundred and second name given it in the *Gangastottara-sata-namavali* – "Roaming About Rose-Apple-Tree Island", which is India.

Note: All diacritical marks which correctly should appear in Indian names have been omitted in this book.

Gangastottara-sata-namavali

(The 108 names of the Ganges)

1	Ganga	Ganges
2	Visnu-padabja-sambhuta	Born from the lotus-like foot of Vishnu
3	Hara-vallabha	Dear to Hara (Siva)
4	Himacalendra-tanaya	Daughter of the Lord of Himalaya
5	Giri-mandala-gamini	Flowing through the mountain-country
6	Tarakarati-janani	Mother of [the demon] Taraka's enemy (i.e. Kartikeya)
7	Sagaratmaja-tarika	Liberator of the [60,000] sons of Sagara (who had been burnt to ashes by the angry glance of the sage Kapila)
8	Sarasvati-samayukta	Joined to [the river] Sarasvati (said to have flowed underground and joined the Ganges at Allahabad)
9	Sughosa	Melodius (or: Noisy)
10	Sindhu-gamini	Flowing to the ocean
11	Bhagirathi	Pertaining to the saint Bhagiratha (whose prayers brought the Ganges down from Heaven)
12	Bhagyavati	Happy, fortunate
13	Bhagiratha-rathanuga	Following the chariot of Bhagiratha (who led the Ganges down to Hell to purify the ashes of Sagara's sons)
14	Trivikrama-padoddhuta	Falling from the foot of Vishnu
15	Triloka-patha-gamini	Flowing through the three worlds (i.e. Heaven, earth and the atmosphere or lower regions)
16	Ksira-subhra	White as milk
17	Bahu-ksira	[A cow] which gives much milk

18 Ksira-vrksa-samakula	Abounding in [the four] "milk-trees" (i.e. Nyagrodha (Banyan), Udumbara (glomerous fig-tree), Asvattha (holy fig-tree), and Madhuka (Bassia Latifolia))
19 Trilocana-jata-vasini	Dwelling in the matted locks of Siva
20 Rna-traya-vimocini	Releasing from the Three Debts, viz. (1) Brahma-carya (study of the Vedas) to the rishis, (2) sacrifice and worship to the gods, and (3) procreation of a son, to the Manes
21 Tripurari-siras-cuda	The tuft on the head of the enemy of Tripura (Siva). (Tripura was a triple fortification, built in the sky, air and earth of gold, silver and iron respectively, by Maya for the Asuras, and burnt by Siva)
22 Jahnavi	Pertaining to Jahnu (who drank up the Ganges in a rage after it had flooded his sacrificial ground, but relented, and allowed it to flow from his ear)
23 Nata-bhiti-hrt	Carrying away fear
24 Avyaya	Imperishable
25 Nayanananda-dayini	Affording delight to the eye
26 Naga-putrika	Daughter of the mountain
27 Niranjana	Not painted with collyrium (i.e. colourless)
28 Nitya-suddha	Eternally pure
29 Nira-jala-pariskrta	Adorned with a net of water
30 Savitri	Stimulator
31 Salila-vasa	Dwelling in water
32 Sagarambusa-medhini	Swelling the waters of the ocean
33 Ramya	Delightful
34 Bindu-saras	River made of water-drops
35 Avyakta	Unmanifest, unevolved
36 Vrndaraka-samasrita	Resort of the eminent

37	Uma-sapatni	Having the same husband (i.e. Siva) as Uma (Parvati)
38	Subhrangi	Having beautiful limbs (or body)
39	Srimati	Beautiful, auspicious, illustrious, etc.
40	Dhavalambara	Having a dazzling white garment
41	Akhandala-vana-vasa	Having Siva as a forest-dweller (hermit)
42	Khandendu-krta-sekhara	Having the crescent moon as a crest
43	Amrtakara-salila	Whose water is a mine of nectar
44	Lila-lamghita-parvata	Leaping over mountains in sport
45	Virinci-kalasa-vasa	Dwelling in the water-pot of Brahma (or Vishnu, or Siva)
46	Triveni	Triple-braided (i.e. consisting of the waters of three rivers: Ganges, Yamuna and Sarasvati)
47	Trigunatmika	Possessing the three *gunas*
48	Sangataghaugha-samani	Destroying the mass of sins of Sangata
49	Sankha-dundubhi-nisvana	Making a noise like a conch-shell and drum
50	Bhiti-hrt	Carrying away fear
51	Bhagya-janani	Creating happiness
52	Bhinna-brahmanda-darpini	Taking pride in the broken egg of Brahma
53	Nandini	Happy
54	Sighra-ga	Swift-flowing
55	Siddha	Perfect, holy
56	Saranya	Yielding shelter, help or protection
57	Sasi-sekhara	Moon-crested
58	Sankari	Belonging to Sankara (Siva)
59	Saphari-purna	Full of fish (esp. Cyprinus Saphore — a kind of bright little fish that glistens when darting about in shallow water — or carp)
60	Bharga-murdha-krtalaya	Having Bharga's (Siva's) head as an abode
61	Bhava-priya	Dear to Bhava (Siva)

62	Satya-sandha-priya	Dear to the faithful
63	Hamsa-svarupini	Embodied in the forms of swans
64	Bhagiratha-suta	Daughter of Bhagiratha
65	Ananta	Eternal
66	Sarac-candra-nibhanana	Resembling the autumn moon
67	Om-kara-rupini	Having the appearance of the sacred syllable Om
68	Atula	Peerless
69	Krida-kallola-karini	Sportively billowing
70	Svarga-sopana-sarani	Flowing like a staircase to Heaven
71	Sarva-deva-svarupini	Embodied in the pantheon
72	Ambhah-prada	Bestowing water
73	Duhkha-hantri	Destroying sorrow
74	Santi-santana-karini	Bringing about the continuance of peace
75	Daridrya-hantri	Destroyer of poverty
76	Siva-da	Bestowing happiness
77	Samsara-visa-nasini	Destroying the poison of illusion
78	Prayaga-nilaya	Having Prayaga (Allahabad) as an abode
79	Sita	"Furrow". Name of the eastern branch of the four mythical branches into which the heavenly Ganges is supposed to divide after falling on Mount Meru
80	Tapa-traya-vimocini	Releasing from the Three Afflictions
81	Saranagata-dinarta-paritrana	Protector of the sick and suffering who come to you for refuge
82	Sumukti-da	Giving complete [spiritual] emancipation
83	Siddhi-yoga-nisevita	Resorted to (for the acquisition of success or magic powers)
84	Papa-hantri	Destroyer of sin
85	Pavanangi	Having a pure body
86	Parabrahma-svarupini	Embodiment of the Supreme Spirit
87	Purna	Full
88	Puratana	Ancient
89	Punya	Auspicious
90	Punya-da	Bestowing merit

91	Punya-vahini	Possessing (or producing) merit
92	Pulomajarcita	Worshipped by Indrani (wife of Indra)
93	Puta	Pure
94	Puta-tribhuvana	Purifier of the Three Worlds
95	Japa	Muttering, whispering
96	Jangama	Moving, alive
97	Jangamadhara	Support or substratum of what lives or moves
98	Jala-rupa	Consisting of water
99	Jagad-d-hita	Friend or benefactor of what lives or moves
100	Jahnu-putri	Daughter of Jahnu
101	Jagan-matr	Mother of what lives or moves
102	Jambu-dvipa-viharini	Roaming about (or delighting in) Rose-apple-tree Island (India)
103	Bhava-patni	Wife of Bhava (Siva)
104	Bhisma-matr	Mother of Bhisma
105	Siddha	Holy
106	Ramya	Delightful, beautiful
107	Uma-kara-kamala-sanjata	Born from the lotus which created Uma (Parvati) (presumably a poetic way of saying that they were sisters)
108	Ajnana-timira-bhanu	A light amid the darkness of ignorance

Chapter One

Long ago on the Ganges

Gange Cha Yamune Chaiva
Godavarai Saraswati
Narmade Sindhu Kaveri
Jale Asmin Sannidhim Kuru

(O Holy Mother Ganges! O Yamuna! O Godavari! Saraswati! O Narmada! Sindhu! Kaveri! May you all be pleased to be manifest in these waters with which I shall purify myself!)

> Prayer to the Seven Sacred Rivers recited by
> every devout Hindu at the time of taking his bath

I love rivers. I was born on the banks of the Thames and, like my father before me, I had spent a great deal of time both on it and in it. I enjoy visiting their sources: Thames Head, in a green meadow in the Cotswolds; the river Po coming out from under a heap of boulders among the debris left by picnickers by Monte Viso; the Isonzo bubbling up over clean sand in a deep cleft in the rock in the Julian Alps; the Danube (or one of its sources) emerging in baroque splendour in a palace garden at Donaueschingen. I like exploring them. I like the way in which they grow deeper and wider and dirtier but always, however dirty they become, managing to retain some of the beauty with which they were born.

For me the most memorable river of all was the Ganges. I had not seen it for more than twenty years since the time when, as a young officer, I had spent six months on its banks at a remote military station some fifty miles from Kanpur.

I arrived there in March, at the start of the hottest season. That summer in the Indian Plain is something which I can never forget, and yet it is something which I find difficult to believe that I ever experienced. I remember a sky like an inverted brass bowl overhead and the earth like an overcooked omelette beneath it.

Through this desiccated landscape the Ganges flowed, not more than a couple of hundred yards wide. It was a disagreeable shade of green and in it floated imperfectly cremated corpses and an occasional crocodile.

All through March and April it was terribly hot but during the second week of May the weather began to change for the better. There were two light showers of rain, the first harbingers of the monsoon, and the midday temperature sometimes fell as low as a hundred degrees fahrenheit.

On 20th May I was standing on the parade ground where I had been teaching recruits to do up their boots. All that day the sky had been overcast. All afternoon it had been very quiet. At four o'clock the recruits were dismissed and they were clumping off to their tents in their great, newly-tied boots when suddenly they began to utter moaning sounds, break their ranks and run for their lives. I wondered if it was another Indian Mutiny.

It was only a dust storm. It came roaring across the plain as black and solid-looking as a cliff. I took one look at it, got on my bicycle and fled.

I reached my bungalow at the same time as the sandstorm and locked the door on it. Outside it was as black as night, the electric light cables snapped, trees were uprooted and a large marquee complete with flailing guy ropes and tent pegs whistled past on the wind. There was a terrible roaring sound. It lasted half an hour, then the wind died away as quickly as it had come, by which time the floor of the bungalow was ankle-deep in sand – one of the windows had been broken by the wind. It was succeeded by a violent rainstorm with thunder and lightning.

When it was all over I put on some old clothes and a pair of gumboots and went down a sunken lane to the river, churning my way through the mud.

At the foot of this lane which was thickly overshadowed by trees, there was a shrine dedicated to the god Siva. There was no temple, just a lingam, a black stone on a plinth at the foot of a pipal tree on which offerings of sweets and marigolds were scattered. Although I went there almost every day and I never saw anyone else, the offerings were always fresh. Buried in the heart of the tree itself, which had grown round it, there was a block of stone with a frieze of figures carved on it. It was a place with a feeling of great antiquity and the magic beauty of a sacred grove in a painting by Claude.

But on this particular day I had come because I wanted to see what had happened to the river as a result of the storm.

The water was no longer green and sluggish. It had been churned until it was the colour of milky coffee and it had spread up over the low-lying bank to the north and was flowing strongly. Overhead, apart from a few egg-shaped clouds which floated across it at regular intervals, the sky was clear and blue. Beyond the swollen river the sand flats on the opposite shore extended as far as the eye could see, to a distant skyline dotted with trees which I had never noticed. Everything in this landscape was brilliant and distinct. It was like the springtime of the world.

Downstream a herd of water-buffaloes was swimming the river. Men and boys were crossing with them, perched on the backs of half a dozen beasts out on the flanks of the main body. They were shouting and laughing to one another and making encouraging noises to the animals which breasted the stream powerfully but slowly. Then they came lumbering out of the water and thundered up into the combe where I was standing, their flanks all glistening, and as they went by the riders waved their sticks at me and shouted that the hot weather was nearly over. Then they all disappeared up the hill, and I was alone by the river. There was something about it, the ability it had shown to change in the space of an hour, to expand and stretch away to distant horizons, to the existence of which I had not even given a thought, that made me long to follow it on and on until it reached the sea. The next day I went on leave to the Hills, and when I came back the rains had come in earnest and the Ganges was itself like a vast, inland sea. A few weeks more and I was sent to the Middle East. Twenty-two years passed before I saw it again.

Chapter Two

The first sight of the river

How magnificent she is when she flows in the valley Rishikesh! She has a blue colour like that of the ocean. The water is extremely clear and sweet. Rich people from the plains get water from Rishikesh. It is taken in big copper vessels to far-off places in India.

Sri Swami Sivananda: Mother Ganges;
Yoga-Vedanta Forest Academy, 1962

Together with Wanda, my wife, I went out on to one of the platforms of the temple. Upstream towards Rishikesh, the river wound between sand and shingle, sometimes hidden from view amongst groves of trees from which long, horizontal bands of mist were slowly rising. Immediately below was the Har-ki-Pairi Ghat with its ludicrous clock tower and, just upriver from it, the barrage at Bhimgoda that channelled the water from the mainstream into the canal reducing the river below it to a trickle among stones that were the colour of old bones. This attenuated stream was the Ganges, the river that we hoped to travel down until we reached the sea. To the south of the Hardwar Gorge, here, at its narrowest, not more than a mile wide, it wound away, a narrow ribbon, reach after reach of it until it was swallowed up in the haze of the vast plain that stretched through all points of the compass from east of south to the extreme west.

Now, for the first time, I realised the magnitude of the journey that lay before us; but I had none of the feelings of the explorer. This was no uncharted river. Millions lived on its banks, regarding it as an essential adjunct without which their existence would be unthinkable, if not impossible; bathing in it; drinking it; washing their clothes in it; pouring it on to their fields; dying by it; being taken into its bosom by it and being borne away.

Even if we succeeded in reaching the end of the river this was no great feat. None of the uncommunicable pleasure that came to the first explorers to look on the great rivers of the earth, the tales of which had meant so much in my youth, would be ours, could ever be. Perhaps it was better so. I had waited many years to make this journey, since as a young man, I sat on the banks of the Ganges at Fatehgarh, and watched the herd of water-buffalo crossing the river. Whatever satisfaction I derived from it and whatever profit I might find, would probably be of the spirit, perhaps uncommunicable to others. Bells sounded and cymbals clashed in the temple. G., our companion, emerged from it, mollified and subdued by his devotions, and together the three of us went down the path to an eggless breakfast at the railway station.

We had arrived at Hardwar from Delhi, at half-past six the previous morning when it was still dark. We were extremely cold – the train had been unheated and the window had remained open despite our efforts to close it. With a retinue of porters that we were already beginning to regard as inevitable, we moved off towards the waiting-room where we were to meet an agent from Shell who had been allocated the unenviable task of helping us to find a boat capable of taking us down twelve hundred miles of the Ganges to the sea.

He had not yet arrived. Soon the light of a grey dawn began to seep in under the roof of the station. It revealed a religious bookstall on which the proprietor was already beginning to set out his stock, and numbers of red-behinded monkeys which, like the cows at the station at Delhi the night before but without the religious sanction wh. allows cows in Hindu India to do what they like, were taking liberties with passengers' baggage.

I bought a guide-book from the bookseller. "Caution", it said. "Hardwar is a dry area, therefore do not keep with you, any intoxicative article along with meat, eggs, etc. Wine, Bhang, Charas, Ganja, Opium, etc., are not allowed here! Those who are addicted to such habits can obtain from Lahksar, Rooorkee, or Dehradun, meat and aggs from Jwalapur (Pick-pockets theives and gamblers). Take every possible care of your valueables from theives and pick-pockets; here you will find them on every step."

With the dawn came breakfast: porridge, tea and toast, brought by a sad-looking waiter in a grimy white uniform and a head-cloth that had seen better days. He was the archetype of all the waiters on all the railway stations on which we were to breakfast. On the walls, prominently displayed, were notices warning visitors that in the sacred area of Hardwar – which included the station – neither fish, nor fowl nor eggs would be served.

Some time later the man from Shell appeared, together with a colleague. They had already tried to find a boat for us but without success. "If we are to do so," they said, "We should set out instantly." We were just getting into their motor car when G., who was going to accompany us on the first part of the journey and who was of high caste, announced that he had not yet performed his ritual ablutions. He disappeared into the station retiring-room for half an hour while the rest of the party waited in the cold, Wanda and I with ill-concealed impatience; the men from Shell with Oriental stoicism. What did Oriental stoicism conceal, I wondered – thoughts of roasting over slow fires, impalements and decapitations? I looked into their eyes, seeking the answer, but in vain. At this moment I formed a high opinion of them that subsequent experience was to enhance rather than diminish; a circumstance which, in India, where the inhabitants tire rapidly of the visitor and the converse is equally true, is contrary to the general rule.

In a silence provoked by exasperation we set off to visit the Irrigation Engineer, whose house was by the headworks of the Upper Ganges Canal, to ask for the loan of a boat. He was away on tour, but we were told that there was a contractor, the master of a temporary bridge over the river, who was reputed to have a boat and we set off in search of him.

The contractor lived in an ancient suburb to the south of the town called Kankhal. It was a pleasant place with grass growing on the verges of the side streets, in which holy men were taking their constitutionals carrying baggy umbrellas. It was a brilliant morning and the air was as invigorating as anything from an oxygen cylinder. Our spirits rose.

His office was on the ground floor of a small building. The room was sparsely furnished with a large divan which was covered with a clean white sheet. The windows, which were glassless, were fitted with shutters, and the light that filtered through them into the room gave it the appearance of being filled with water. The five of us squatted untidily on the divan which was awfully hard, and I tried to detect some sign of interest or compassion in the flinty eye of the contractor who addressed himself, without any of the customary enquiries about one's health and strength, exclusively to the men from Shell. He was a Brahman. He wore a little white cap, a high-buttoned jacket of village homespun with a stand-up collar and a dhoti. Normally a dhoti looks rather ludicrous when worn with socks, suspenders and brown shoes; but there was nothing comical about this man of iron. He did not offer us tea.

"He says he has a boat that he will sell you."

"We don't want to buy a boat. We want to hire one."

"He says he will sell you a boat."

It was obvious that no good would come of pursuing this particular line any further.

"*Yih kisti achcha hai?*" Even after a lapse of more than twenty years I was determined to speak the language, however deplorably.

"Is it a good boat?"

So far as the contractor was concerned I might not have been there at all.

"He says that it is the only boat in Hardwar. He is indifferent to whether you take it or not. He also says that if you do not wish to have his boat why have you come to ask him for it? He is a villain."

"Can we see it?"

"He says that you can see the boat but as there is only one he asks why it is necessary for you to see it. However, if you wish to do so he will accompany you. It is at his bridge."

"We don't have to thank him, do we?"

"It is unnecessary."

The bridge was at a place called Chandi Ghat,* some little way downstream from the town. As we drove over the embankment built by the British on the right bank, we had our first view of the Ganges.

It was a bit of a shock. It was December, the dry season, and the river which in the rains would have been a mile wide now ran sluggishly through a wasteland of sand and stones. Although it was already so far from its source, it was no more than 70 yards wide. Most of the water was being drawn into the Upper Ganges canal which takes off just below Hardwar.

It was a wooden bridge supported on piers of rough dry stone, and the roadway across it was covered with coarse grass. Bullock-carts with huge wooden wheels were creaking over it, towards us, loaded with bamboo from the jungle on the east bank and the drivers sat high up in the front of their vehicles like ships' figureheads.

Moving across the bridge in the opposite direction were hill people on their way up to Garhwal, carrying pack frames with enormous loads lashed to them. With their snub noses and slant eyes they were as different from the bullock-cart drivers, who were from the river bank, as visitors from outer space. Upstream from the bridge a number of flat-bottomed country craft, like small barges, were moored to the bank. Nowhere was the water more than two feet deep. Of the boat that we had come to see there was no sign.

At this moment a number of men arrived at the water's edge pushing a hand-cart on which there was a dead cow covered with a

---

* *Ghat*: From the Sanskrit word *ghatta* meaning "a landing place", "steps on a riverside", "a mountain pass", "a range of hills". Used in this book in the first two of these senses.

red cloth. They began to off-load it, intending to dump it in the river. Now, for the first time since we had met him, the contractor showed signs of emotion. It was obvious that if they succeeded in getting away with this ill-conceived burial the cow would remain stranded there, a source of embarrassment, until the end of June when the monsoon would come and wash it away and the bridge with it. He rushed to head them off. Soon the air was rent by angry cries and an interminable wrangle began.

"You are Brahman. This is a sacred animal. She must go to Ganga!"

"I am Brahman but you must take your sacred animal somewhere else!"

While we were waiting for the dispute to end, we sat on a log outside the bridge-keeper's hut which was made of reeds, and looked upstream. To the right, over the river, the jungle that once had teemed with wild animals – tigers, leopards, herds of elephants, sloth bear, wolves, nilgai, antelope, black buck and the terrible wild dog – jungle in which the Indian lion survived until the beginning of the nineteenth century – and which was still well stocked with poisonous snakes, cobras and karait – broke at the foot of the hills in a green hazy sea; while far to the north, seen through the deep trench that the Ganges had dug for itself through the foothills on its way to the plains in which we now found ourselves marooned, an impressive, snow-covered peak rose, shining in the sun.

I asked what it was.

"It is called Triyugi."

"What is Triyugi?"

"Triyugi is from *Treta Yuga*."

"What is *Treta Yuga*?"

"It is one part of *Yuga*."

"What is *Yuga*?"

"*Yuga* is one age of the world. There are four Yugas and each is named after one god. There is *Krita Yuga*, *Treta Yuga*, *Dwapara Yuga*, and *Kali Yuga*. Age is preceded by period not light, not dark, called *Sandhya* and after it a further period called *Sandhyansa*, also not dark, not light. Each is equal to one-tenth of *Yuga*. *Treta Yuga* is three thousand years but with not so light, not so dark period, three thousand six hundred years. In *Treta Yuga* Ganga is most sacred. Altogether *Yugas* are twelve thousand years."

"Twelve thousand years isn't all that long. The Ice Age was before that."

"Yes, but one year of god's life in *Yuga* is three hundred and sixty years of man. Whole period is called *Maha-Yuga*. There are four million three hundred and twenty thousand years in *Maha-Yuga*."

"That's still not very long."

"Ah, but two thousand *Maha-Yugas* make *Kalpa* and in *Kalpa* I am counting eight billion, six hundred and forty million years and *Kalpa* is only one day and one night of *Brahma*. After one day of life of *Brahma* world is consumed, except for wise men, gods and elements. Next day he recreates world and so on for hundred years until he too expires. His daughter is *Sandhya*, of the not light, not dark period, and with her he has much intercourse and in this way is father of all men."

"How long is that?"

"I am not counting that number of years."

On the far side of the river, lying on its side on the stones, there was a rusty tin boat. It was sixteen feet long, and the bottom was as full of holes as a colander. It was like a lifeboat thrown up on the shore, the harbinger of a greater disaster. The thought of travelling 1,200 miles down the river in such a craft would have been laughable if any other boat had been available.

"The contractor says that he will sell you his boat for fifteen hundred rupees." This was more than a hundred pounds.*

"What about the boats upstream?"

"They only draw one foot but they are too broad and too heavy. Further down the river is very difficult, besides they cannot pass under this bridge."

"But you can see the daylight through this one."

"The contractor says that he will have it repaired; otherwise, he says you can have one built."

"How much will that cost?"

"About three thousand rupees."

"How long will it take?"

"About a month, perhaps more. It is difficult to say. He is not a friendly man."

For what seemed hours they haggled with him while he looked with far-away flinty eyes at the disconsolate little party of cow-buriers, now specks on the shingle downstream. Finally, due to their pertinacity it was agreed that we should hire the boat to take us as far as Garhmuktesar, a place 100 miles downriver. This, together with the hire of boatmen and a lorry to send the boat back again (apparently it was impossible to travel upstream by boat), would come to more

---

* There are 16 annas to the rupee, which before devaluation in 1966 was worth about 1/6 (7½p).

than 500 rupees. If each hundred miles of the journey was going to cost the equivalent of forty pounds in boat hire, we would be penniless long before we reached Calcutta. The alternatives were to buy the boat, abandon the first part of the journey, or walk it – all three were unthinkable.

Chapter Three

Life at Hardwar

For very long time only yogies, holy sages, Richies and munies used
to live here for meditation, in order to please almighty, for his mercy
for sinners and also for the prosperity of human peace. It is assumed
that God was instructing these good men from time to time and was
showing light for their guidance. In the past the sages from all parts
of the world used to assemble here on certain astronomical stages for
the announcement of such directions from Gods side. In fact it was
Bradcasting Station of God's orders for General Public and rulers of
the time. These occasions were celebrated at Kumbh Fastival especially held in Basakh or April at the interval of Twelve years. Thus
wis real fact of fame of Hardwar. Although now people performe
every thing like that but it is for forme actuality.

A Tourist's Guide to Hardwar Rishikesh;

At Hardwara the capital of Siba the Ganges flowed amongst large
rocks with a pretty full current."

Thomas Coryate to Chaplain Terry:
A Voyage to East India, 1655

To dispel the memory of this exasperating encounter, we decided to
bathe at the sacred ghat. Even G., scarcely dry from his ritual ablutions
at the railway station, decided to accompany us; for Hardwar is one
of the founts of Hinduism, and one of the seven great places of pilgrimage of Hindu India and the Har-ki-Pairi Ghat is particularly
sacred because the footprint of Vishnu is preserved there.

The ghat was at the head of an artificial cut — a remarkable work of
nineteenth-century engineering — which diverts the Ganges from its
course into the Upper Ganges Canal. Here the stream ran very
strongly, compressed between the shore and a small artifical island in
the middle of which there was a municipal clock tower presented by an
Indian motor manufacturer that looked rather odd at this place where
the Ganges enters the plains of India. "Tower clock installed by
Swadeshi Electrical Clock Mfg. Co." said a notice. This was the prin-

cipal bathing-place. Above it, almost deserted at this late hour and at this season of the year, loomed tier upon tier of meretricious buildings, some of them partly obscured by advertisement hoardings. They included an unspeakable hotel and the palace of the Maharaja of Kashmir. Above these constructions rose the hills of the Siwalik range, uncultivated, almost completely uninhabited, dotted with sal* trees, and topped by a white temple, gay with flags.

Down where we were on the waterfront, limbless beggars moved like crabs across the stones; on the offshore island which was joined to the land by a pair of ornamental bridges, non-ritual bathers, intent only on getting clean, soaped themselves all over before lowering themselves into the stream; men wearing head-cloths swept downriver on tiny rafts of brushwood supported by hollow gourds; large, silvery cows excreted sacred excrement, contributing their mite to the sanctity of the place; while on the river front the nais, the barbers, regarded by the orthodox as indispensable but unclean, were still engaged in ritual hair-cutting under their lean-to sheds of corrugated iron, shaving heads, nostrils and ears, preparing their customers for the bath. The wind was still cold; it bore the smell of burning dung, mingled with the scent of flowers, sandalwood and other unidentifiable odours. Everything was bathed in a brilliant, eleven o'clock-light. It was an exciting, pleasant scene.

Reluctantly, because it seemed unlikely that we would ever see them again, we gave up our sandals to an attendant at the entrance to the bathing place, who filed them away out of sight in what resembled the cloakroom of a decrepit opera house, and went down the steps to the sacred pools past touts and well-fed custodians who were squatting on platforms under huge umbrellas which were straining in the wind, and which threatened to lift them and their platforms into the air and dump them in the river. All three of us were wearing the costume of the country; Wanda and myself in the fond hope of diminishing the interest of the inhabitants in us. For G., there was no need of such subterfuge; he was one of them already.

These men were called Pandas. Pandas are debased Brahmans, and other Brahmans consider them to be of low status. Most of them are rich; many are almost illiterate. They perform various functions. Male bathers usually deposit their belongings with them while they bathe, a necessary precaution for anyone who wishes to leave the ghat with any clothes at all. They supply anointing oils, powdered sandalwood and a kind of clay of a pale yellow colour, said to be obtainable only

* Shorea robusta.

from a tank at Somnath in Gujarat in which some of the 16,000 wives of Krishna drowned themselves after his death. This they grind on damp stones to make a paste with which they make the tilak, the mark on the forehead which is reputed to cool the bather's brain, if it has not already been frozen solid.

Pandas also inscribe the vital statistics of their clients' lives in great books: the date of birth, the day of the week, the star under which they were born; the sign of the Zodiac, the hour, and if it is known, the precise second, so that, when the need arises, an accurate horoscope can be cast without delay. For a consideration, which is always exorbitant, they perform the ceremonial worship called the Ganga-Puja. Some of them were engaged in it now; droning on in Sanskrit while the celebrant shivered on the steps: *"Jambu-Dwipe Bharate Varshe Uttarakhande Pavitra-Ganga-Teera ..."* ("In Jambu-Dwipe,* in the northern part of Bharata-Varsha,† by the side of Holy Ganges ..." and so on.)

There were two temples at the water's edge. Both had the curious, pyramidical towers characteristic of Hindu temple architecture. They looked like shaggy caps, the edible fungi that one finds on waste land in England.

The temple on the bank was dedicated to Vishnu and his wife; the other, which stood in the water, to the river. Here the bathers offered small, green, boat-shaped baskets made from stitched leaves, filled with marigolds, rose petals and white sweets which tasted like Edinburgh Rock, placing them carefully in the water. The Ganges whirled them round for a bit in the lee of the temple until one by one they upset and their contents were carried swiftly away.

We dabbled our feet in the water; it was dreadfully cold.

"Embrace it! Only good can come of it," croaked an elderly holy man. He told us that until the previous year he had been a guard on the Metre Gauge Railway. Now having discharged his commitments to his family he had left them and the world to pursue his own salvation. Unlike His Holiness Sri Swami Sivananda who, according to G., had attained Union with the Godhead on 14th July 1963 and is buried upstream at Rishikesh, his salvation will come later after a succession of re-births.

"I am going to die by Ganga", he said.

There are thousands of old men like him in India. The majority generate no great spiritual force, but they at least receive a little res-

---

* *Jambu-Dwipe*: one of the seven islands of which the world is made up.
† *Bharate-Varshe*: South of the Himalayas—India.

pect. It is a pity that the climate is against such a scheme in Britain. It is better than waiting for the end on a street corner.

The Swami Sivananda at Rishikesh was a remarkable man who could have made his mark in other fields. He was not only interested in his own salvation as his biography shows:

On the 17.2.47 Swamiji saw some printed pamphlets of the society (The Divine Life Society) being thrown in the Ganges by some inmate of the Ashram.

Swamiji: "Om Nijabodhaji, I saw the printed pamphlets being thrown into the Ganges. We are sending several parcels daily of books and medicines to several people, why can't you see that each packet from here carries at least one pamphlet?"

Secretary: "Yes, Swamiji, I shall see to it."

Here is one more instance in which Swamiji corrects his disciples. In December '46 the winter in Rishikesh was very severe. On 11.12.46 Swamiji saw me taking a hot-water bath in the bathroom attached to the Ashram. After two or three days, when I happened to be in the League-hall, Swamiji began thus and spoke to a by-stander.

Swamiji: "People from far and wide come to Rishikesh to have Ganges bath but the Ashramites here who live on the very brink of the Ganges have recourse to hot-water baths and thus lose a fine opportunity given them by God."

This talk settled me. I took the hint and began to take the bath regularly in the Ganges itself. This habit has invigorated me a good deal and put splendid and clean ideas into my mind and I had a healthy time of it. Here is another instance in which Swamiji corrects his disciples. It was on 17.8.46 when Swamiji saw that I was using a toothbrush to clean my teeth in the Ganges. After five days when Swamiji and myself were both climbing up the steps leading to the Bhajan Hall, Swamiji began: "Om, Swagyan, there is tooth-powder called 'Sadhu's' tooth-powder in our league for sale to the public; it is highly efficacious and when used twice daily will relieve anyone of Pyorreah etc.' This I took as a hint to me to discard the use of toothpaste which is costly and old-fashioned. . . . Swamiji knows the nature of ignorance." *

Whatever else this old man generated he was an extraordinary figure. It was the fifth of December; winter had set in and the wind was

* *Biography of Swami Sivananda—by one of his disciples*; The Sivananda Publication League Rishikesh.

blowing straight off the Himalayas. He was wearing a leather helmet
that made him look like the wizened pilot of an early flying-machine,
and he carried a pair of bedroom slippers. Everything he had — his
helmet, the cloths in which he was wrapped, his quilt, the sack in
which he presumably kept his other possessions — were all dyed the
uniform dark yellow, bordering on orange, the colour of the sadhus.
This dye is made from a special mud which has the unusual property
of keeping the wearer warm as well as holy-looking; a property which
it shares with cow-dung ash.

"Embrace it! Only good can come of it!" he repeated. To tell the
truth he was becoming a bit of a bore. He had bathed already, long
before first light, and he was too full of beans, like some old man at
the Serpentine. The only way to escape from him was to go in ourselves.

It was so cold that it was like stepping into a fire. The water was
very clear and remembering that no harm could come of it I drank
some and it tasted good, while great speckled fish called mahseer,
anything up to thirty pounds in weight, made insolent by over-
feeding, nipped me. It was necessary to keep moving. I wondered how
G. was getting on. He was standing in the slack water in the lee of
the temple of Lakshmi-Ganga, completely immobile, with only his
upturned face showing above the surface. A little upstream Wanda,
having emerged from the ladies' bathing establishment, which was a
cross between an Edwardian boathouse and a lock-up garage, in the
dim recesses of which modest ladies were splashing unseen, was having
trouble with her sari. She looked like someone handling a spin-
naker in a strong breeze; finally it unwound completely and she was
left up to her knees in water "the cynosure", as Milton wrote, "of
neighbouring eyes", like a freshly peeled plum. In order to dis-
associate myself from her, I went on foot up to the top end of the
island and dived in there. The water was quite shallow, but the
bottom was lined with stone-flags which were slippery with weed.
The current lifted me high out of the water, and bore me down in a
series of surges past a large smooth rock in mid-stream; past the
ladies' establishment with its admonitory notice in Hindi — "Non-
violence is the Greatest Duty. Where there is Religion there is Victory" — to which Wanda was now retreating in disorder; down into
the main pool where G. still floated in the shadows of the temple;
under the lower of the two bridges, in the shade of which a young
Vishnuvite sadhu smeared with cow-dung, his hair a beehive of mud,
was sleeping off the effects of a dose of hemp. Here I grabbed one of
the chains that hung down from the arch, the bather's last chance of

stopping before being swept into deep water and the headworks of the Upper Ganges Canal several miles downstream.

This bathing ghat has frequently been the scene of heavy losses of life. In 1760 two rival sects of sadhus fought a pitched battle here in which nearly 2,000 perished. In 1795 Sikh pilgrims killed 500 of the religious mendicants called Goshains. Until 1820 it was only 34 feet wide at the top and there were only 39 steps. In that year 430 pilgrims and a number of sepoys were crushed to death on them, after which the ghat was enlarged. In April or May, at the beginning of the Hindu year and on the birthday of Ganga herself, as many as 400,000 persons gathered there at the fair called Dikhanti for the bathing, and as it was considered a good thing to be the first to enter the water as soon as the propitious moment arrived, it is a wonder that there were not more casualties. Every twelfth year when the planet Jupiter is in Aquarius (Kumbh) — a particularly auspicious time — the numbers of pilgrims increases vastly. In 1796 and again in 1808 onlookers supposed to be reliable estimated that two million attended. In 1904 the number had fallen to 150,000; but at the Kumbh Mela of 1962 on April 13th, the principal day, two million people are said to have bathed.

Later as we crouched together on the lowest step, dripping and very cold (all three of us had forgotten to bring a towel), a young, evil-looking panda began, unasked, to recite the Ganga-Puja over our heads, having first ascertained our names. *"Vede Aham Erric Nubi Vona Nubi Pavitre Ganga Mataram ... Aradhanam Kalpayami Tharpanam Kalpayami Ganga Mataram Maduyam ... Ayurarogya Sampat Samrithim Kuru..."*. The-*am* endings, *Mataram Maduyam Aradhanam Tharpanam* imparted a mysterious quality to it. This is what it sounded like.

"Give me what you please" he said, unasked when he had finished, lowering his eyes like a bashful girl.

"Give him 10 naye paise", G. said.

"What, for three of us?"

"We did not ask for Puja. These Pandas are rotten fellows."

We had already paid an exorbitant amount to a particularly venal old man in order to see the footprint of Vishnu. He had veiled it completely when we approached, and had refused to uncover it until we gave him what he asked. It was a singularly unconvincing carving; one that might have been produced by a monumental mason in South London, rather than the footprint of a being capable of striding through the seven regions of the Hindu Universe in three steps. As an American shoe manufacturer, whom we met later on the water-front at Banaras, said, when confronted with a similar pair of footprints:

"If that's Vishnu's footprints, then he's got fallen arches."

"What's this?" said the panda when I gave him the ten naye paise. "Give me ten rupees." His voice rose to a shriek.

"You should be ashamed to be panda", said G., severely. "A strong young man like you".

Together with a kinsman of one of the men from Shell, we visited such a large number of temples that eventually it became a test of sheer endurance for all of us, including the guide. He was a man of strikingly handsome appearance and unusual attainments.

"I am Samudrika," he said when we were sitting drinking tea, exhausted. "I am, therefore, able to know what you are thinking. I have been watching you and I know many things about you. Think of your favourite flower," he said.

I thought of my unfavourite flowers, bronze wallflowers in a municipal bed; decided that this was unsporting and concentrated on roses. He handed me a piece of paper on which he had written the word "rose". The performance of such a feat was more impressive here, at the foot of the Himalayas, than it would have seemed in Wimbledon. "Between the ages of sixteen and twenty-six you were very poor," he said. "You are still poor but you would like to be an extravagant man. When you are angry it is not for long, but when your wife is angry she seethes like a pot. You will be always together."

"It sounds like a death sentence," Wanda said. She was not pleased with the way he used his talents. I asked him if he was a Sivite or a Vishnuvite.

"I am a worshipper of Sakti — female energy of Siva," he said. "It is a very intellectual worship."

That night I looked up Sakti worship in a book called *Bhattacharya's Hindu Castes and Sects*. According to Bhattacharya, if he was a Sakti worshipper he must either be a Dakshinachari or a Bamachari, a Sakta of the right or the left hand, or a Kowl, an extreme Sakta. If he was a Dakshinachari, a right-handed one, then his devotions would be comparatively conventional; if he was a Bamachari, a left-handed Sakta, then he might possibly use wine as an offering to the female organ of generation. A Kowl would engage, according to the book, in ceremonies of "a beastly character". The next day when I asked him which of the three he was, he only smiled.

Hardwar was swarming with sadhus. The Namadaris, the followers of Vishnu, had mud-packed cones of hair like the young man asleep under the bridge. On their foreheads they wore three vertical stripes, the centre one blood red the outer ones of white clay. They carried iron rods and little braziers of hot coals for kindling incense, and they wore long Chanel-like necklaces of black nuts. The Sivites also wore long necklaces of rudraksha seeds and their arms and foreheads were smeared with burned cow-dung. Some carried gongs; others carried conch-shells which they blew into, making a disagreeable high-pitched noise. Both sects handled this multiplicity of gear with the same assurance as an experienced party-goer who, equipped with wrap, handbag, cigarette-holder, lighter, vodka and tomato juice, still manages to take the offered canapé.

The female sadhus were less remarkable. They were mostly grey-haired, beardless, stout, and school-marmy. And there were American girls wearing holier-than-thou-expressions and an elegant parody of the sadhus' uniform, made from re-embroidered saffron silk organza, who were down for a day's shopping from one of the Ashrams at Rishikesh, with their Retina cameras at the ready.

In the temple of Gangadwara three priests were chanting Vedas before a stone lingam. They continued hour after hour, taking it in turns. Siva had been discovered in bed with his wife Durga by Brahma, Vishnu and other gods. He had been so drunk that he had not thought it necessary to stop. The majority, all except Vishnu and a few of the broader-minded, thought them nasty and brutish and said so. Siva and Durga died of shame in the position in which they were discovered; but before they expired Siva expressed the wish that mankind should worship the act manifest in the form which he now took to himself, the lingam. "All who worship me," he said, "in the form of lingam will attain the objects of their desire and a place in Kailasa!" Kailasa is the paradise of Siva, a 22,000-foot mountain in the Himalayas, north of the Manasa Lake in Tibet. Death for a Tibetan on the shore of the Manasa Sarowar is as meritorious as that on the banks of the Ganges for a Hindu.

"What is the water for?"

"Water to cool organ, because it is passionate", said one of the men from Shell.

"Water is in memory of water Siva had poured down his throat after drinking poison that would have destroyed the world," said G.

Our friend who had conducted us round the temples and who knew that I liked roses said nothing. Only Siva knew what he was thinking, but I was convinced that if he had chosen to do so he would have been the nearest of the lot to interpreting correctly the significance of the water and the lingam — perhaps there was no significance at all. In Hinduism, as in most other religions, there is a remarkable lack of unanimity amongst the devotees.

The temple of Daksheshwara at Kankhal, into which we were con-

ducted by a boy with no roof to his mouth, was under repair, and
the spire was enclosed in bamboo scaffolding. A sadhu sat outside on
the river front under an enormous pipal tree and on the bank of what
was now, at this season, a backwater of the Ganges, elderly pilgrims
were having the Ganga puja recited over their shaven heads.

This place was the scene of an ill-conceived sacrifice to Vishnu
offered by Daksha, a son of Brahma, to which Siva, Daksha's son-in-
law, was not invited. Uma the mountain goddess, Siva's wife, was so
enraged by this slight that she urged her husband to assert himself,
which he did, producing a monster called Vira-Bhadra from his
mouth. Vira-Bhadra had a thousand heads, eyes and limbs which
swung a thousand clubs. As if this was not enough he carried a fiery
bow and battle-axe, had a vast mouth that dripped blood and was
clothed in the skin of what must have been a very large tiger. When
Vira-Bhadra went into action the mountains tottered, the earth
trembled, the wind howled and the seas were whipped to foam. What
followed was like a Saturday night brawl in a saloon. Indra, the god
of the air, was trampled underfoot; Yama, the god of the dead, had
his staff broken; Saraswati, the river goddess and goddess of learning,
and the Matris, the divine mothers, had their noses removed; Pushan
the nourisher, multiplier and protector of cattle and possessions – also
the patron of conjurers – had his teeth rammed down his throat;
Mitra, the ruler of the day, had his eyes pulled out; Chandra, the
moon, was beaten; the hands of Vahni, the fire god, were cut off;
Bhrigu, one of the great sages, had his beard pulled out; the Brahmans
were pelted with stones; the sons of Brahma, the Praja-patis, were
soundly beaten; innumerable demi-gods were skewered with swords
and arrows, and Daksha's head was cut off and thrown on to the fire.
At the same time Sati consumed herself by spontaneous combustion.
When these pyrotechnic efforts had subsided and with it Siva's rage,
he restored everyone to life, even Daksha who emerged as good as
new except that he had the head of a goat, his own having been burnt
up. Only Sati was beyond recall.

It was pleasant by the river at Daksheshwara. In a quiet valley
behind the town, in a grove of dusty mango trees there was a small
temple with several outbuildings, skeleton structures without walls in
which the iron tridents of the sadhus stood, the three prongs of
which symbolise bodily, worldly and heavenly suffering, planted in
the still warm ashes of the fires of the previous night. It was as if the
occupants had just fled.

Higher up the valley, where it narrowed between sandstone cliffs,
a small stream came purling down. On one side protruding from the

cliff was a wooden construction with walls of wire mesh. Reluctantly, because it seemed a gross infringement of privacy, we crowded at the entrance. Inside there was a sadhu, a youngish man with a brown beard. He was preparing vegetables and putting them into a pot. His only visible possessions were a stone pillow, a pile of sacred books and a drinking vessel made from a huge black sea shell. "He is the Moni Babar", said our friend. "He never speaks." The sadhu looked at us for a moment with his great brown eyes before resuming his task and feeling ashamed and flattened we went away.

We spent the nights at Hardwar in a dharmsala on the river front, downstream from the great ghat. It was a rest-house for poor pilgrims, now, with the onset of winter, almost deserted. Originally, we had intended to stay in one of the hotels above the sacred ghat but although we were prepared for discomfort, the place was so repulsive that we all three shrank from it, leaving the proprietor genuinely perplexed. It was a labyrinth whose emptiness only accentuated the all-pervading air of decay. The walls of the corridors were covered with eruptions of dark green lichen, and the sheets on the beds bore the impress of former occupants. To me it was reminiscent of another, similar hotel, seen years before on the shores of the Bosphorus. It seemed to set at nothing all the pious works of purification we had witnessed and the efforts of the municipal authorities to make Hardwar a clean place, which on the whole it is.

Late each night we hammered on the huge carved double-doors, with the words *Dharmsala Bhata Bhawan-Der Ismail Khan* inscribed above them, the name of a pious family from Der Ismail Khan, a town west of the Indus in the former North-West Frontier Province, who had endowed it originally; until a small, sleepy boy of ten or eleven, who seemed to be in sole charge, opened them up and led us into the main court. The courtyard had cells on three sides of it for the accommodation of pilgrims and at the far end a pink-washed, fretted archway led down to a bathing ghat at the water's edge. Dark stair-cases led to other levels with more cells and to a platform which overlooked the river, furnished with rows of lavatories open to the sky. Up these stairs we lurched behind the small boy who, although he had a lantern, was always a flight ahead, bruising ourselves on the sharp angles where the stairs took a turn to the left and right. The two dimly-lit rooms which we occupied were bare except for a pair or charpoys — beds which were nothing more than a couple of wooden frames with a mattress of woven string. They were simple but they were clean.

In spite of the simplicity of the arrangements at the dharmsala, we contrived to make a shambles of them with open trunks and unstrapped bedding rolls, their contents half-disgorged, over all of which hung a stench of kerosene which boded ill for life in the more restricted space of a rowing-boat; but to us it seemed like paradise, and we blessed the Bhata Bhawan family of Der Ismail Khan and all their descendants for ever, for their beneficence and the kindness of the warden of the dharmsala who allowed us to stay there – for, although we were not bona fide pilgrims, it was completely without charge.

I was too tired and too excited to sleep much. Both nights I went out on to the platform above the river. It was very cold and clear and the moon was in the last quarter. It shone down on the waters which poured down past the ghat, like molten metal on an inclined plane. On either side of the dharmsala, so close that I felt that I could almost touch them, spires and pyramids of shrines and temples rose gleaming in the moonlight. On the other side of the gorge through which the river flowed, the continuation of the Siwalik hills rose in a dark wall. The only sounds apart from the rushing noise of the river, were those made by the night-watchmen in the narrow streets far below, alternately groaning, and blowing their whistles, as if to prove to themselves that they still existed, for no one else was about. In one cell of the dharmsala, behind a window of red glass, a light still burned. I, too, wondered whether I existed, standing here on a roof-top on the banks of the Ganges, as incongruous as a Hindu on a pier on the south coast of England in the dead season, to which the dharmsala bore a remarkable resemblance.

On the first night before he went to bed, G. said that he must have a ritual bathe the next morning.

"We can bathe, here from dharmsala," he said. "If you wish to come I am bathing at five-thirty."

It was impossible to sleep after five a.m. anyway because of the sounds made by the other guests who already, at this early hour, were clearing their throats and wringing their noses out in preparation for another day. There were not many of them, but they made up for their weakness in numbers by an incredible volume of sounds that resembled massed bands of double bass and trombones with an occasional terrifying eruption of noise that obliterated all the others, the sort of noise small boys make when pretending to cut one another's throats.

When I went to his room at five-thirty, G. had finished clearing his passages. He was doing his Yogic exercises, alternately sucking in huge gouts of air and then releasing them with a hissing noise like a gaggle of angry geese. Together we went down the staircase, across the court and under the archway to the ghat. The moon was down and it was very dark. All one could hear, standing on the steps, was the deep sighing of the river rushing past. It was bitterly cold. For some moments neither of us spoke.

"I think," G. said at last, "that at this moment I am not bathing. In such circumstances there can be danger to health."

Silently we crept up the stairs and back to bed.

When we rose again at seven, it was still very cold and we peeped round the front gate as apprehensively as mice. Wanda had decided to come with us. The sun had risen some ten minutes earlier but the streets were still in shadow and the wind whistled down them, raising little eddies of dust on the cobble-stones. The only other people who were up were two cha-wallahs, sitting by their smoking tea-engines on either side of the gateway, and we each drank a cup. It was hot, weak and milky and tasted of nutmegs. Then we set off up the road. It was a street of dharmsalas. Some of the more ancient ones with eyeless windows, protected by rusty iron gratings and doors bolted and barred and locked with corroded padlocks, seemed as if they were closed for ever, and one could imagine the interiors with room after shuttered room in which skeleton pilgrims slept for ever on charpoys of worm-eaten wood and rotting string; others dating back to the twenties were painted in faded blues. With their elephant-ine pilasters and heavy lintels they resembled the exhibition buildings at Wembley which I remembered as a child; while some, more modern still, were painted an indigestible *sang de boeuf*.

We groped our way through the bazaar, at this hour as dark as the grave. Most of the shops were still bolted and barred. Only the food merchants were preparing for opening time, heaping up great mounds of sugar and rice which glowed luminously through the murk. Then, suddenly, we emerged from the darkness on to the waterfront and into the light of the sun that was shooting up across the river, blinding the Sivite sadhus who squatted, coated in ashes, in the alcoves below the temple of Gangadwara, still warming themselves before the smouldering tree-trunks with which they had seen the night through. Here we turned inland, away from the river, and began to climb a steep path at the back of the town which led to the temple of Manasa-Devi.

At the temple, nearly 2,000 feet up, the air was gelid. G. asked the priest to recite the Lalita-sahasra-nama, the thousand names of Vishnu.*

---

* "A prayer or chant to attain the ultimate combined with great power (Sakti) ... The highest plane of consciousness in one's head" (Dr. C. Suryanarayanamurthy: *Braham-andapurana Commentary*; Madras, 1962). Lalita is another name for Lakshmi or Sri, the wife of Vishnu, used in the sense of "Mother".

"I do not know the Lalita-sahasra-nama", the priest said, equably and went back to his own protracted devotions.

"It's disgraceful," G. said. "He ought to know it. It's like priest in Church of England not knowing the Lord's Prayer."

Chapter Four

Down the Ganges

From the hills to Sookerthal on the Ganges, the navigation is restricted entirely to rafts of timber and to the passage of boats which, being built in the valley of Deyra, are with some difficulty and great danger floated, empty down the rapids.

Col. Sir T. Proby Cautley: *The Ganges Canal*, Vol. 1

A list of suggestive articles which are needed on the journey is given here but the pilgrims may have all or some of them as desired and needed.

Religious	*Cloths*	*Medicines*	*Utensiles*
Japalma	Rugs, Blanket	Amrutanjan	Canvas bucket
Agarbattis	Muffler	Smelling Salt	Cooker
Camphor	Dhavali or	Vaseline bottle	Oven
Dhup Powder	Silk Dhoti	J & J De Chane's	One set of
Kumkuma	Dhoties 2	Medical Service	stainless steel
Sandalwood	Shirts 4	set with its	vessels
Powder	Baniyans 2	guide book	Ladle
Wicks soaked in	Uppar	Homeopathic Box	Spoons—3
ghee and kundi	clothes 3	& a guide Booh	Fraid pan
Asanam	Towels 3	Diarrhoea Pills	Tiffin Carrier
Bhagavad Gita	Waterproff	Dysentery Pills	Tumbler
or any re-	cloth (2	Indigestion Pills	Glass
ligious book for	yards)	Malaria Pills	
daily use	Rotten cloth	Boric Powder	
Bhajan Songs or	(pieces 4)	Cotton	
Namavali	Coupeens 2	Cloth (Plaster)	
Sri Ramakoti	Cloth bag for	Bandage cloth	
Book	money to	Aspro Tablets	
	keep round	Purgative	
	waist	chacklets	
	Bedding	Tooth powder or	
	Mosquito	paste	
	Curtain		

Miscellaneous

Looking Glass and comb	Tongue Cleaner
Soaps for bath and wash	Suit case or hand jip bag
Nails of all sizes	Lock and chain
Locks 2	Pandari bag to carry things on
Cloth bags for food stuffs	shoulder
Pen knife	Safety pins
Small gunny bag for coal	Change for Rs. 10–00
Wrist Watch	Setuvu from Rameswaram
Umbrella	Ganges from Allahabad
Hand stick	Haridwar or Gangottari
Visiting Cards	Rail and Road Maps
List of departed souls	Battery light with spare
and their Gotras	Batteries
Hand bags 2	Thermos Flask
Note book	Hurricane Lamp
White Papers	Match box
Fountain pen and pencil	Calendar both Telugu and
Candles	English
Needles and thread	News Papers
Railway Guide	Ink bottles
Pilgrim's Travel Guide	Postage stamps and cards
A small hand axe	
Good Camera with flash	
Movie (Cene) Camera	

from *A Pilgrim's Travel Guide*

At six-fifteen the following morning we were at the bridge, ready to embark. A bitter wind was blowing and against a pink sky flights of teal and mallard were rocketing upstream towards the Hardwar gorge.

The boat was moored ready for us alongside one of the piers of the bridge on the upstream side and the current was grinding it against the stones, emphasising its tinniness. It was as full of holes as it had ever been and there were eight inches of water in the bottom. Because of its lightness it had somehow achieved a balance between floating and foundering; but if any further weight was imposed on it, it would certainly scuttle itself.

Of the crew whom we had interviewed the previous day, a pair of terrible ruffians with mops of greasy hair, there was no sign. We had told them to be ready to leave at six and we had arrived at a quarter past, hoping to start within an hour or so, this being the custom of the country, but now it was evident it did not matter at what time they arrived; there would be no sailing in this boat today or any other day.

We were prey to all the violent, unworthy emotions that have con-

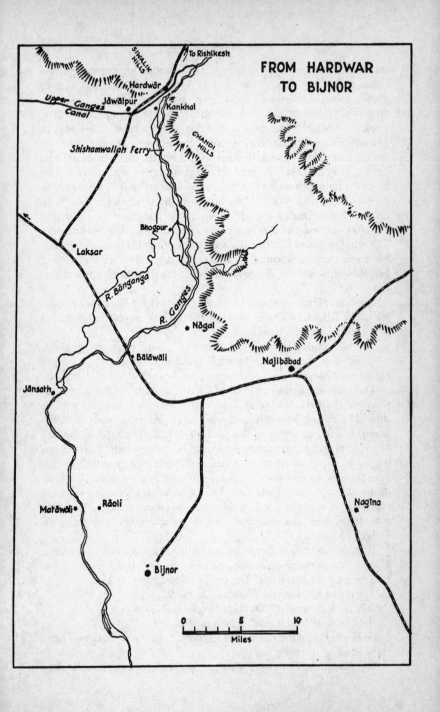

FROM HARDWAR
TO BIJNOR

SIWALIK HILLS

To Rishikesh

Hardwār

Jawālpur

Upper Ganges Canal

Kankhal

CHANDI HILLS

Shishamwallah Ferry

Bhogpur

Laksar

R. Banganga

R. Ganges

Nāgal

Balāwali

Najibābad

Jānsath

Matāwāli

Rāoli

Nagina

Bijnor

0   5   10
Miles

sumed visitors to India from time immemorial: impotent rage; the desire that Timur Leng, the terrible Tatar, knew and was able to gratify; to make hecatombs and raise great towers of skulls (he made a sanguinary detour to the banks of the Ganges in the Year of the Hare, 1399, and entered Hardwar and sacked it sometime at the end of January that year); but for us there was no such way to vent our spleen, except by allowing it to evaporate. For the inhabitants of India have a simple genius for concocting exasperating situations which, however long he may have lived in the country and however much he may have anticipated them, burst on the victim each time with pristine force. One of the pre-requisites of real exasperation is that there should be no one to vent one's anger on, and there was no one. The wind whistled through the reed walls of the bridge-builder's hut but there were no dormant figures inside it to rouse from sleep and galvanise into activity. We were alone on the river bank under a vast sky.

It was at this moment that G. announced that the Executive Engineer of the Irrigation Works, who had been away on our first morning in Hardwar, had come back.

"He has returned from Tour," he said. "Now he is giving us his boat. But first we are speaking with Assistant Engineer. He is feeling kindly towards us."

The Assistant Engineer lived in a bungalow that was almost completely shrouded in bougainvillaea. It was difficult to imagine why he should be feeling well-disposed towards us. After an interval he appeared in a dressing-gown. The patience of Indian Officials in the face of requests that must appear to them to be either lunatic or frivolous has to be experienced to be credible. What we were doing in this instance was the equivalent in Britain of waking a fairly senior officer of the Metropolitan Water Board at a quarter to seven on a winter's morning, in order to ask him to wake a yet more senior official and request the loan of a boat from one of the reservoirs in order to go down to Southend.

"I think Executive Engineer is lending you one boat," he said, when he explained the situation to him and he called the Executive Engineer on his telephone. The conversation was very brief.

"He is not lending you his boat," he said.

"We must now visit Executive Engineer," G. said.

"But he's just said he isn't going to lend it."

"Yes, yes," said the Assistant Engineer. "Now you must visit him. He is lending you his boat."

The Executive Engineer, who was in even greater déshabillé than his assistant, lived in a vast building close by the headworks of the Canal.

"I have no boat," he said without preamble.

"You have two boats."

"I am needing two boats. I have no boat that I can spare."

We showed him a letter from the Prime Minister. In Delhi it had had all the magic of a pre-war British passport. "We, Edward Frederick Lindley, Viscount Halifax, Baron Irwin, Knight of the Most Noble Order of the Garter, a Member of His Majesty's Most Honourable Privy Council, Knight Grand Commander of the Most Exalted Order of the Star of India, Knight Grand Commander of the Most Eminent Order of the Indian Empire etc., etc., etc., His Majesty's Principal Secretary of State for Foreign Affairs, Request and require . . ." Here, in the sticks, the impact was visibly diminished.

"You must go to Delhi," he said, brightening momentarily. "The Prime Minister is in Delhi."

"We have just come from Delhi. He is in good health. We spent some time with him." This last tossed in carelessly.

"Then you must go to Roorkee. At Roorkee there is Army Bridging Unit. They have many boats. It is only 30 miles."

For what seemed ages the fruitless conversation butted backwards and forwards.

Finally, Wanda had a brilliant idea. She has developed a great capacity for overcoming disaster. Not that she has ever been without it.

"You have two boats," she said. "It is obvious from what you say that you must be having two boats" (effortlessly she slipped into the vernacular). "There is a boat in the river by the bridge which although unsuitable for a long journey is excellent for your canal. Lend us your boat and if you need two boats during the next two days use that one."

Only in India could such an illogical argument have had any chance of acceptance. The boat that Wanda was offering the Executive Engineer was not even hers to offer. I tried to picture the scene in which the Executive Engineer tried to borrow the Contractor's boat, and having succeeded, watched it sink in the canal. But suddenly he capitulated. Perhaps because he was even more alarmed by G.'s suggestion that he should close down the Upper Ganges Canal and divert its waters into the river, thereby allowing us to rush headlong downstream in a boat of really large draught.

The boat had most probably been built in the time of the British. Perhaps the prototype had been designed in a moment of nostalgia by an engineer who was an exiled rowing man. It was a five-oared skiff fitted with swivel rowlocks. It resembled what used to be known as a ran-dan, only in a ran-dan bow and stroke have oars and two uses sculls, and this was even larger. A few rare examples of ran-dan are or were employed until recently at the two Universities for conveying dons about their occasions and they are still used on the Thames by swan-uppers; but instead of being built of varnished mahogany this boat was constructed from mild steel plate put together with rivets. It was twenty-five feet long, had a five-foot beam and to show its official status it was painted battleship grey. Loaded it drew eighteen inches; and it needed thirty-two men to lift it.

We set off down the Ganges at two o'clock in the afternoon. It was 6th December, my forty-fourth birthday. Our immediate destination was the Balawali Bridge, twenty-five miles as the crow flies from Hardwar, a journey which we believed would take two days. The boat was deep-loaded, so deeply and with such a quantity of gear that only three of the five oarsmen's benches could be occupied. Besides the six occupants (we had recruited two more boatmen and the Irrigation Engineer had sent one of his own men to ensure that his boat was not misused) there was the now augmented luggage, plus further purchases we had made in the bazaar at Hardwar; sacks of chilli powder and vegetables; namdars — blankets made from a sort of coarse felt; teapots, kettles, hurricane lamps and reed mats. I had even bought an immense bamboo pole from a specialist shop in the bazaar as a defence against dacoits (robbers) whose supposed whereabouts were indicated on some rather depressing maps which G. had annotated with this and similar information, in the same way as mediaeval cartographers had inscribed "Here be dragons" on the blank expanses of their productions. G. himself had made an even more eccentric purchase from the same establishment — two officer's swagger-canes about a foot and a half long which now, as he stood in the middle of the boat directing its final trimming with them, made him look like an old-fashioned sailor semaphoring. Our bills were paid. We had left a hundred rupees for a lorry-man to come to collect the boat downstream. Prudently we had put this into the hands of the men from Shell who by this time, together with the one who had told me that I had liked roses, were the only people we trusted. We had paid the thirty-two men who had come tottering barefooted across a mile of hot shingle with the boat upside over their heads all the way from the Canal to the Ganges; we had shaken hands with everybody — some, whom we had never seen before, had wept; and for the second time in two days we had advanced money to boatmen for them to buy provisions for the journey (we never saw the first two boatmen again). We were ready to go.

As we crouched low in the boat while the current took us under the bridge, an old bridge-builder who was wearing spectacles as large as the headlamps of a Rolls Royce, dropped sacred sweets on us as a provision for the journey. His tears wetted our heads. The boatmen put their oars in the rowlocks and rowed off smartly. We were off.

Two hundred yards below the bridge and some twelve hundred miles from the Bay of Bengal the boat grounded in sixteen inches of water. This was no shoal. There was no question of being in the wrong channel. At this point the uniform depth of the river was sixteen inches. I looked upstream to the bridge but all those who had been waving and weeping had studiously turned their backs. The boatmen uttered despairing cries for assistance but the men at the bridge bent to their tasks with unwonted diligence. As far as they were concerned we had passed out of their lives. We might never have existed.

We all got out, including Wanda, who was wearing an ingenious Muslim outfit which consisted of peg-top trousers of white lawn and a hieratical-looking shift. She simply took off her trousers and joined us, still apparently fully dressed, in the water.

The bottom of the river was full of rocks the size of twenty-four-pound cannon balls which were covered with a thin slime of green weed. The water was absolutely clear. It frothed and bubbled about our calves. Fifty yards below the place where we had gone aground, the shallows terminated in a waterfall down which the river cascaded. We began to dig a passage towards it with our hands, lifting the great slimy stones and plonking them down on either side of the boat. Under them were more stones of equal size and even greater slipperiness.

It is difficult to describe the emotions that one feels when one is aground on a twelve-hundred-mile boat journey within hailing distance of one's point of departure. It is an experience that has fallen to the lot of some blue-water sailors who have grounded when setting off to sail round the world. But about them there was something of tragedy which derived from the grandeur of the design. To be stranded in a river sixteen inches deep is simply ludicrous.

At the head of the fall to which we finally succeeded in dragging the boat, it became stuck with its forepart hanging over the drop. It would go neither backwards nor forwards, but suddenly as we redoubled our efforts it overbalanced and began to go downhill at a tremendous rate with everyone sprawling over the gunwales, vainly trying to get aboard.

The only one who succeeded was Karam Chand, the chief boatman, the young man who had been let to us by the Executive Engineer, to ensure that he got his boat back in one piece — at this moment it seemed a faint hope. Fortunately he managed to take the tiller, otherwise it would have broached-to and probably capsized. The rest of us were half in and half out of the boat.

It was like descending an escalator on one's back. The noise made by the boat as it bounced from boulder to boulder was terrifying. Finally it plopped into a deep pool, watched by a little band of country people who stood high above us on a concrete spur, part of the out-works of the canal.

It was a lovely day. Overhead, infinitely remote in a pale blue sky, streamers of cirrus were being blown to tatters in a wind that was coming off the deserts of Central Asia. On the left, a small solitary white temple winked in the sunlight. Below it there were terraces and silvery-looking cliffs of sandstone and at the foot of them where the jungle broke in a green sea the light shimmered and danced in a haze of heat. On the river itself the wind tore at the surface of the water, throwing up little arcs of spray which formed rainbows against the sun. There was the pleasing sound of rushing water as the Ganges poured down eagerly over the stones in innumerable small rivulets on its journey towards the Bay of Bengal. It was travelling much faster than we were. It had taken us three-quarters of an hour to cover three hundred yards.

In the next hour we covered eight hundred yards. The pool in which the boat floated, apparently undamaged, opened out and seemed to give promise of becoming a navigable reach. Ahead of us a man came down to the shore from the jungle, picking his way delicately among the stones. He wore a long sleeved white shirt and its whiteness gave him the appearance of being disembodied. Only his dark head and spindly limbs showed. On his back he carried a raft made from orange-coloured gourds. He placed it in the river, spread-eagled himself on top of it and began to paddle some distance downstream and set off towards the right bank which was invisible from where we were deep in the bed of the river. The sight of this man gave us hopes that we might be coming to deep water, but they were vain ones. Soon the grumbling, bumping noises began again and once more we were aground and over the side, pushing the boat, slithering from rock to rock, watched by cows which stood at the water's edge, sticking out their thick, pink tongues at us and lowing derisively.

We excavated another channel, a hundred yards long, and another of fifty; both were followed by rapids. By now there was a lot of water in the bottom of the boat but there was so much gear on board that it was impossible to tell whether the hull was holed or not. To the right a mile or so away, the spires of the Temple of Daksheshwara, the scene of Siva's godly brawl in the suburbs of Hardwar, rose against the evening sun, mocking us with their nearness. It was four o'clock.

The next hour was a duplication of what had gone before, except that the rocks on which we slipped and slithered grew larger and more difficult to lift and more painful to stand on. At five we rumbled down into a deliciously calm stretch of water in which the stream ran sluggishly. Here a bridge was being built, a twin of the one upstream. A country boat was crossing piled high with shisham wood from the jungle, and on top of it were perched the woodcutters themselves, bundles of off-white rags, more like scarecrows than human beings. This was the Shishamwallah* ferry. This reach was succeeded by a brutal stretch of shoal water in which the stones stuck up like fangs and which ended in a waterfall over which the boat hung, immovable, threatening to break in two. By the time we had negotiated this obstacle the sun was setting and it was time to make camp. I was in favour of stopping, as one place seemed as good as another, but an insane urge to press on seized the rest of the party. "If we are to reach the Balawali Bridge in two days it is necessary to go on," G. said, and when Karam Chand added his voice it was useless to argue. Perhaps they were goaded by the sight of the Temple of Daksheshwara which, by some cruel twist of the river, seemed far closer than it had an hour and a half previously.

The sky was now a brilliant saffron. On the stony shore, trees that had been brought down by the river in flood and stripped of their bark on the way, gleamed in the last of the light which was draining away rapidly. Myriads of winged insects swarmed about the boat, attracted by the light of the torches that were being wielded improvidently as we flashed them into the water searching for a navigable channel. As instruments of navigation our eyes were now useless to us; the water reflected the last light in the sky and its depth could only be determined with the aid of torches and poles or simply by getting out and standing in it.

Now the boat became immovably stuck. It was as if it were glued to the bottom. With infinite difficulty, swearing in a variety of languages, we unloaded the luggage piece by piece: the huge tin trunks, the great bouncy bedding rolls, the stove and the cans of

* Shisham: Dalbergia Sissou

kerosene, together with the boatmen's modest gear, and started to drag the boat to the head of the next fall, leaving Wanda to guard the luggage alone on the foreshore, with only a torch to defend herself from the beasts of the jungle which here loomed above her like the Wild Wood.

The rapid was more than four hundred yards long, and the last we saw of her as we shot downhill was a despairing figure dressed in a jungle hat, a leaving present from a Major-General in Delhi, and a bathing costume, scrabbling for warm clothes in one of the tin trunks, haloed by a swarm of insects that had been attracted to her by the light of the torch.

There was a further interminably long delay while we returned upstream on foot to make a portage of the luggage. While we were lugging the trunks over the stones I wondered how much more of this treatment the boat could stand without being irreparably damaged. The thought of being marooned here, almost within sight of the places from which we had set off, with a piece of Indian Government property with its bottom torn out, which had been lent to us under duress, was more than I could bear to contemplate.

It was now quite dark and very cold. Shivering, we poled across to the right side of the stream, for we were all unanimous about not wanting to sleep on the edge of the jungle, and edged the boat in as close as possible to the shore. The water was so shallow that there was still a gap of several yards between the boat and the beach when it finally grounded and the unloading of the gear we needed for the night was a miserable, cold business. By good fortune there were two small patches of sand among the stones and on these we made our camp. The boatmen disappeared, in order, so they said, to look for firewood. I would not have been surprised if they had not returned. But they did, dragging with them one of the barkless trees. Soon a big fire was going and we made strong, sweet tea for everyone.

Now Wanda began to cook rice, watched by the boatmen who squatted round the fire smoking the vile cigarettes called bidis and sipping tea from a pannikin. They seemed to be in no hurry to prepare their evening meal.

Finally, embarrassed by their unblinking gaze, she asked G. when they were proposing to start cooking.

"They are not eating," he said.

"Why not?"

"They are not eating because they have no food."

"But they were given money to buy it. You gave it to them."

"They are saying that there was no time to buy it."

"Well, what are they going to do?"

"Now they are awaiting your instructions."

"Can't they get some from a village?"

"Now I am asking them."

An animated conversation ensued.

"They have never been so far from their homes before. If there is a village they do not know it. They know nothing. It is difficult for me to understand these fellows," G. said.

We were in a fix, really the last of a succession of fixes, but the overcoming of insuperable difficulties is, of course, one of the unspoken reasons for travelling in remote places. Nevertheless it was a bore. We had anticipated living simply, and purposely we had brought with us simple things, for there is nothing more disagreeable than eating copiously in the presence of people to whom a square meal is an unknown pleasure. Now the whole lot of us were faced with the possibility of being without any food at all if the journey to the Balawali Bridge was unduly prolonged, for this was the nearest point at which we could be certain of getting any. We had bought what seemed a lot of rice in Hardwar, but not enough to feed everyone. We had chilli powder, sugar, tea, biscuits, a few tins of sardines and some Indian tinned meats. I was determined that we should not have recourse to the tinned meats unless we were forced to. Although there are numerous secret cow-eaters and a host of overt pig-eaters in India, the mere possession of tinned beef and bacon was enough to label us as cannibals so far as the Hindus were concerned, and as unmitigatedly filthy persons to any orthodox Muslim. To tell the truth, I was far less worried about the stigma that attached to its consumption than I was about the possible indignities to which it might have been subjected in the course of its preparation. Both beef and pork, according to the labels on the tins, emanated from the same factory. It was difficult to imagine any Indian sufficiently debased to can beef and bacon indiscriminately; it was equally difficult to imagine Hindus and Muslims both working under the same roof, each, in one another's eyes, committing sacrilege. Did they, I wondered, have separate production lines or did they spit ritually in each tin before sealing it, in order to square themselves with their respective gods? But these were useless speculations. The boatmen had worked well, all three of them. There was nothing to do but give them food and hope that something would turn up.

Among our stores was a bottle of Indian whisky and a bottle of rum, which we had procured from Jawalapur, the place which the guide book referred to as being infested with thieves and pickpockets. It seemed as good a moment as any for a drink, but with only two bottles between three of us, in a land be-devilled by prohibition, either partial or complete according to where one found oneself, and no prospect of being able to buy any more, I jibbed at sharing it with the boatmen.

"We don't have to give them drinks as well, do we?"

"Certainly not," G. said. "These men are not drinking. It is against their religion."

A special journey had had to be made by bicycle ricksha in order to buy these two bottles. Because it was outside the sacred area, two miles away on the banks of the Ganges Canal, Jawalapur was the place of pilgrimage for those in search of forbidden pleasures. This was the rendezvous of secret drinkers, eaters of fish and fowl, eggs and meat; while across the canal in a sad area of mud-filled lanes and mean brick buildings were the stews to which the pandas came to stretch themselves after long hours of squatting on their wooden plat-forms, puja-chanting, casting horoscopes and making the tilak marks on the foreheads of the faithful.

The place was a great hive of whores. It was late afternoon when we arrived and they were just beginning to stir after the long sleep of the day. Bleary-eyed, the older ones leaned against the door posts in narrow alleys choked with sewage, babies at their slack breasts, while bigger daughters still too young to be broken to the trade, wearing frilly western dresses and with their hair in red ribbons, peeped round their skirts; others, younger women, crouched in door-ways that were so low that they were more like entrances to a rock tomb than to a brothel, smoking cigarettes, and one could imagine the clients, emerging in the early dawn, half stupefied with hemp, hurting themselves dreadfully. Some were as stern and forbidding as the Goddess of Destruction herself, with long thin downturned mouths. Some had the broken-looking snub noses and the slightly bulbous foreheads that seem to be universally esteemed by men. All were heavily bangled; jewels shone in their noses, their eyes were set in black rings of shadow that proclaimed an intense fatigue. One needed courage to lie with women like this, to put out of mind the awful smells in the lanes; to banish the thought of their mothers and grandmothers who hovered behind them, too old for further service and an earnest of what they themselves would one day become, and of their husbands/keepers/fathers, whatever they were, still snoring, stretched out on charpoys under the washing that hung lifelessly in the airless courts, but they were in no real mood for business, and those that were offered their services without enthusiasm. In a little while they would begin to prepare themselves for the night's work, but this was their quiet hour and they were making the most of it.

Wanda put on a lot more rice to cook, gave Karam Chand a wooden spoon and left him in charge of it. Then the three of us paddled out to the boat. Hidden from view behind the open lid of one of the trunks, as surreptitiously as any panda, we drank whisky that had been distilled with the aid of Scottish technicians, using Indian ingredients and Indian water.

At dinner we ate a mountain of boiled rice, heaped with chilli powder. In addition the three of us shared a tin of sardines and some slices of rather nasty cut loaf. We had difficulty with the sardines as there was no opener. Later, as we crouched round a gigantic fire that the boatmen had kindled I had the first real opportunity of observing them as individuals. Karam Chand, their leader, was about twenty years old. He was thin and intelligent-looking. He had shown himself an excellent navigator when there had been any water to navigate. The other two had more primitive countenances which, in the case of the elder one, Bhosla, verged on brutality. Jagannath, the youngest, was more animated. From time to time our eyes met, and I wondered what their feelings were, these men who had never left their native place, embarked on a crazy journey with no avowed purpose and now marooned with three foreigners (for them G. was as foreign as any of us) on a bank of stones in the middle of the Ganges. My heart, made mellow by whisky, warmed to them.

While the three of us were drinking more tea and smoking Trichinopoly cheroots, two men appeared and stood at the edge of the fire. They had been overtaken by night while in the jungle, they said, and had come to recruit their spirits by the fire before setting off for their village which was a couple of miles to the west. We gave them tea and cigarettes and, after ascertaining that we were outside the sacred area of Hardwar, ordered a dozen eggs from them to be delivered early the next morning.

We slept close to the fire cocooned in our bedding rolls, buoyed up by the rubber mattresses which we had cursed because they were so cumbersome. Before we went to bed, shamed by the inadequate coverings that the boatmen had brought with them, we gave each of them one of the blankets we had bought in the bazaar; but they were not in the mood for sleep and they remained hour after hour droning on about new masters while I lay listening to the sound of goods trains concertina-ing in the sidings at Hardwar and the water rippling over the pebbles. Overhead the sky was a great blanket filled with innumerable holes through which shone innumerable stars. To the north the lights of the town loomed above the mist that hung low over the plain.

At six o'clock the next morning the sky to the east began to glow. Soon it was fierce red. It was as if someone was stoking a furnace. Against it the Siwalik hills undulated away to the east-south-east as far as the eye could see, like a giant switchback. Flight after flight of duck streamed up the river towards the north. Across the water the stranded trees were like sea monsters hauled out on the shore.

Then the sun rose over the Plains. Three spotted deer came out of the jungle which was still in deep shadow and crossed the river towards us, while a fourth emerged from a belt of long grass that fringed one of the tree-clad islands a quarter of a mile downstream. Seeing us it remained motionless until we got up to look at it. Then it took fright and went off together with the others. The nearness of the temples on either side of the Ganges gorge showed us how far we had really come. One of the two men whom we had met the previous evening arrived with the eggs but it was too late. We had already eaten our breakfast.

Chapter Five

Through the Bhabar

For a considerable distance below Hardwar the bed of the Ganges is composed of boulders ... The stream has a far from stable course ...
District Gazetteers of the United Province, Vol. III, Saharanpur;
Allahabad, 1909

We set off at nine o'clock. It was hopelessly late but it is always like this at the beginning of a journey. Even when we had bailed the boat dry, and carried out an anxious inspection of the plates and rivets and loaded it up again, there never seemed to be a quorum for the actual departure. Apart from some dents that showed through on the inside as large, ominous swellings, the hull seemed sound enough. Whether or not it was capable of enduring another day of similar battering was another matter.

Although at this point the Ganges was about seventy feet wide, it was still not more than twenty inches deep; but the pebbles which were covered with weed of a greenish-bronze colour seemed smaller and, foolishly, thinking that they would soon vanish altogether, we congratulated ourselves on having done so well.

As soon as we set off we went aground. This was a bad patch. There were three rapids one above the other, each preceded by its own dreary shoal through which we manhandled the boat swearing monotonously. Half way down the third rapid, a fast exciting ride, we hit a large rock head on; the stern reared in the air, a bedding roll went over the side and was rescued by Jagannath as it started to go downstream; the boat broached-to; the gunwales went under and it began to fill with water. We slithered out, righted it, pulled the head round and went down the rest of the way with our stomachs on the gunwales and our feet dragging on the bottom; ending up as we always did in a deep, calm pool of cold water; this time in the lee of an island under a high steep bank of silt and sand to the edge of which a number of stunted trees clung by the last of their roots.

We were in the tract called the Bhabar (the porous place). Here the torrents from the Siwaliks lost their steepness and flattened out, depositing the rocks and boulders which had been making life such hell for us ever since we set off. All the time, on its passage through the Bhabar, the Ganges, already enfeebled by the loss of the vast quantities of water that were drawn from it into the Upper Ganges Canal, was being deprived of even more of its strength as a proportion of it sank into the dry limestone and percolated away. Somewhere further downstream, the water would emerge again to give fresh impetus to the river, but we needed it here and now. With the onset of winter and the dry season the water coming down from the Himalayas was diminishing rapidly. Each day the level of the river fell an inch or more. In a week's time there would be no water at all in some stretches we had passed through. We were engaged in a race with a dying river which threatened to leave us high and dry, a race which we might have lost without knowing it.

At the end of a short reach in which we were able to use the oars, we went aground in a place where the stream divided itself into three parts. All were equally uninviting. They all began with waterfalls; none gave any indication of which was the principal one, or, whether it bore any relation to the others. It was a problem that from now on was to be with us constantly.

For the purpose of navigation the map was useless. The scale was a quarter inch to the mile. The original survey had been made in 1917 by the Survey of India, and it had been published in 1924 with corrections up to 1950 but only so far as roads, railways, tramways, canals, car tracks and tube wells were concerned. "The course of the Ganges River is liable to continual change owing to the shifting of the river bed," a note on the map stated. Because of the fighting with China the Indian Defence Regulations were so stringent that it was impossible to buy a large-scale map of any kind in India — I had brought this one with me from England. We could scarcely be accused of being unprepared but for all we knew the right hand channel might be the Banganga, another river altogether. There was no way of knowing. The jungle on the left bank which up to now had extended to the water's edge had receded and was invisible as was the bank itself; the right bank was equally so. We were somewhere in the middle.

The Banganga is really a backwater of the Ganges; it is said that in ancient times it may have been its bed. Completely unfordable in the rains, it takes off from the parent stream about four miles south of Kankhal on the right bank — we were still not more than four miles from the temple of Daksheshwara — and from this point meanders inconsequentially through the Khadir, the lowland of Saharanpur, in which the principal crop is unirrigated wheat, and through wastes of sand, savannahs of tall grass and marshland before rejoining the

Ganges some thirty miles downstream, in the district of Muzaffar-nagar, during which it covers at least three times this distance. If we ended up in the Banganga, which at this season must have already reached a point nearing extinction, it would take more than the thirty-two men whom we had employed at Hardwar to carry the boat from the Canal to the Ganges to put us on our way again.

The Ganges Canal was the brain-child of Captain Proby Cautley of the Bengal Engineers. He was convinced that it was possible to get water out of the Ganges and into the Doab*, the land between the Jumna and the Ganges, an immense area which suffered from frequent and terrible famines. He made his first survey in 1836.

Every kind of difficulty had to be overcome: orders and counter-orders came from the authorities, civil and military, in bewildering succession. One moment it was to be an irrigation canal, next for navigation only. Then it was not to be built at all; notwithstanding the fact that the East Jumna Canal which had originally been built by the Mughals in the eighteenth century had been extremely successful in combating famine in the country which it passed through. It was said that earthquakes would destroy the viaducts, that miasmas would hang over the irrigated land, that malaria would become rife and that the navigation of the Ganges would be affected. (The last objection was the only one that proved to be right.)

The builders laboured under the most fearful difficulties. Rain destroyed the brick kilns and the unbaked bricks along the whole line of works. Often the wooden pins which marked the alignments on which the excavations had to be made were knocked down by cattle or else stolen by the local inhabitants. There were also the problems of working so far from the base at Calcutta, 1,000 miles away. There was no railway in those days. It was found, for instance, that the steam engine which had to be sent to them at Roorkee had been manufactured the wrong way round for the building into which it was intended to fit.

Nevertheless, twelve years after its commencement the Ganges was finally admitted into the canal at Hardwar in April 1854. It was still some time before it was finally finished but when it was it watered the whole tract between the Jumna and the Ganges, bestriding it like a colossus extending to Etawah on the Jumna, and to Kanpur on the Ganges 350 miles downstream. By the eighties it had been extended as far as Allahabad and the irrigation of the Doab was complete. Its completion marked the end of serious famine in the region.

*

* Doab: literally, two waters, the land between any two rivers.

There was only one person to ask the way from, an old man sitting alone on the shingle, but he was not very helpful. "I don't know where I am," he said. "Nor have I heard of the Banganga."

It was Karam Chand who discovered the proper channel; rather he divined which was the correct one.

"Sahib," he said. "This is the way of Ganga." None of us believed him; but fortunately we decided to take his advice.

Once more we started our miserable excavations and once more, having reached the head of the fall, we tipped over it and roared down-hill watched by the old man, the solitary spectator, who had moved down to the foot of it and was squatting there, happily anticipating disaster, in much the same way as an inhabitant of an outer suburb who takes his ease on a bench at a dangerous corner on a warm August afternoon.

But this was only the beginning. At the bottom there was yet another fork. Here, however, the choice was a simple one. A pro-longed reconaissance showed that the two streams joined again a mile lower down. It was only a question of which was the least disagree-able. The one on the right had four separate waterfalls; the one on the left had three. The difficulty lay in the approaches. There was not enough water in either to float a cork, let alone a twenty-five-foot boat, drawing eighteen inches of water, and it lay on the stones as incongruous as a rowing-boat on a gravel drive after a sharp shower of rain.

Far away to the right, four men appeared and began to fish using weighted nets. G. set off to interview them. We saw him flourishing one of his swagger-sticks at them; then we saw them turn their backs on him and take up their nets and make off.

"These men are not knowing anything," he said when he returned. "And, what is more, they are not helping us."

"You might have got some fish," I said — tempers were becoming frayed.

"They were catching fish," G. said sadly. "They were catching Rahu but they were not giving me any."

The boatmen set off in search of a village, a temporary place in-habited only during the dry season, which the fishermen had told G. existed not far off, where they hoped to buy food and get help. We waited for them to return and time, which we were in the process of learning to disregard, ceased to have any meaning at all. A black and white pied kingfisher with a beak shaped like the pick of an ice-axe and equally deadly, hovered motionless over what little water there was. Occasionally it hurled itself into it with its wings tight against its body, emerging with something which might have been a small fish or a tadpole which it walloped savagely on a stone in order to make it more digestible, before swallowing it. High overhead bar-headed geese flew purposefully in long, undulating ribbons wing-tip-to-wing-tip on their way to some distant feeding-ground.

Eventually the boatmen returned. Although they had phrased it differently the villagers had given the same reply to their requests for assistance that the fishermen had given to G.

"We spoke to them for some time," said Karam Chand. "Huzoor, all that they would say was that their work was not with water."

Both he and the others had also failed to get any food; whether by accident or design it was impossible to say.

We removed all the baggage from the boat and stripped it of everything we could; the rudder, the oars, the bottom gratings, and the stretchers. Without all these things it was still immovable. Our only hope lay in recruiting extra help but there was no one to give it.

We started to carry the gear a mile downstream to the place where the falls ended, through wastes of sand and stones that were now so hot that it was impossible to remain standing on them barefooted without dancing up and down. Bent under the weight of tin chests, oars and gratings, with hurricane lanterns held improbably in the crooks of our arms, we resembled the survivors of a shipwreck on the coast of Namaqualand, all except Wanda who, wearing a bathing costume of Helanca yarn, high wellington boots and her General's hat on top of which she balanced a tin full of kerosene, was a fantastic figure, more like a drum-majorette in some Middle Western town than a memsahib on a serious excursion, and the boatmen regarded her with awe.

Suddenly, by the kind of miracle which all true travellers regard as inevitable and almost unworthy of remark, three men appeared. They were on their way to cut wood in the jungle, but when we asked them for help they said, as the others had, that their work was not with water. Nevertheless we pressed them into our service at a colossal wage of two rupees a head and although they were poor, emaciated, gentle creatures, with their unwilling help the boat began to move over the stones, making a noise like an old tram.

But it was only for a short while. At first the air resounded with encouraging cries. *"Challo!"* (Oh, move!); *"Shabash!"* (Well done!); *"Aur thora!"* (A little more!) but in the face of the almost overwhelming difficulty of the operation, the noises soon died away and our efforts were concerted by a succession of unintelligible grunts. I could think of nothing but my bare feet, which, as I pressed them down on one rounded stone after another, felt as if they had been bastinadoed. I only possessed two pairs of shoes, one for social occasions and one for walking. The size and shape of my feet made it certain that, unless I was able to remain in one place long enough to have them made-to-measure, I would never find another pair however long I remained in India. I was very reluctant to ruin my shoes by using them underwater, but in the course of the next hour I was forced to put them on, for it took an hour to get the boat to the top of the fall. Even then it was not just a question of leaping into it or holding the gunwales and careering down as it had been previously. The water was too shallow. It was not until the boat was part way down the second rapid that it suddenly floated. It now gained such a momentum that it shot right through a large pool, over the top of the third fall and down it into a beautiful open reach. We had managed to transport some of the gear from the boat this far, but the rest was spread out in small dumps over a mile of beach, dropped at the whim of whoever had been carrying it, and while Wanda boiled the kettle for tea we went back to retrieve it.

We drank our tea and set off again. We were very tired. It was a beautiful river; but it was destroying us. Almost at once we heard the sound of more rapids. To our diseased imaginations they sounded like the Victoria Falls. We were hungry now. It was three o'clock. Since breakfast, a thin meal, we had eaten nothing except some hot, white radishes that Wanda had produced artfully from a mysterious-looking bag. Now she began to cook in a space which she cleared for herself in the bottom of the boat and when we finally came to the next rapids she refused to be off-loaded and separated from the stove. "If I stop cooking now we'll never eat," she mumbled doggedly.

But this time there was no need for any of us to get out. There was a superabundance of water in these rapids and we went down at a terrific rate, clasping the seething cooking pots as if they were sacred relics. Safe at last we stopped to eat alongside an island that rose steeply out of the river. The water had cut away the banks, exposing stratas of smooth oval stones embedded layer on layer in the silt, like the flint wall of an old English house. The island was thickly wooded with shisham trees whose trunks and lower branches were closely wrapped with band upon band of coarse grass brought down by the flood waters and bleached white by the sun. It gave them a strange surrealistic appearance as if they had been bandaged. It was a sinister place; even the sandbanks in the river which had now begun to supplant the shingle seemed to float on its surface, and although I tried to rid myself of the image they reminded me of the bodies of long-dead, bloated animals that had lost their hair.

We set off again at four, and immediately, conforming to a ritual to which we had long become accustomed, came to another fall. These were the longest, most hazardous rapids we had so far encountered; but fortunately we did not know this. With the last dreary portage behind us we had hoped that we had turned the corner, crossed the high pass. Certainly the character of the river was changing. Boulders had become stones and now, where previously there had been shingle on the bottom of the river, there was sand with chips of mica in it that glittered in the afternoon sun.

There was no difficulty about entering these rapids. The top end was like the mouth of a large funnel. Into it the water was being sucked with a singularly powerful motion which gave the surface an oily appearance. For a moment the boat remained almost stationary at the top; the next moment it was thundering downhill. There was barely time to ship the oars. The channel was not more than a dozen feet from side to side, but in it the current was running between steep banks of gravel which accentuated the feeling of speed. As we went down a cloud of small white birds enveloped the boat uttering indignant cries. It was terrifying but at the same time it was wonderful. It was as I had always imagined the descent of the Cresta Run on a bob sleigh. High in the stern, Karam Chand was grasping the tiller with both hands and uttering cries of exultation. The two boatmen, Bhosla and Jagannath, were leaning on the bedding rolls ecstatically chanting something that sounded like a triumphal hymn. Wanda, as devoted as the boy on the burning deck, was grimly trying to finish the washing-up. G. was in the bows, at look-out. It was a superfluous office. We swept on. We were all set for a spectacular disaster.

It came. The water ahead was curling back on itself. Under it there was something dark. G. uttered a despairing cry of warning, but it was too late. There was a tremendous crash as we hit the rock and everyone was thrown forward on their faces. Cooking pots erupted from the bottom of the boat. It reared in the air; Jagannath, the young boatman with the moustache, shot clean out of it, presumably into the water. At this moment, irrationally, Wanda could be heard asking to be put ashore. It was like an old print of a whale-boat with a whale surfacing underneath it. But there was no time to worry about Jagannath, even if we had wanted to. The bows came down again on the water with a resounding smack and now we were approaching the bottom of the fall at an appalling rate. At the bottom there was a bend so sharp that it gave the impression of being a dead end. It was, in fact, a right-angled bend with a twelve-foot-high bank of sand and shingle across the bottom of it, but there was nothing anyone could do about avoiding it. Karam Chand had as much chance of turning the head of the boat from its course as the driver of an express train who sees the gates of a level crossing closed against him. The boat simply ignored his efforts at the helm. It cut straight across the right angle of the turn and buried its head with enormous force in the sand and shingle which exploded about our heads like shrapnel. For the second time we were thrown on our faces, then the current took hold of the stern and slewed the boat round so that it lay across it, with its starboard under water. For a moment I thought it was going to capsize, but the bows broke loose from the bank and it began to gather way and shot stern first into deep, comparatively still water. We had made it, and so had Jagannath who came limping down the bank towards us. In one hand he carried an aluminium saucepan. Through the bottom of the boat two stiff jets of water were rising like an ornamental fountain.

We put into the shore and unloaded everything, and Karam Chand caulked the two holes in the bottom — the shock of hitting the rock had started two rivets. So far as we could ascertain, apart from the boat being full of sand and stones, this was the extent of the damage. It was a remarkable testimonial to the men who had built it. It was more like a battleship than a rowing-boat.

High on a sandbank above the pool in which we now floated, a solitary figure was crouched over a small fire in front of a grass hut. It was like one of those constructions that harbour beings, part human, part animal, part vegetable, in the paintings of Hieronymus Bosch. Although the exciting events of the last few minutes must have been abundantly visible, whoever it was gave no sign of being aware of our existence. "Sadhu," said the boatman. "Mahatma Ji." And uttered a prayer as we went down past his dwelling.

It was five o'clock; time to stop. Slowly we paddled a few hundred yards down a quiet reach, looking for a place to camp. On the left bank the trees on the outer edges of the jungle loomed redly, illuminated by the setting sun. No one wanted to camp on the left bank.

As we dawdled, four ragged-looking men loaded with wood came out of the shadow of the trees and down the beach towards us at a quick lope. "Oho!" they shouted. "Thou with the boat. We have many kos to travel before night. Take us over!"

We ferried them over, one at a time because of their heavy loads. They came to gather fuel every day in the dry season, they said. At other times the river was a great sea, miles wide. Their village was far away on the right bank. If what they said was true then a great part of each working day must have been taken up in this way collecting wood. According to them there were two more rapids below this place and then one came to a village. They did not know its name. These men were full of fears: of other men, of the beasts of the jungle, of evil omens and portents of disaster that on many occasions made them turn back and pass the day in the shelter of their houses; but most of all they were afraid of being in the jungle with night coming on. To us their fears seemed perfectly legitimate ones.

We chose a camping-place on the foreshore of what seemed at first to be the right bank of the river (a place as sandy as the previous night's had been stony), but was really one of a series of islands overgrown with grass and shisham trees a few feet higher than the dried-out bed of the river. As the light failed the long bands of wind-blown cloud that all afternoon had floated high in a pale sky turned first to bronze and then a leaden colour, all except the ragged edges which were tinged a daring shade of pink. The sky itself became darker and more opaque until it was a deep navy in which the evening star shone brilliantly and alone. To the west, over the line of false shore, the long, plumed grass waved in the dying wind, black against the last conflagration of a rather vulgar sunset. It was a memorable scene.

With the light gone from the sky, squadrons of *Pteropodidae*, fruit bats, began to pass silently overhead in horrible, undulating flight on their way to ravage some fruit garden. We counted them in dozens, then in hundreds and finally, when we reached four figures, we lost patience and gave up. In the morning, just before first light, they returned and later we found one dead on the shore. Perhaps the excesses of the night had been too much for it. Close-to it was even more loathsome than it had been in flight. It had a shrunken foxy head with long upstanding ears, in each of which there was an additional lobe of skin the shape of a small willow leaf, probably some kind of extra navigation aid. In death the mouth gaped displaying long indrawn teeth, deeply grooved to assist it in its orgies of fruit eating. Its wings had a span of more than four feet which, when the membranes were extended on their elongated, rib-like fingers, were like some ghastly surrealistic umbrella made of flesh and bone. The only member that was free from the membrane that embraced the three fingers, was the thumb which was split into two parts, each of which was furnished with a sharp claw.

While the boatmen were banking up a great fire we set off to see the sadhu. "He is very holy man," G. said as we lurched through the deep sand. "We must profit by meeting him. Now he is telling us many things." He was entranced at the prospect but I was oppressed by the thought of meeting yet another sadhu, most probably under a vow of perpetual silence, who would do nothing but stare at us until we went away.

Fortunately, the sadhu was not a sadhu at all, but an emaciated old man planted in the sand by God knows what authority to scare off poachers from the jungle on the opposite bank. It was difficult to see how he could do this as he was on the wrong side of the river and there was no means of crossing. He lived here, alone in his grass hut, all through the dry season from October to March. Now he was squatting outside it over a fire that was so minute that it barely gave off any heat at all, with a dish of water-chestnuts before him that looked as old and shrivelled as he was.

"Yours is the only boat I have seen," he said when he had recovered from the rather extravagant greeting that G. had given him while still under the impression that he was a holy man, at the same time politely offering us the water-chestnuts of which there were only three. "Here I am very solitary but I have four sons and a wife in my village. It is a long way off and there is little to eat there, only gram.*"

"She must be a difficult wife; otherwise no man would live alone in such a wilderness," Jagannath said, unkindly, when this conversation was reported to him. It was more probably that the old man remained there because he was very poor and fit for nothing else. We gave him some rice and chillies but he scarcely looked at them.

"It is sufficient that you have come to visit me," he said. "Once there were many wild animals, but now there are many poachers. Few of the true hunting people, the real *shikar* log, come here any more."

"Well, if there are poachers why don't you report them to the authorities?"

"Huzoor," he said, simply, "How can you report a poacher to himself?"

It was a comfortable camp. We lay in the sand with all our goods and chattels heaped about us, like the defenders of Rorke's Drift in

* *Pulse*: the edible seeds of leguminous plants, as peas, beans, lentils. (*Shorter Oxford English Dictionary*).

a reproduction that hung in one of the corridors at school. There was a big fire. Dinner was rice and the awful tinned sausages that we were now forced to broach, thanks to the improvidence of the boatmen. It was fearfully cold. By eight o'clock we were all tucked up in bed, like naughty children. Genuinely afraid that the boatmen might die of exposure, we gave them two more blankets.

A fish leapt in the river and sank once again with a dull plop. Bhosla was supposed to be the expert on fishes, but as he was not a forthcoming sort of man the process of finding out what sort of fish it was was a tedious one.

"*Mauli hai?*"

"*Nahin!*"

"*Kotha hai?*"

"*Nahin!*"

"*Rahu hai? Tengena hai? Lachi hai? Saunl hai? Gaunch hai?*"

"*Nahin! Nahin! Nahin! Nahin! Nahin!*"

"Blast! *Bam hai?*"

"*Hai!*"

"Elephants come here in the rains," Karam Chand said helpfully, sensing my exasperation.

Sometime in the dark watches after midnight he woke me. He was in a state of alarm.

"SAHIB! Tarch *hai?*"

After some fumbling I found it in the bottom of my bedding roll.

"*Ek nilgai bahut nazdik hai,*" he said. In the beam of the torch two brilliant eyes regarded us unwinkingly.

Three parts asleep, unwilling to do so, but because Karam Chand wanted it we blundered about in the sand looking for the nilgai, the blue cow, a most inoffensive but destructive animal held sacred by the Hindus for its imagined relationship with the domestic cow – which, not unnaturally, had vanished. As a result I could not sleep any more.

At four it was fearfully cold. In spite of wearing skiing underwear, a woollen shirt made from a piece of sixty-year old Welsh flannel that had been one of my father's bequests to me, a fisherman's jersey, thick whipcord trousers, and being rolled in two thick blankets inside a bedding roll, I was frozen. I had read somewhere that the more clothes one wears the colder one feels, but this was no time to start stripping. Karam Chand, Bhosla and Jagannath had the felt blankets we had given them at Hardwar, the two extra blankets we had issued to them before we went to bed, a thin piece of carpet and a miserable quilt — and they wore cotton clothes; nevertheless they all three slept soundly.

At five the fruit bats began to go over. The men continued to sleep like logs.

"They must be used to cold," I said to Wanda, who lay in bed with her teeth chattering.

"They must be," she said picturesquely, "otherwise they'd bloody well be dead."

It seemed as if the dawn would never come. The moon, a pale hemisphere, was churning its way through a sea of cirrus that was moving away, high over Garhwal. There was no wind and the river between the shoals was like sheets of black glass. At about six the sky to the east became faintly red; then it began to flame and the moon was extinguished; clouds of unidentifiable birds flew high overhead; a jackal skulked along the far shore and, knowing itself watched, went up the bank and into the trees; mist rose from the wet grass on the islands on which the shisham trees stood, wrapped like precious objects in their bandages of dead grass. Frozen stiff and full of sand we waited for the kettle to boil. It was only the second day of our voyage but the stubble on G.'s chin was beginning to sprout prodigiously.

The old man appeared, picking his way towards us through the sand on his painfully thin legs like a ragged heron. On one of his shins there was a deep, festering sore which Wanda had insisted needed attention. He had filled it with sump oil from a motor bus and underneath it was all rotten. "The nearest village is Bhagmalpur," he said as she probed about in the huge cavity, watched enviously by the boatmen who wished that they too, could attract some sympathy and be the centre of attention. 'It is a place of little consequence, but it is my village," he added, deprecatingly. The only place on the map of the area in which we found ourselves that had a name at all was Bhogpur.

"Bhogpur is two kos from Bhagmalpur," he said.

If Bhogpur was two kos from Bhagmalpur then it might be possible to make a reasonable guess at our position. It depended on what he meant by a kos.

"There are seventy rassis in one kos," Karam Chand said.

"There are twelve hundred laggis in one kos," said Bhosla in a sudden garrulous outburst.

"There are three thousand six hundred gaj in one kos," said Jagannath, the youngest boatman.

"Now I am telling you," said G. "If one kos is three thousand six hundred gaj, there are two miles and eighty yards in one kos." If this was so, then we had not travelled more than five miles since the previous morning.*

We left the old man standing on the bank with a parting gift of boracic lint, penicillin powder and biscuits, and carried the gear two hundred yards downstream to a place where the shoal ended; here we loaded the boat. It was now a quarter to eight. What the boatmen called Zirrea, small ringed plovers, compact little birds with neat scarves of black feathers round their necks and yellow legs, rose from the shingle in which they had been pecking, almost invisible, and wheeled over us, uttering despairing cries while a pair of orange-coloured Brahminy duck watched us warily from the shallows on the far side of the river.

In slow succession we dug our way through the sixteenth shoal and descended the sixteenth rapid and so on through the eighteenth and nineteenth, up to twenty-one. It would be tedious to enumerate them all but as we proceeded downstream, literally step by step, I made a note of them. It seemed unlikely that I would pass this way again and I knew that if I kept no record, for the rest of my life I would suspect that my memories of the Ganges below Hardwar were the figments of a disordered imagination.

Even when we had completed our excavations there were only nine inches of water over the twenty-first shoal, but by rare good fortune, four men appeared and without being asked helped us to work the boat through to the accompaniment of a lot of "*challo*'ing" and "*shabash*'ing" while all the time covertly regarding Wanda who was a remarkable figure in red woollen skiing underwear rolled up to the knees: for the sun had temporarily vanished behind some clouds and it was unusually cool.

"You are by Bhogpur," they said; but it was little comfort to us. We had thought ourselves by Bhogpur two and a half hours ago, and it was now a quarter past ten.

As we came to the head of the rapid a line of bullock-carts came out of the jungle on the left bank and began to rumble down over the foreshore towards the very place through which we had just hauled the boat. There were so many of them and we were so unused to traffic of any kind, that we decided to watch them cross. There was no need to anchor, we simply stopped pushing.

As the leading bullocks entered the water, possibly because it was

---

* There is also a *gaukos*, a rather vague measure – the distance a cow's bellow can be heard.

cold or because the stones with the water running over had a different feeling, they halted. The driver did not lash them. He simply waited perched high in the bows of his cart until they had become accustomed to the new element. The carts were piled high with grass. They were of the kind called chhakra, the heavier sort of bullock-cart, but not the heaviest. They were as simple as a jeep and yet, in their own way, as complicated; machines that could go anywhere; the despair of western economists because of their maddening slowness, the destruction which they wreak on unmetalled roads, and their great weight, grossly disproportionate both to their capacity and to the pulling power of the under-nourished beasts which draw them.

Nose to tail with squeaking wheels and the groaning of stressed timbers, the carts lumbered across the river and, as they went, the drivers exhorted their beasts: "*Mera achcha beta!*" (My good son!) "*Aur thora!*" (A little more!) "*Jor se challo!*" (Get on with it!) Soon they disappeared behind one of the islands on the other bank and once more we were alone. For the first time we noticed that the Siwalik Hills to the east of the Hardwar gap were invisible. The river was running to the south and parting company with the whole range.

Now we entered a reach that was perhaps a mile long and a hundred yards wide down which we paddled until we came to an open expanse of shingle on the left bank which extended inland towards the forest. "This is our village," said the leader of the four men who had been helping us. "It is by the Rawasan Nala," and when he invited us to visit it, although Karam Chand and the boatmen were reluctant to stop, the thought of our food box with its diminished contents hardened our hearts, and we forced them to go ashore with us.

Leaving Jagannath to guard the boat we set off across the shingle which was covered with dry, silvery mud, shooing our unwilling little force before us in the direction of the village which was hidden behind a thick bed of reeds and tall grass. After a quarter of a mile we came to an inlet of brackish water full of frog spawn, the bottom of which consisted of thick, glutinous mud into which we sank up to our knees. On the far bank thousands of hairy caterpillars were exercising in the sun. Here a young man and an old woman were making a grass rope, using a flat stone with a hook on it and a piece of bamboo with three holes in it through which the strands passed. The entrance to the village from the river side was by a narrow path that wound through the grass which was very high.

From beyond this plantation came the sounds of activity; the clinking of chains and weird snatches of song, and I had a feeling of pleasurable expectation which turned to terror as a horde of savage curs with sharp, brown teeth came pouring down to meet us. There was no question of saying "Good dog," or extending a friendly hand to beasts like these, and we laid about us with our bamboos with a will until they turned tail and vanished.

The village was in the form of a rough rectangle. It consisted of about forty mud huts with thatched roofs which sagged under the weight of the orange-coloured gourds which grew profusely on them and whose broad-leaved tendrils and yellow flowers seemed to bind them to the earth. In front of each house there was a platform of well-swept dried mud on which the female inhabitants were squatting until the moment when we came into view when they took to their feet and retreated indoors uttering little cries of alarm and mock modesty.

The place was divided down the middle by a straggling path on either side of which emaciated cattle were hobbled in rough pens made from the branches of trees. At the north end was a larger, open-fronted building with a space in front of it, the meeting place of the elders of the village council. It was furnished with a couple of kulphidar, communal pipes with clay bowls and jointed wood stems, which helped them in their deliberations. Everywhere, on the uneven but smooth surfaced ground that had been moulded by the passage of innumerable bare feet, lay the simple machinery of village life: the wooden ploughs which have to be light enough for the cultivator to carry them on his shoulders to the fields; mattocks with iron heads bent at a sharp angle to the hafts; harrows that were nothing more than flattened logs; sowing baskets made of slips of woven bamboo; bigger baskets for feeding cattle; small, wooden-handled reaping sickles; a potter's wheel and broken potsherds ("The potter sleeps secure for no one will steal clay," Karam Chand said, sententiously); open-ended sieves, that looked like dustpans, made from reeds; a grinding mill, the kind that is worked by two women, one of whom turns the upper stone while the other pours in the grain; a cast-iron chaff-cutting machine with a flywheel; filled water pots sweating moisture; ropes and chains and halters and small children with black-painted eyes; all together in the thin dust. Above the village a solitary great shisham tree that had given shade to the village longer than anyone could remember was dying now. Its branches were filled with vultures. For the most part they remained motionless but from time to time they raised themselves, turning

arrogant heads to show off their profiles and flapped their
great wings, displaying white back feathers as dingy-looking as an
old vest.

Through a gap in what was otherwise an almost continuous wall of
houses I could see the fields of wheat and gram that lapped the
village on three sides like a sea in which men and women, bent
double, were weeding and loosening the soil around the young plants
with wooden-handled knives. This was the Rabi, the crop that had
been sown in November. All through the winter, from December to
February, it would be weeded and watered, and sometimes between
the middle of March and the middle of April the harvest would
take place. From April to mid-May the villagers would thresh it – first
it would be trodden out by six bullocks yoked together moving round
and round a central post; then it would be winnowed and a cake
of cow dung placed on top of the heaped grain to avert the evil
eye. In June or July, after the monsoon rains had begun, the Kharif
crop would be sown – rice, maize and millets; and in early October
there would be the harvest and then the land would be ploughed and
the Rabi would be sown once more. Another important crop, not here
but in irrigated land, was sugar cane, now more important than
cotton. The land in which it was to be planted might need as many
as twenty ploughings before it was ready to receive it, lots of manure
and constant weeding. This was the cycle in the State of Uttar
Pradesh in the Ganges Plain. Floods, drought, blight, pestilence, the
incursion of wild animals into the standing crops, any of these might
destroy them and often did. They might fail from lack of fertilisers
or the land might fail from excessive cropping; or because the sub-
division of the property between all the sons made it impossible to
farm it economically. This was the law of inheritance carried to the
ultimate limits of absurdity; by it the individual holding might be
reduced to the size of the back yard of a slum property. But
whatever happened to it this was the cycle and had been for two
thousand years.

The other crops were mustard and tobacco. At one time, as the
result of the efforts of two British officers, tobacco grown in the
forests of Bhogpur, a town somewhere to the south-east, had been
so esteemed that, mixed with Latakia and Manila leaf, it had been sold
in tins, but this like so many other ventures had eventually come
to nothing. In the fields round about the village, stood the machans,
rickety constructions in which watchmen sat at night to scare off
wild animals, principally wild pig and nilgai that would play havoc

with any crop if they succeeded in entering it. Armed with a pot containing a smudge of fire they passed the hours of darkness groaning apprehensively and calling to their neighbours in other machans in order to keep up their spirits.

The Headman, an old-looking man but probably not more than fifty, spoke with nostalgia of the days when the British were still in India.

"Your honour," he said, "this village is often flooded and at such times we are in great misery. We have asked the Government to provide us with an embankment. That was more than a year ago and so far nothing has happened. In the time of the Raj such a thing would not have been allowed. A Sahib would have come on his horse and quite soon all would have been well."

"I wonder," G. said, "why they did not ask the Sahib for an embankment when he was coming here on his horse."

In the circumstances this did not seem to be a good time to produce Mr Nehru's letter which asked for assistance on our behalf, rather than proferring it. Instead we bought some potatoes and some stunted eggs for the boatmen, and the Headman gave us a bunch of green bananas. This was the extent of our shopping, for this was all they had to offer us. The Headman was genuinely sorry to see us go, as were the other inhabitants and we left watched by the women. They were wraith-like, swaying figures dressed in the lugri, the poor woman's version of the sari, and wrapped overall in yet another sheet called the chadar. There are some 450,000 villages in India similar to this, all with less than 500 inhabitants, all with similar problems. Who can know what it is like to live one's life in a village such as this with its 300 inhabitants and its 5,000 bighas* of land, except those who are born there and live in it all their days? Not even the most assiduous anthropologist or the most devoted social worker. The windowless front that this village presented to the world seemed to be a symbol of the inhabitants: turned in upon themselves by its very layout, as if in a hall of mirrors; still, in spite of legislation, inhibited by consideration of caste; still, in spite of legislation, the victims of moneylenders paying off their never-to-be discharged debts at an interest of anything up to 25 per cent; desiccated by the summer sun;

---

* Under British administration the standard bigha was equal to one-third of an acre. There were also *pakka* bighas and *kachcha* bighas. In 1962 the use of metric weights and measures was made obligatory in India; but a transitional period of three years was allowed, in the case of metrical units for land areas, during which the existing units were still recognised.

ploughing through a Passchendaele of mud in the rainy season; creeping into the fields to put out a black pot to ward off the evil eye. Poor ignorant people, living on a knife-edge between survival and disaster.

Chapter Six

The way to the Balawali Bridge

The river is not navigable until it reaches the vicinity of Nagal in pargana Najibabad.

District Gazetteer of the United Provinces
Vol. XIV, Bijnor; Allahabad, 1908

Back in the boat I began to feel better. The weather was fine and warm, like a beautiful summer's day in England; the sort of day I remembered, or thought I remembered, as being commonplace when I was a child and now only half-believed had ever been. To the north the Siwalik Hills had reappeared once more, wrapped in a haze which gave them an agreeable air of distance. Behind them rose a cluster of snow peaks, while downstream and far below the level at which we were, the jungle on our left extended eastwards to the foot of the mountains like a great green rug.

In spite of all the difficulties everyone, including Bhosla, whose lugubrious appearance and taciturn manner concealed and belied an optimistic nature, was in good spirits. I myself had not felt so well for years. Hard exercise and short commons, as my father would have called them, and minimal quantities of alcohol were all conspiring to do me good. Even my feet, now that I had decided to sacrifice one of my two pairs of shoes to the river, no longer hurt. It was fortunate that this was so, as we were now faced with the task of digging yet another channel for the boat, this time thirty yards long, to the head of the next fall, down which we plunged into a deep pool of green water in which the bottom could only be dimly seem. Here we let the boat drift aimlessly while we each ate half an orange, a surprise treat which Wanda produced from her useful bag.

The next rapid, the twenty-seventh since leaving Hardwar, was a long narrow race between banks eight feet high, two vertical slices of silt marked with long scourings, one below the other, the lower ones not yet dry, a reminder if we needed any that the water level was sinking fast. "Much more than two inches a day," said G., gloomily. But whatever was happening to the water level, the appearance of the river bed itself was changing too. Westwards it broadened out in huge expanses of sand and shingle. There was a feeling of great loneliness in this place, borne out by the map which gave no indication of any settlement or habitation.

We entered a wide lagoon in which there was no perceptible current and went aground in it. By now our sense of well-being had deserted us and we felt weak and disinclined to face new difficulties, for it was now one o'clock and so far we had had little to eat. Languidly gnawing giant white radishes, we splashed ashore and set off, each on a different course, to try and find a usable channel, leaving Wanda to curry rice and potatoes for the boatmen.

After twenty minutes during which the only living thing I saw was a crab too small to be worth eating, we reassembled. All reports were bad: the lagoon ended in a trickle of water with a short fall to the next reach; somewhere in the centre there was another, longer fall, but it was almost as feeble as the first; far over to the right there was a third that was deeper than the others, but very long. This was the one that Karam Chand favoured. After a good deal of wrangling and a frugal lunch – a tin of sardines, three cream crackers, two sweet biscuits and jam and a mug of tea – not much of a meal on which to push a boat through India (for that is what we seemed to be doing) – we decided to try it. We unloaded the boat, leaving Wanda to guard the gear, and pushed it back the way we had come and round a promontory to the head of the fall.

After all the business of lightening the boat it was enraging to find ourselves making an easy descent in ghostly silence by a narrow sluice-like run with a sandy bottom. It was a journey of only half a mile, but by the time we had carried everything down from the lagoon to the boat, we had each covered four times the distance.

The whole operation had taken nearly three hours; but it seemed worth it. Before us stretched what appeared to be the longest, most inviting reach we had so far encountered. There were no sandbanks and there was no sign of any rapids. To me, in one of those moments of insane optimism which no amount of experience was capable of shattering, it seemed that we might, with a little luck, reach the Balawali Bridge by nightfall; but no sooner had I expressed this hope than we were grounded again – this time in quicksands which quivered underfoot in a particularly horrible manner, as if one was walking on a blancmange.

At four-thirty we came to a place where four men were sitting marooned in mid-stream on four grass rafts on which they had been attempting to float downstream to their village which was somewhere near a place called Nagal on the way to Balawali Bridge. As we came abreast of them they appealed to us to take them aboard. "We, too, are watermen," they said. This was an admission so rare in our experience on the Upper Ganges, where everyone we had met had hastened to dissociate himself from it, that we would have taken them with us if for no other reason.

It was unfortunate that we chose this moment to run aground ourselves and we now found ourselves in the ridiculous position of having to ask the raftsmen for help before we could help them. These men were in a terrible state. They were wet and shivering and dressed in nothing but sodden loincloths that were mere vestiges of clothing. Now they abandoned their rafts and joined us in the boat, wrapping themselves from head to toe in long damp sheets, more like corpses exhumed from the tomb than living beings. "We have come from the jungle, northwards of the Rawasan Nala," they said. "For two days we have eaten nothing."

We gave them sugar and sweets, all that we could lay our hands on without unloading the boat; but their pleasure was short-lived. We were now approaching the fifteenth rapid of the day, the twenty-ninth of the journey, a particularly frightening one, and the boatmen, whose sympathy for the newcomers was of a less demonstrative order than our own, made them disembark and stagger along the bank for half a mile on foot, while we descended the long run of water in comparative comfort.

The long day was drawing to a close — far too rapidly for my liking — although I had had more than enough of it. We would never reach the Bridge, that was certain; what seemed equally certain was that we would not even reach Nagal before nightfall. Already the plumed grasses and sugar cane on the islands to the west were silhouetted against the sun which was sinking at an unseemly rate and deep in the bed of the river we were already in cold shadow.

As the boat entered the thirty-first rapid down which it careered silently, rocking from bow to stern on the powerful stream, we had a respite from the oars and now for the first time we had the feeling of being carried on the bosom of a great river. This was what I had imagined that the descent of the Ganges would be like.

The sun had gone now and for those who were not at the oars the air was very cold; but in spite of everything it was a lovely time and I felt strangely contented rowing like mad down this long reach, stripped to the waist, with the wild duck rising in hundreds and the Sarus Cranes, tall grey birds, standing in the water on long, bare, red legs, trumpeting to one another; while in the after glow sky and water became blood-red and a long line of cliffs to the east which were now closing with the left bank of the river were the colour of canyons at sunset in the *National Geographic Magazine*. It was very calm and very impressive, but when we asked the raftsmen how far it was to Nagal — *"Wuh kitni dur hai?"* They said — it was *"Bahut dur"*, (very far), and wrapped themselves closer still in their wet rags. These men were remarkably vague about their whereabouts. All they seemed to know was that their village was somewhere near Nagal, a small market town of 2,000 inhabitants, which lay somewhere to the east of the Ganges.

Now we went aground in the last of the light. Nine men and one woman hopelessly lost in a maze of shoals; blundering about in the darkness probing for a channel with bamboo poles; at one moment up to our waists in water, the next with it barely covering our calves. When eventually we did find a way it led through quicksands in which it was impossible to let go of the side of the boat for an instant for fear of disappearing for ever; attempting to move the boat in these circumstances, with no solid substance underfoot, was rather like pedalling a unicycle in a circus.

As we went slowly on, Karam Chand interrogated the raftsmen about the whereabouts of their village. "Three miles," they said at first, and then much later, "Two miles", from which distance, however far we travelled, they refused to be dislodged. Finally, even Karam Chand became exasperated. "It is my opinion," he said, "that their village is nowhere near Nagal at all."

The water shoaled still more and we stuck aground below a bank of steep crumbling earth. Here, before we could stop them, the raftsmen, fed up with the slow progress we were making, leapt ashore and began scrambling up it, heading for home on a breast-high scent.

"Laut ao!" I shouted after them in my best Hindi. *"Joh main kahta hun woh karo!"* (Come here! Do what I tell you!) And when they showed no signs of complying and had, in fact, already disappeared, "Bastards!" forgetting that apart from some sweets, a few mouthfuls of sugar and some biscuits which Wanda had succeeded in extracting with great difficulty from the provision box, they had eaten nothing for two and a half days and were in no mood to listen to anyone.

There now seemed little chance of finding a village at which to stay the night, let alone Nagal, so we decided to remain where we were and make a camp on top of the bank. The foot of it was a nasty place to disembark in almost total darkness. The water through which we splashed with the baggage was unnaturally warm and very dirty. Up to now, whenever we were thirsty, we had followed the example of the boatmen and simply scooped up a handful from over the side; this water would have to be boiled. Worst of all, the foot of the bank was thick with human excrement into which we plunged with trunks and bedding rolls on our backs. We had hoped to find an inhabited place in which to spend the night and it looked very much as if we had succeeded. Civilisation was not far off.

At the top of the bank we found ourselves in a stubble-field. It was dark and misty. The raftsmen had disappeared and there was no sign of any village, but, exercising some sixth sense, Karam Chand led G. and myself through a plantation of sugar cane to a small hamlet of reed huts close under the cliffs which here began to run inland away from the river. In it everyone seemed to be asleep; there was not a light anywhere. By good fortune we met a young man who was on his way home. When we told him that we needed bread, milk and firewood, he led us into one of the huts where he lit a lamp and began to shake what looked like a bundle of old clothes on a charpoy. From it emerged a small boy, not more than eight years old.

"Your honours," said the little boy, "I shall bring milk in the morning. Wood you may have now for a rupee, although there is not much, and as for bread there is none, but if you wish to have the half of the chapati that remains to me I shall be happy to give it to you," producing a half of one of the round pieces of unleavened bread that was a little the worse for wear, from inside his shirt. Shamed by this display of generosity, we declined the bread and gave him a rupee. He led us to a place where there was a small pile of wood which the three of us would have no difficulty in carrying back to the camping place; so small a quantity that, seeing on the way back a large, shiny piece of timber, far superior to anything that we had just bought, I picked it up, only to be told when I reached the camping-place, where the rest of the party had already made a quick blaze with rice stubble and the roots of a tree, that it was a bullock's yoke. The burning of such a vital piece of equipment was not likely to raise our stock in the village, and I slunk away to put it back where I had found it. On the way back I found an even larger, more desirable piece of wood, but this turned out to be a harrow of the same sort that we had seen that morning in the village by the Rawasan Nala.

Back at the camp things were not going at all smoothly. The entire contents of a tin of condensed milk, which Wanda had attempted to seal with a splinter of wood after opening it at lunch time, had spilled in the provision box. It was the sticky, sugary kind. Now the boatmen were helping her to clean it up. It would have been better if they had left her to do it alone, for they had little domestic sense and as soon as their hands became sufficiently sticky, they smeared them on whatever was nearest to hand — in this case the rest of the luggage. Soon everything we possessed was covered with condensed milk (a state of permanent stickiness is one that, in my opinion, is more likely to lead to mental breakdown than any other) and we were forced to crawl up and down the bank with pots full of Ganges water until we had more or less got rid of it.

This was by no means the end of our troubles. Now that we were on dry land Jagannath and Bhosla began to complain of sore throats. They had been excited by the brief glimpse of the interior of the medicine chest when Wanda had opened it that morning to treat the old man. Now, although her medical knowledge was of the slightest, she proceeded, in spite of my protests, to dose them with dangerous drugs of a kind that are normally reserved for patients in extremis. At this moment we were not a "happy ship".

To make peace, and because we really needed it, the three of us drank whisky, while crouching out of sight behind our only refuge, the open lid of the provision box. None of the boatmen were taken in by this absurd subterfuge which, in fact, destroyed any pleasure that the whisky was giving us, and when Karam Chand asked in a rather pointed way, if we had any brandy — although we had none — I felt so ashamed of our secret drinking that I gave each of them a large tot of rum which they swallowed as they had the one I had given them the previous night in one improvident gulp, like Russians.

They now began to cook their dinner: rice and potatoes with chillies and parathas (chapatis fried in ghee — clarified butter). This took an unconscionable time and, worse, they were using our cooking pots — not only had they set off without food or proper clothing, but they had also omitted to bring their own utensils. Fortunately there was a good fire and from time to time we received propitiatory offerings of delicious, greasy parathas.

Much later, while we were sitting by the fire digesting our own dinner, Karam Chand approached me secretly and asked if he might accompany us to Calcutta. It seemed an extraordinary ambition. To me the journey seemed to leave a lot to be desired from the point of view of comfort; but he was quite serious.

"You are a government servant," I said. "We have promised the Irrigation Engineer to send you and the boat back to Hardwar when we reach the Balawali Bridge. If you go further you will lose your job." But Karam Chand, like the Water Rat in *The Wind in the Willows*, had become enamoured of distant horizons, and it was difficult to make him see the folly of giving up his job which was, at least, a secure one and with the promise of some kind of pension, however lowly, at the end of it. "I have experienced great kindness in your service," he said, his eyes filling with tears. "Kindness to which I am unaccustomed, and I wish to continue to be with you both."

I found it difficult to recall any act of kindness that we had rendered Karam Chand, apart from feeding him our rations, which was an act more likely to be equated with feeble-mindedness by anyone who knew the country, and I attributed what he said to Oriental hyperbole. I was embarrassed by his display of emotion but, at the same time, I did my best to dissuade him.

I had almost succeeded in doing so when G., who had been listening to this conversation, began to tell him that if he did make the journey downstream it might be possible for him to transfer from the Irrigation Department to the Ganga and Brahmaputra Water Transport Board — which concerned itself with inland water transport on the two rivers. G. now began to play the part of the adventurous Seafaring Rat depicting a rosy future for a person of Karam Chand's watermanship and general ability if only he followed his inclinations.

I listened to this with a growing sense of depression. I knew that G. really believed what he was saying, at least while he was saying it. I also knew that if it came to the point at which the actual transfer had to be effected, it would never take place. On the other hand, it was difficult to know whether Karam Chand really believed what G. was telling him or not. Both were Indians; both might be playing the same Indian game. I was almost tempted to tell Karam Chand to come to Calcutta just to see what he would say; but then I decided that it was too risky. He would almost certainly accept. I therefore decided to say nothing at all. It was a mistake and one that I was to have occasion to regret. Even after such a short time in the country what critical faculties I possessed were beginning to collapse.

We made our beds on the spiky stubble with our feet towards the fire so that we radiated from it like the spokes of a wheel. Overhead, in a sky filled with stars whose brilliance was dimmed by the glare of the fire, Orion shone boldly, like an illuminated tennis racquet. Across the water in the great expanse of the dried-out river bed, invisible in the mist that enveloped it, jackals howled dismally and their howlings were taken up by similar bands on the plateau behind the village, who echoed them with dreadful fidelity.

Each night I seemed to be doomed to be woken by somebody, and always in the small hours. This time it was Wanda. It was three o'clock in the morning. Everything was swaddled in thick fog. "I have heard voices and seen figures", she announced in a sepulchral, Middle-European accent which only comes to the surface in moments of stress.

I peered into the fog. It was like trying to see through cotton wool; but after gazing in one direction for several minutes on end – the one infallible way of summoning phantoms, as anyone who has been a sentry in a lonely place at night will testify – I, too, thought that I could make out some indistinct shapes which seemed at times to hover above the ground, and at others to dissolve into nothingness.

I decided to delegate the responsibility for deciding what to do to Karam Chand who, in his newly assumed office of faithful companion, slept on my left. Everything that was happening on this journey was conforming to a rigid literary framework. The source book of most of what had happened up to now was undoubtedly *The Wind in the Willows*; but this was a situation from a novel about the war – either war. The faithful old Sergeant-Major – "I was with your father at Ladysmith" – whose loyalty was unwanted and unrequited until the cowardly, not now-so-young officer, evaded his responsibilities: "Carry on, Karam Chand!"

It was more difficult to delegate responsibility than I had imagined. Karam Chand appeared to be dead, and it was only with great difficulty and by pressing firmly behind his ear – "an old hunter's dodge" – that I succeeded in waking him. But I hardened my heart. After all, it was he who had woken me the previous night; and only to see a nilgai. "Sahib," he said. "Have your knife ready!" He seemed delighted by the way things were going. It was a Wilkinson's fighting knife – part of a bulk purchase years before when we had gone to the Hindu Kush. They were intended as presents for "headmen" but the headmen had rejected them; knives might have been all right for their fathers or grandfathers, they wanted German or Japanese binoculars. I unsheathed it with visions of spending the rest of my life in a jail in Uttar Pradesh if I misued it. Wanda, having roused us, and ensured that she was protected, was already asleep.

Eventually, after three-quarters of an hour, during which the pair of us goggled into the fog, three white-clad figures appeared and squatted down by the remains of the fire without saying anything. "Men such as these, abroad at such an hour, can only be thieves and robbers," Karam Chand hissed in my ear. It seemed to me that they were more probably lunatics, but whatever they were I had no intention of playing Quixote to Karam Chand's Sancho Panza at a quarter to four on a cold, foggy morning. Besides, to me, they looked like a trio incapable of taking anything by force, and leaving Karam Chand to make what he could of them I followed Wanda's example and went to sleep. When I woke again at a quarter to six, they were still there by the fire which was now more lively.

"We are sorry," one of them said, "that we alarmed you" ("alarmed" was an inadequate word to describe my sensations). "And we are even more sorry not to have offered you hospitality in our village, but when you arrived we were already asleep. Our day begins early." He could say that again.

All three now began to speak about our future movements — apparently the object of their visit to us in the first place. "It will be impossible for you to reach the Balawali Bridge without our help," they said. "The way is a difficult one." (What the devil did they imagine it had been up to now, I wondered.) "If you pay us two rupees each we will go with you."

"Good idea!" said G., who had just woken from an uninterrupted sleep.

"What are these men?" I asked Karam Chand.

"They are drivers of bullock-carts."

I immediately rejected their offer. Not because I thought their terms were exorbitant, on the contrary; but simply because the little experience we had had of the Ganges indicated that life on its banks and life of the water itself were two separate entities. The driver of a bullock-cart would be as much out of his element in a boat as a boatman would be in a bullock-cart.

"Then we will go for nothing," they said, neatly turning the tables and making me feel mean.

"What do they know of the river?" I asked Karam Chand.

"They know nothing at all about it," he said. "It so happens that, today, they have to go to the Balawali Bridge."

"I think we should go in those bullock-carts," G. said.

I asked him what he proposed to do with the boat, scuttle it?

"We can wait at the bridge for the boatmen to bring it down and while we are awaiting we can telephone Hardwar," he said.

At six the fog lifted a little. Overhead the moon shone down from a clear sky but the river was still invisible.

The field in which we had been sleeping now revealed itself as a rectangular plot of rice stubble, forty yards by fifty, on which we had been reclining like holy men on beds of nails. Each field was separated from its neighbour by a low earth embankment. Behind the village were the cliffs which here turned inland away from the river. The ravines were filled with swirling vapour; stunted trees clung to their

sides. There was an almost entire absence of colour. It might have
been a landscape by an artist of the Sung dynasty. The village, or what
one could see of it, was a collection of low thatched huts from
which the smoke of cooking-fires was rising. The river was
invisible, buried in the fog.

While we were sharing a delicious breakfast of porridge with the
boatmen who were enjoying it for the first time in their lives, quite
suddenly the fog lifted, leaving long, tattered remnants of vapour
trailing above the water. It was like a lull in an artillery engagement.
The river was full of sandbanks and the sun shone down through the
murk overhead in a single shaft of brilliant light, illuminating a
bullock-cart that was crossing the river towards the other shore. It
was being pulled by two white bullocks and two more were tethered
behind it. Sitting on the front of the cart was the driver, wrapped in a
black blanket. The cart was preceded by a man who carried a long pole
with which he sounded the water. Every so often he called out the
results of his findings in a high sing-song voice. Then the fog came
down again, as thick as it had ever been, but for some time we
could hear the driver calling to his bullocks, the squeaking of the
wheels and the cries of the leadsman as he plodded on across the river.

At a quarter to eight we put to sea. There was no question of going
aground as we already were; wet to our waists we lugged the boat
through the freezing shallows parallel with the bank, watched by a
silent man who was sitting under a banana tree. The fog was still
thick. Above us on the bank strange surrealistic objects loomed
through it – irrigation levers for lifting water from the river into the
rice fields; long bamboo poles with a bucket at one end and a counter-
poise weight at the other, supported in the fork of a tree. Between
these constructions, lapwings ran up and down the stubble calling
frantically to one another. They seemed as lost and desperate as we
were.

We poled out towards the middle of the stream into a maze of
quicksands from which the topmost branches of trees which had
been almost engulfed by them reached out skeleton hands towards us.
It was not an altogether far-fetched simile. In a moment of pioneering
enthusiasm when he left the side of the boat to search for a navigable
channel, Karam Chand sank to his waist in sand, and up to his neck
in water, and it needed our combined efforts to withdraw him from it.
Meanwhile, the sun forced its way through the fog creating strange
atmospheric effects, arches of dark grey vapour, rainbows without
colour.

Somewhere ahead of us in this desolation we could hear the sound of an engine, but it soon died away. There was no question of digging a channel in such a place. As soon as we began to excavate one it silted up. The only way was to rock the boat from side to side until it made a passage for itself through the sand.

By nine-thirty we seemed to be clear of the worst of it, and we poled down past long, firm promontories in which small white shells were embedded. The fog was now in full retreat before the growing heat of the sun, and soon it shone down unobscured on the river. There was not a breath of wind and, apart from the last trails of vapour that were streaming away low over the sandbanks, everything was very still. We came to a place on the left bank where there was a reed hut and moored close to it, a flat-bottomed boat with upturned bows. It was a clinker-built boat about twenty-five feet long, broad in the beam, and it had a red and white band painted round the gunwales from stem to stern. This was the ferry boat from Nagal to a place called Jaspur Ranjitpur on the right bank, and this was the first boat, apart from the dilapidated ferry at Shishamwallah, that we had seen since leaving Hardwar. Beyond it the little town of Nagal could just be seen on the high ground above the river.

On the bank, close to the ferryman's hut, men with pack ponies and foot passengers with large bundles done up in brightly coloured cloths waited stoically for the ferryman to make up his mind to take them across. There were many bullock carts and their drivers were crouched together in twos and threes over small fires. This was a place where people halted, whether they needed the service of the ferryman or not, to pass the time of day.

As we passed the ferryman shouted at us, asking where we were going.

"To Calcutta."

"Ho! Calcutta! The Balawali Bridge is four miles and it will take you two hours," he said. "Of Calcutta I cannot speak."

Ahead of us a barrier of sand appeared to stretch across the whole width of the river, but we had been so excited at our brief contact with civilisation, and the ferryman's directions had seemed so straight-forward that we had forgotten to ask him where the channel lay.

We were now half a mile below the ferry, and rather than turn back we decided to communicate with him by word of mouth. It would have been quicker to have returned. It took about ten minutes to attract his attention and another twenty minutes of screeching by Karam Chand, which reduced his voice to a hollow croak, to establish that there were four channels through the sands of which only the centre one was navigable. We pondered this strange advice and eventually decided to follow the one on the extreme right. As we went whirling down it clouds of greylag rose into the air, uttering hoarse cries and flew off in a long, loose V-shape formation towards the north.

We saw two turtles, one lying on the bottom and another hauled out on the bank; and we heard a train. Sugar cane and maize were growing on islands in the river and every so often whole sections of bank with the growing crops on them fell into the water with a booming noise and were carried away; while to the right there was nothing except a waste of dried-out sand as far as the eye could see.

At eleven o'clock the factory chimneys at Balawali station came into sight. At a quarter to twelve we got our first sight of the Bridge – a girder construction on piers with electric pylons at either end carrying the cables across the river, that seemed huge even in this vast land-scape. On the left bank men were ploughing and burning stubble in the fields of silt below the cliffs which were the continuation of the ones in the lee of which we had camped the previous night. High in the air small white birds fluttered like pieces of silver paper, and brown Pariah Kites hung motionless whistling eerily.

At twelve forty-five we suffered our thirty-fifth major stranding since leaving Hardwar and bumped down the thirty-fifth major rapid just as the factory hooter at Balawali sounded the dinner break. We, too, had had enough for one morning. We took the boat in towards the left bank, moored it to a convenient stone and without delay set off for the town, leaving Jagannath and Bhosla to guard the boat.

Chapter Seven

A short halt at a railway station

Strung out in line ahead, each engaged with our thoughts, we plodded towards Balawali — first through a waste of dried mud in which cows and goats nibbled at some miserable sprouts of vegetation; then through fields of winter wheat and an orchard of guava trees. Finally we reached the high spur of the railway which carried the line out to the bridge. At the foot of it there was a pond half-choked with lotus plants, in which laundry men were walloping the washing, each on his personal stone.

We climbed the embankment and stumbled along the tracks until we reached the railway station. It was a small place, little more than a halt, its principle raison d'être being the glass factory. On a wall there was a notice in English which read:

GOODS SHED REMAINS OPEN FOR THE RECEIPT AND DELIVERY OF GOODS AND LIVESTOCK FROM 10 A.M. TO 4 P.M. ON SUNDAYS, INDEPENDENCE AND REPUBLIC DAYS, WHICH ARE DIES-NON, IT WILL REMAIN OPEN FOR THE DELIVERY OF LIVESTOCK AND CINEMATOGRAPHY.

Standing at the platform was a giant, brand-new, seventy-five-ton crane, built by a firm in Dusseldorf. It formed part of a breakdown train which seemed capable of dealing with the most spectacular disasters and in the excitement engendered by its arrival our own went practically unnoticed.

The stationmaster was a gentle, kindly man but the news he gave us was not good.

"Now this lorry that you are ordering from Hardwar can never arrive here," he said. "And I am telling you the reasons. The first reason is that there is no bridge for motors, and the second reason is that if the driver, knowing that there is no bridge, is crossing the river at Hardwar and coming by jungle route, then he will never arrive, because he will be lost. So your lorry is not arriving. This is two reasons why you should continue in boat to Raoli, which is by Bijnor. There is another reason. Now I am telling you that there are no boats at Balawali of any kind, so I am advising you to continue down Ganga to Bridge of Boats at Raoli. It is only eighteen and a half miles," he went on apparently unconscious of the effect he was having on his audience. "That is the place to which your lorry is now going and I am telegraphing to Laksar on other side of Ganga and telling them to relay message to Hardwar to this effect."

While this agreeable and practical man went off to implement his suggestion, we sat apathetically under a corrugated iron canopy in front of the station entrance and let the flies swarm over us. Of the four of us, two, Wanda and myself, were convinced that however well-intentioned the stationmaster was, his message would never get through and if it did, that it would be so mangled in the process that it would be unintelligible to its recipients. Both of us had been born and brought up in a world in which incompetence and disaster were hand in glove with one another. Of the others, G., who still believed in mankind's capacity to organise itself, believed that the message would arrive. The only one of us who looked completely happy was Karam Chand, who didn't care. All that this meant to him was that for the moment he was reprieved from returning to Hardwar.

Both Wanda and myself were worried about the Irrigation Engineer at Hardwar. We had borrowed his boat on the understanding that we would return it to him at the end of the second day, by which time we had presumed that we would have reached the Balawali Bridge and been able to find another one in which to continue our journey. It was now the afternoon of the fourth day. The Irrigation Engineer had been more than reluctant to lend us his boat in the first place. By now he must be thinking us a trio of villains who had obtained his boat by false pretences. He would have other pre-occupations too. Behind every official — and this is not something peculiar to India alone, but displays itself there in its most refined and demonic form — there is his shadow who is waiting to supplant him, together with a whole horde of attendant relations, who are themselves like a shadow cabinet preparing him, egging him on and sustaining him during the long period of waiting. It often takes years before such efforts are successful; sometimes they never are. In this particular instance the business of the boat might, in the hands of a cunning and unscrupulous plotter, be the cause of untold trouble to the Irrigation Engineer. It might even bring about his downfall. To cover himself he might even now be setting in motion machinery for our apprehension. Only G. seemed confident that there was no cause for alarm.

"Chief Irrigation Engineer is not worrying about his boat," he said cheerfully. "He asked me who would be responsible for it and I have told him that you are holding yourself entirely responsible."

I found precious little comfort in this. Neither was the immediate prospect one to elevate the spirits. Across the square from the station there was a refreshment house, a terrible-looking place full of flies. Next to us, squatting on the brick pavement, a hairy old man was gnawing sugar cane and spitting the butts out round him; horrid curs whose tails looked as if they had been worried by rats lay, comatose, in the sun, all except one whose hindparts appeared to be paralysed, which was dragging itself towards us leaving a trail behind it in the dust. To our right a man was asleep, flat on his back on a disused well-head. His head hung down over the outer edge and flies were walking in and out his open mouth. The only redeeming figure in this scene of squalor was a man on a ladder who was thatching a roof and at the same time singing at the top of his voice. He gave an impression of cheerfulness and energy that was so much at variance with his surroundings, that he seemed the figure of industrious man conquering sloth in some mediaeval allegory.

In such circumstances, although we were hungry and thirsty, it was not difficult to resist G.'s suggestion that we should eat in the shop across the way; but while he was there himself ordering tea, the stationmaster reappeared and invited us into the waiting room where he had a delicious spread laid out for us — tea, cauliflower fried in light crisp batter made from gram flour, golden-coloured ring-shaped sweets filled with syrup and translucent sweets like large musket balls, made with milk, sugar, flour and a pinch of bicarbonate of soda. It would have been difficult to imagine a meal more nicely balanced between sweetness and lightness for persons as exhausted as we were.

"You were very wise not to eat at teashop," he said. "This teashop is a dirty, filthy place." And he despatched a small boy to fetch G. from it. When we thanked him for what he had done for us all he said was "It is nothing. It is my duty."

Still trying to imagine what an official of British Railways would have done with a party of Indians under similar circumstances, we took leave of the stationmaster after ascertaining that it would be a waste of time if we waited for a reply to the message he had sent up the line, and set off across the tracks and down a dusty lane flanked by low red brick constructions, the houses in which the workers at the glass factory lived, every bit as dreary as their counterparts in the Midlands. At the end of it there was a little shop, very dark inside, which sold Sunlight soap, matches, bidis, exercise books, oranges and things in sacks that looked like dog biscuits.

To us, ill-prepared for civilisation by the lonely, untainted country we had passed through, Balawali seemed a sad place. Nothing we had seen on the way had prepared us for its particular kind of squalor. It was redeemed by its situation on the splendid river and by the huge, red painted bridge which spanned it, over which long freight trains rumbled, whistling mournfully as only Indian trains can, as if they were drawing attention to the condition of humanity.

On the way back to the boat a violent wind rose and the air was filled with flying sand. The sandbanks shimmered in the heat and on them the solitary figure of a fisherman working in a little compound that he had made from his nets which were flailing about in the wind, only accentuated the loneliness of this part of the Ganges.

Chapter Eight

An encounter with a bridgekeeper

According to the stationmaster, the distance to Raoli was eighteen and a half miles. We set off at three-thirty, by which time the wind had dropped, but three-quarters of an hour later we were still footling about above the bridge. The way to it was a labyrinth of channels through the sandbanks, and we went aground many times. On them fishermen were repairing their nets, but just as the stationmaster had said there was not a boat to be seen.

The bridge itself was an immense structure and a remarkable testimonial to Victorian engineering skill. It was more than half a mile long. Between the huge piers which were sunk a hundred feet in the bed of the river, there were strong rips and whirlpools in which the boat spun as the current took us through, and we narrowly avoided crashing into one of them. High overhead among the girders wood pigeons made thick gooey noises. Here at the bridge the Ganges was already only about 450 feet above sea level. At Hardwar it had been 1,024 feet. The distance between the two points was about twenty-five miles in a direct line — a fall of about twenty-two and a half feet a mile.

The stream took us swiftly down, bubbling and muttering to itself in a way that was almost human and bore us away from the bridge, south-south-west. It was a hundred yards wide now and for the first time there was only one channel. Away on the left hand to the east, beyond a stretch of low, alluvial flood plain, the cliffs on the edge of which the town of Balawali was built began to close with the river; while to the west there was nothing but a vast, sandy waste which extended as far as the eye could see. Somewhere beyond it was the Banganga which was now, if the map could be believed, preparing to rejoin its parent stream. Close under the banks in the shallows, a number of furtive-looking pariah dogs were wrangling over a tightly-wound white sheeted corpse with a pair of Pharaoh's Chickens — repulsive, dirty-white scavenger vultures with bald, yellow heads and yellow beaks, which were waddling about on the foreshore close to it. The dogs snarled at them, displaying teeth that were like rusty nails, but the birds were unimpressed and as we went past, one of them lifted itself into the air and came down on the bundle in the river with a sickening plop.

The light was going fast. It was time to make camp. Karam Chand steered the boat across the river to the west. "It is better to sleep on the sands than on the shore," he said. He and the other boatmen, it seemed, were only happy when they slept far from the haunts of men. In this instance the vast expanse of sand was haunted by only one man, an elderly Muslim fisherman with strange, web-toed feet, who was sitting in front of his grass hut warming himself over a fire made from an infinitesimal amount of dung.

When asked if there was any wood to be had, he laughed hollowly and waved an expressive hand towards the wastes behind him, in which nothing but a few coarse grasses and little scrub could be detected, and that half buried in sand. "You are welcome," he said, "to any wood that you can find, and I have no fish either."

In spite of what he said we began a frantic search for fuel. Further upriver we had found as much wood as we wanted. Now we were in a tract where even the real bank of the river to the left was so sparsely wooded that we did not dare to break off a single branch for fear of upsetting the inhabitants; while here, on what was not really terra firma at all, the sand for miles around had been scoured for driftwood by the fishermen so that none remained.

Each of us on his own course we set off across the sands towards the west, where the last conflagrations of the afterglow were taking place. Eventually I reached an island of silt that rose a few feet above the level of the surrounding sands. It was covered with a dense jungle of grass that was twice the height of a man and it was riddled with narrow, muddy backwaters which had not yet dried out completely. I followed one of them; I was barefooted and the mud underfoot was dank and sticky after the sand that was still warm from the sun. The grass met over head and made it into a dark tunnel. I had the disagreeable feeling that the grass was closing in behind me and covering my tracks. Suddenly I felt very frightened. It was now quite dark. I thought of snakes — I was in no state to realise that they were in all probability hibernating miles away on dry land, not coiled up in the mud in the middle of the Ganges. I thought of old, badtempered tigers with toothache. I turned back, trying hard not to start running. All the way to the hut I felt as if there was something close behind me with a giant hand that, without exerting any effort, would press me into the sand and smother me. At this moment with my primitive fears I was one with the inhabitants of the river valley.

Our combined efforts produced only sufficient scrub to make a single, impressive flare-up. Perhaps the others had felt as I had about going into the interior. The effect was similar to that produced by burning magnesium ribbon but, short-lived as it was, Jagannath managed to burn his fingers and once more, to everybody's delight, Wanda broached the medicine chest. Much later we all ate curried eggs, including the non-egg eating members of the crew — "What eggs?" they asked innocently on being asked if they had enjoyed them — and rice and parathas all prepared on the fisherman's expiring dung fire, which somehow never expired completely. The river, as exasperating as it was holy, still refused to yield up to us even the minutest fish.

The fisherman said that he was one of a syndicate who worked the reaches below the bridge. They had to pay the government for the fishing rights and they were indignant about this. "In the time of the Raj," he said, "we paid nothing. Now all is changed," and he looked at me reproachfully as if I was responsible for this new state of affairs, but I refused to accept the Imperial burden.

"We sell our fish for between two and four rupees a kilo according to the season," he said. "Between us, when all is decided, we each make a profit of four rupees a day." They sold their catch at Balawali and most of it went to Calcutta, an insatiable market.

"He asks how old you think he is," Karam Chand said.

It was a difficult question. I knew that the answer I would give would be the wrong one. It all depended whether he wanted to be thought old or young. He had a white beard and to me he looked as old as Methuselah.

"Seventy-five," I said. He looked displeased.

"According to his own reckoning he is only fifty-five," Karam Chand said. "And he is unhappy because, he says, by the time he will be seventy-five he will already have been dead for eighteen years."

That night G. and the boatmen slept in the hut with the fisherman, while Wanda and I slept in the open. It was a clear night. The sky was full of stars and there was a bitter wind from the north. At intervals a train lumbered over the bridge; otherwise, apart from the howling of the jackals, the silence was complete. Not even the river, now that it was flowing over a bed of deep sand, made the smallest sound.

At half past three in the morning, a time that we were coming to accept as a commonplace one for visiting on the Ganges, three men arrived and crouched down over the place where the fire had been. Mistrusting them, the fisherman, taking his duties as host more seriously than I would have done, resuscitated his fire and spent the rest of the night crouching over it with them, "in order", as he said in the morning, "that you might not be robbed."

At first light everything was hidden in mist; but by six-thirty it began to roll away majestically downriver. Bar-headed geese honked overhead going upstream.

I had a row with Wanda. It was about something so ludicrous that after it had been going on for some minutes neither of us could remember the reason; but it was no less bitter for that.

"I shall leave you here," she said. "Boo-hoo!"

It was not a convenient place to leave from. Besides what the devil would I do without her?

"Where will you go?" I said, really alarmed.

"I shall go back to my country and my people," she answered, majestically.

At this moment G., who had been hovering in the background, decided that it was time for him to intervene.

"Everything about this journey is impossible," he said. "Mathematically it is impossible. Boat floats in no water and men five and a half feet tall sleep in hut five feet wide. It is a rotten journey."

Listening to this tragic cri de coeur it was impossible to remain angry for long, and after Wanda had had a good cry behind the fisherman's hut, she cooked us all a lovely breakfast of porridge, eggs and tea with sand with everything. Before we set off we treated the old man for a nasty cough which probably came from too much smoking of his dirty old hookah, rewarded him for his kindness to us, and then left him alone on the sand surrounded by crows. It was a lonely place, and the trains whistling on the distant bridge did nothing to abate the feeling.

We left at eight-fifteen. Under the cliffs on the left bank the current was strong and once we got into it we made about five knots without any assistance from the oars, shooting down through water that was chocolate-coloured over a slippery runway of hard black mud. To the west the featureless desert that stretched away ten miles to a similar line of low cliffs which formed the right bank of the river, was enlivened, at a great distance, by a solitary tree. In the shallows flocks of snow-white egrets prodded scientifically for frogs.

At nine o'clock Karam Chand said that he had left his shirt at the camping-place. To save time I said that he could have one of mine. Then, remembering that I only had two, I retracted the offer and said that he must go back on foot and fetch it. Awed by the thought of such a journey he discovered his own in the bilges. He seemed pleased by my severity.

The strength was going out of the stream now. It was taking us down at not more than three knots through a series of vast bends. "Perfect sine curve," G. said appreciatively, "Ganga is also mathematician."

We passed a ferry and the ferryman who lived in a tent which was suspended on a ridge rope between two poles shouted to us that, in his opinion, we might reach the bridge of boats at Raoli that evening but that we would not have much current to assist us. Then once more we were in the wilderness, out in the middle of the river. The sun was hot on our backs. The only sign of human activity was a number of dark, cone-shaped stacks of reed that were like punctuation marks on the dazzling sand. There was in fact so little to excite our attention that we became disorientated and the energy seeped out of us as if we were a lot of leaky buckets. In order to keep awake Wanda began to fish, using some gear that the proprietor of the refreshment rooms at Hardwar, a sporty Sikh, who took no notice of the prohibitions in force there, had given her, using a part of the lid of a condensed milk tin as an enormous spinner.

"The only thing that the lady will catch with that will be the Gaunch," Bhosla said, gloomily, "and if she does, that will be the end of us all."

"What is the Gaunch?"

"The Gaunch is a great fish."

Two hours after setting off we passed three men sitting on top of a bullock-cart in the middle of the river. One of its axles had collapsed and it was lying on its side in the water. They had unyoked the bullocks and tethered them to a stake on the bank and were now smoking bidis placidly in midstream. They seemed perfectly content in this extraordinary situation, and brushed aside our efforts of assistance. "You are by Manwala," they said. If this was true then we were making painfully slow progress. Ahead of us was a choice of three channels, but knowing that it was useless to ask the drivers which was the best one, we made our own decision and chose the middle one. It was not a good choice and we suffered a prolonged stranding, the fifty-seventh of the voyage.

The sun was now high and hot and we became the victims of the mirage. To the west long lines of cattle seemed to float in mid-air; trees manifested themselves in what was a treeless waste, detached from mother earth and hovering upside down on their doubles. Ahead of us was a village. At one moment its component parts were solid and integrated, the next there were two identical villages which overlapped one another. It was like looking through a range-finder that was out of focus. According to the map it might be a place called Jansath. In this expanding and contracting landscape we felt like drunken men who had boastfully announced that they were able to drive and were now regretting it. Lifelessly, in a stream that was as heavy and inert as lead, we poled down towards the village, which had now begun to wobble like a jelly. Over it a long skein of geese which was also subject to the general distortion, undulated in an alarming fashion.

"I think I'm going to be sick," Wanda said.

The village was on an island of silt. It was in a state of ruin. The houses were roofless. The largest, which had probably belonged to a landowner of some substance, overhung the bank; the next monsoon rains would probably see the end of it. As we dropped down past this melancholy settlement the inhabitants crowded to the bank, emerging from their grass huts which they had set up amongst the ruins and offered us a mass of conflicting information. This, they said, was not Jansath but the village of Burra Semla. The first place of any size we would reach was Sukarthal, and after that we would arrive at the bridge of boats at Raoli. It was not far. We were heartened by what they said and increased our efforts. The river was full of birds: great pale bar-headed geese with black flashes on the backs of their heads; and out on the sand there were orange coloured Brahminy ducks, gulls and shag and there were a couple of pied-kingfishers, perched on stones from which they looked at us unafraid. It was noon. We went aground for the fifty-ninth time.

Now Karam Chand, who up to this moment had never deserted his post as helmsman, took the stroke oar and increased the rate of striking to an almost unendurable pitch as a result of which after three-quarters of an hour he had not only rowed us out but himself too. Nevertheless, we were all agreed that we would not eat until we reached Raoli. There was really very little choice. The only food we possessed in any quantity was eggs, and three out of the total boat crew were not prepared to eat eggs unless they were so heavily disguised as something else that they could lay their hands on their hearts and say that they were not aware of what they were doing. To keep ourselves going we ate guavas. They were delicious. "Guavas," said G., "are excellent fruits." He sounded like the paterfamilias in the Swiss Family Robinson, and I thought that he was about to embark on a disquisition on their various qualities, but all he said was, "Very good for clear motions," which was not what a Swiss Pastor would have said. "I haven't been for four days," Wanda said, "and you talk about clear motions. I'd be glad to have any motions at all."

We alternated between extremes of elation and despair. Instead of swallowing them I threw my guava skins over the side. "Ashes to ashes, dust to dust and unto dust thou shalt return," G. said disconcertingly. "Those skins are rich in vitamin C."

We were now aground again. Around us small unidentifiable birds stood up to their ankles in water. It was a disheartening sight. A hundred yards further down a vigorous stream flowed into the river from the right, seething and bubbling where the confluence took place, and we hauled the boat towards it through the pitifully shallow water until suddenly we were up to our necks in it. Was this the Banganga, emerging from its tortuous wanderings through the back-blocks of Saharanpur and Muzaffarnagar or was it just another channel of the Ganges itself, this all-devouring river? It was impossible to tell. At this point the map ended in mid-stream and we had not got the adjacent sheet. To the east it marked a village called Semla. Was this the same as Burra Semla, the collapsing village which we had passed an hour before, or was it one of a series of villages whose last name was Semla, like the Wallops in Hampshire on the edge of Salisbury Plain? If it was, then the river had changed its course radically since 1907. But what was a mile or two either way to the Ganges when Timur Leng's bridgehead over it at Tughlaqpur now lay twelve miles inland? If the village was Burra Semla then we must be quite close to Raoli; on the other hand, if the river was the Banganga then we would never reach Raoli by nightfall. We were lost.

The only consolation about being lost on a river is that if you go on downstream you are bound to arrive somewhere different, unlike being lost in a forest, when you are quite likely to end up where you started at the beginning of the day.

On the bank there were a couple of goatherds with whom Karam Chand had a long conversation from which even he, used to the ways of the country, emerged exasperated.

"They say that they do not know the name of this other stream or where it comes from. They have never heard of Burra Semla and they have no knowledge of Sukarthal, the place spoken of by the station-master," he said. "Either they are persons with weak minds or else we have already passed these places."

Whatever this new river was, the strong current picked us up and sent us on our way and a few minutes later we saw, stretching across the horizon, from west to east, a long dark line of something that looked like a wall but which, as we drew nearer to it, proved to be thickly wooded high ground. On the foreshore, a small girl who was looking after a flock of sheep and goats said that Raoli was at a distance of two kos.

Half a mile further on we passed four fishermen asleep on a sandbank in the shadow of their nets which were drying on poles. With a lot of hollering we managed to wake them. "Raoli," they said, looking down at us grumpily, "is three kos. With such a boat you may reach it in two hours," and lay down again. A quarter of an hour later some men loading a country boat with sugar cane said that Raoli was four kos. We rowed down an interminable reach with the woods looming more and more distinctly. We could see a large temple with its spire shining in the sun, and a number of smaller buildings half hidden among the trees; and ahead of us, forming an impassable barrier, a bridge of boats with lines of bullock carts crossing it. We could only feel amazement that we had succeeded in arriving at our destination. It was a memorable moment.

There were twenty boats strung across the river with a roadway of timber and straw laid on top of them. Long guy ropes extended upstream from the pontoons to buoys anchored in the channel, and they were reinforced by other cables which held the boats steady when the current was strong; at this time of year it was almost non-existent.

We rowed the boat so hard into the bank that it stuck in the silt and there was no need to tie up to anything. Although we were happy to have arrived, it was not an attractive spot. Because the current was so sluggish the bridge formed a sort of dam and the channels between the boats were clogged with grass and the broken branches of trees. The water was very dirty and it was covered with a layer of ashes from the cremation places upstream. There were masses of flies, and as the bullock carts thundered down on to the bridge from the bank they raised dense clouds of dust which settled on us thickly. Both G. and the boatmen were anxious to set off to eat and look for the lorry and we let them go. We had both had more than enough of the company of our fellow men for a bit; besides we suspected that the eating arrangements in the town, if there was a town, would be similar to those at Balawali, perhaps worse. Also we were convinced that the lorry would not be there.

When they had gone off I took the boat a little way upstream and Wanda cooked a delicious lunch of fried eggs with rice and chillies. Then we drank tea. The heavy traffic across the bridge had ceased. In a whole hour the only vehicle to cross it was an ekka, a small pony cart with a canopy over it and side curtains, which came dashing across the sands from the east. As it went up the steep bank the rear curtain was lifted and revealed a lady of quality, swathed in dazzlingly white silk which just showed the crimson hem of an expensive sari under it, who glowered at us with a pair of immense eyes. The only other company we had were a number of turtles which stuck their heads out of the water and remained motionless with their mouths open like a lot of floating beer bottles.

The landing party reappeared. They were in ill-humour — the eating arrangements had been even worse than we had imagined they would be — and it was with some satisfaction that they gave us the bad news. This was not Raoli but the elusive Sukarthal. "We must find the bridge-master and make him open the bridge," G. said.

The bridgemaster was asleep in a grass hut; but although he was a dapper figure in khaki jodhpurs and a clean white shirt, he was not an attractive individual. He addressed us in a hectoring manner and spoke of us collectively as "*Tum*," which was not a polite form of address. Perhaps it was from habitually addressing people whom he considered to be his inferiors, but we thought none the better of him for that.

"I shall not open the bridge until the morning," he said. "I have not enough men."

To anyone who was not on his way to Calcutta this might have seemed reasonable, but we were in no mood to be thwarted. I had never seen G. so angry.

"This man is supposed to keep enough men to open his bridge," he said. "He is making one hundred and fifty rupees a day and now he is saving money by not employing men. Now I am asking him for his complaint book and I shall write a complaint."

The bridgemaster was completely unimpressed.

"I have no complaint book," he said.

"You must have complaint book. It is the regulation."

For some time the battle raged with this obdurate, bloody-minded man. To me bridgemasters seemed an ill-tempered lot, like army cooks. "Tell him that if he doesn't open it we will do it ourselves," I said.

"He says that is contrary to regulations."

"Show him Mr. Nehru's letter," Wanda said. She had great faith in the Prime Minister.

The bridgemaster pored over it. "And don't make it dirty!" she said, in a menacing way.

"He says it is no letter of authority to open bridge. It is a letter asking for assistance to be rendered. What is our hurry," he says. "There are many things of interest in this place. There is the temple of Sukra and the temple of Viswa-Karma. It is a place of pilgrimage. He will be happy to show them to you." At least he was no longer calling us "*Tum*"; but this was a courtesy that was lost on Wanda.

"Tell him that if he doesn't open his bridge we will telephone the Prime Minister."

By now I was almost weeping with vexation. It was late afternoon. On the bank men were ploughing and harrowing. Already they and their beasts were casting long shadows. Finally we accepted defeat, unloaded the boat; pressed a number of men who were in the service of the bridgemaster into our own by the promise of money, and together with them dragged the boat overland and into the river below the bridge. It was complete defeat because, as Karam Chand observed, most of the money which we were giving to these men would end up in the pocket of the bridgemaster.

It was a quarter past four before we finally put to sea again, watched impassively by the bridgemaster who sat in the cane chair by a little table outside his hut. More than happy to leave Sukarthal behind us, we went off at a great rate. As we cleared the narrows and the river opened out, at the head of an impressive promontory we could see the temple of Sukra, the planet Venus, and the lesser one of Viswa-Karma standing in the shade of an immense tree. Viswa-Karma, in addition to being omnificent, is the great architect of the universe. He is the engineer-god — operator of a lathe so powerful that with it he cut off an eighth part of the sun's brightness, the shavings of which fell on earth and were formed into the discus of Vishnu, the trident of Siva, the weapons of the God of Wealth and the complete armoury of the God of War. At this moment I wished that they would take them up collectively and strike down the bridgemaster. But there was no time to pursue these bloodthirsty speculations. With Karam Chand at stroke we rowed at a ferociously high rate of striking, down long, wide reaches, like a school crew at Henley coming up past Remenham Barrier while the sun went swiftly down until it sank in to a bath of cloud that rose like steam about it.

It was at this moment with the light almost gone, when it seemed that we must be benighted and have to spend another night in the open, that we suddenly saw a bus.

It was an extraordinary sight in such a place. It was lurching along the left bank, following a line of leading marks through the sands. Heartened we put in a last sharp burst, rounded a bend and saw a bridge of boats with a couple of huts silhouetted against the brilliant red of the afterglow. Then we shot down into the pool above the bridge all cheering madly, and I did what I had wanted to do all day while I had been sweating at the oars, dived over the side and swam the last forty yards or so. It was the most delicious swim I can remember.

A number of men came running across the bridge towards the boat. "Is this Raoli?" Karam Chand shouted. "Yes, yes," one of them said. "We have been expecting you. This is the bridge at Raoli."

Chapter Nine

Terra firma

When the body is afflicted by senility and diseases, the holy water of Mother Ganga is the medicine, and Lord Narayana, from whose feet Ganga emanates, is the great physician.

Lord Dhanwantari

The bridgemaster at Raoli was a very different sort of man from his miserable counterparts at Sukarthal and Hardwar. "You will sleep in my hut," he said without preamble, and when we said that he must not put himself out, protestations that were dictated partly by politeness and partly by reluctance to accept his offer without first seeing what we were letting ourselves in for, he looked so down-cast that we hastily accepted. Bridgekeepers on the Ganges appeared to wield such despotic powers that it seemed to us he might evict an entire family from its dwelling in order to please us. In Asia it is usually best to accept the hospitality that is offered, however rudimentary it may be; failure to do so will almost certainly be the cause of acute discomfort to a number of people whom you have never seen. In fact the bridgekeeper was a kindly man.

We need not have worried. After what we had grown used to in the last five days his hut, which was perched on top of the bank above the bridge, seemed a place of unimaginable comfort. It was fifteen feet by twelve and about eight feet high and could easily contain us all. It was made of grass. Small, white birds were roosting in the thatch of the roof, but after inspecting us they soon settled down. The mud floor was so smoothed by use that it was more like polished wood than mud. The back part of the hut which formed the sleeping quarters was slightly higher than the front, and was covered with straw mats.

While the luggage was being brought up by the boatmen and some of the bridgemaster's minions, an operation in which we, the so-called passengers, were not allowed to take part as being beneath our dignity (God knows what they thought we had been doing on the way down from Hardwar) we heard the sounds of a band of music coming from some way off — quavery flutings, the braying of a trumpet, interspersed with the booming of drums and strange noises made by unidentifiable instruments. There was going to be a wedding and the band was getting into shape for the following day.

Led by the bridgemaster, who was both surprised and pleased that we were interested, we set off down a deeply rutted track which ran between dense plantations of sugar cane. Mist had already blotted out the stars. It hung above us ten or twelve feet in the air like the roof of a marquee. Ahead, where the village was, it was tinged with orange rather like the night sky over a great city except that here the light sometimes increased in strength and sometimes died away. It was an eerie scene. The combination of the outlandish music with the noise made by the myriad frogs in the fields, the gigantic shadows cast by the pressure lantern which the bridgemaster was carrying, the flicking light projected on the fog and the novelty of finding ourselves on terra firma bound for an unknown destination all combined to produce the same sort of feelings of excitement and apprehension that one has when visiting a place of entertainment in the disreputable part of a city.

Now the croaking of the frogs reached a crescendo and we walked past a pond straight into the centre of the village where a big fire was burning. As we approached someone threw a bundle of straw on to it so that it flared up, illuminating a large crowd of people who were gathered round it in a half circle.

Facing this audience on the other side of the fire was the band, four men and one small boy whose head was almost completely snuffed out by a man's western-style felt hat, the sort of hat worn by sahibs in "mufti" in the early thirties. He wielded two black instruments which were made from some kind of gourd and which emitted a curious clicking sound. One man was blowing a trumpet, another was blasting away on the clarinet, and the other two were walloping drums. Everyone seemed delighted to see us; great eyes flashed and teeth gleamed. We were presented to the Headman. A wooden bed was brought on which we were all four installed; the fire was heaped up and the bridegroom was produced. He had a crew-cut and looked more like a college boy than someone destined the next day to set off in a chariot drawn by bullocks to fetch his bride for the consummation of his marriage from a village two miles away.

This is the extent of the ceremony. The family of the bride-groom sends a present of sweetmeats to the house of the bride, and the following evening, when it is dark, he sets off in the chariot, accompanied by the rest of his party on foot. At the house of the bride the parents bury a plough-shaft in the ground; another is buried outside the house of the groom. This day is chosen after long consultation with astrologers, as being an auspicious one.

At the bride's house there is a feast which lasts most of the night and the next morning, at dawn, she sets off with him for his village. Before leaving, their nails are cut by the village barber. With them the bride's parents send a return present; one or more painted pots containing sweets, and when the pair enter the house of the bridegroom, his sister demands yet another present — only if it is given will the bride be allowed to pass. They then worship the family god. This is the extent of the ceremony. They have sometimes already been married for years.

While G. and I sat with the men, Wanda went off with the women. Soon they were engrossed in an inspection of one another's clothes and jewellery. The women were wrapped in saris that were either vivid red, or else a particularly brilliant king-fisher blue. Their jewellery had a wonderful, rough-hewn quality. They wore bracelets and anklets which looked as if they were carved from ingots of solid silver, and their necklaces of coloured glass or crystals were of such barbaric splendour that if they had been displayed on black velvet in the Rue de la Paix, they would have satisfied the most sophisticated taste.

Food was produced — a mixture of rice, sugar and clarified butter, at which we pecked apprehensively. There was something a little grubby about its appearance which gave promise of stomach trouble ahead. Heavily swaddled babies like well-packed parcels, their eyes ringed with lamp black, were handed up for inspection; the Headman bemoaned the demise of the Raj.

The village was about the same size as the one we had visited up-river, but less primitive. The walls of the houses were covered with curlicues and strange designs in red and umber. Taking a lantern, the Headman led us into one of them. It was a sort of village guest house. Inside a number of men were lying on charpoys under quilts. With the din outside sleep must have been impossible, and when we came in they all sat up. It was a large room and on the back wall under the thatched roof there were more designs worked in the mud, shapes that were half-human, half-animal, and impressions of palm trees and houses.

"Why don't you say something to them?" Wanda said.

"What do you want me to say?" I said. "That the evenings are drawing in?"

"We shouldn't have come into their bedroom," she said, unreasonably, as if it had been my idea.

We were shown the wedding chariot, a splendidly antediluvian vehicle. It was constructed on similar lines to the little pony-carts called ekkas, but it had a domed canopy and red side curtains. On an impulse Wanda asked if we might ride in it. The Headman was delighted, and in a short while a pair of pale, impassive bullocks dressed in dark coloured blankets were brought out and yoked to it. Inside it was a close fit, even for two persons, but with the curtains drawn it had the air of a *cabinet privé*. The dome had chunks of coloured glass set in it of the same sort as was used in making the women's necklaces. The suspension was made from curved pieces of wood, covered with chased brass, as unyielding as that of a bullock cart but more elegant. As we lurched through the mist, thrown from side to side and bouncing up and down on the seat of woven cords which acted as a trampoline, the rest of the party followed on foot, guffawing and making lewd remarks to one another.

Back in the hut we had a splendid, end-of-term, vegetable curry (I was just about to eat the first paratha when a nasty, sharp-toothed little dog snatched it out of my hand and ran off into the night); rum was issued to the boatmen; cheroots to the bridgemaster who did not drink. We gave ourselves whisky. What a week it had been! The distance from Hardwar to Raoli is only about thirty-five miles as the crow flies; by river it is much more. We had been stranded sixty-three times and crossed thirty-six rapids. The journey had taken five and a half days. It seemed more. By nine o'clock we were asleep.

The next morning, as there was no need for anyone to get up early for the first time since leaving Hardwar, the boatmen did. At a quarter to five they started threshing about in their bedding like baby whales, clearing their throats, praying and stumbling over us. Outside it was as black as pitch and there was thick fog. At five o'clock bullock-carts began to cross the bridge, making a tremendous noise. They passed so close to the hut that I expected them to demolish it. It was like being dead and in hell.

At seven the fog was still thick, but now the sun was trying to force its way through. It was bitterly cold. Overhead, a thin sliver of moon was fading in a sky that was becoming, every moment, a deeper shade of blue. The carts were still coming. There were dozens of them. They came lurching out of the wastes on the left bank and down to the bridge, their drivers muffled to the eyes in white cloths, and there they remained, jammed head to tail, until the leaders got their beasts moving up the steep cut in the right bank where our hut

was. Then the whole lot began to move forward and surge past it
blaspheming and cajoling, and out into the stubble around the bridgehead where the fires of those who had arrived earlier gleamed through
the fog. Then the sun began to come up and everything was tinged
a dull bronze. It was like an engraving of the crossing of a Russian
river in the war of 1812.

By eight o'clock the fog had almost disappeared, and the sun was
warm on our backs. I set off upstream to a lonely place where I
bathed, only to find when I emerged from the river that Karam Chand
was hovering on the sand with my towel, waiting for me, an Indian
Jeeves. Unasked, he had constituted himself my personal body-
servant, but I was embarrassed by his attentions and I rejected them.
He was deeply wounded but, although he succeeded in making me
feel brutish, I knew that it was best that I should do so. I was unused
to being cosseted, and I found it impossible to step back twenty
years or more to a time when I had had to accept such treatment
because it was part of the system. I had always detested it. To me
it seemed ridiculous that an able-bodied man should need help in
putting on his shoes. Now it seemed doubly so.

As Wanda and I had predicted there was no sign of the lorry;
worse still, there were no boats in which to continue the journey,
and, naturally, no boatmen. However, there was a bus; the number
937, which would take us to Bijnor, the principal town of the district,
ten miles away on the left bank. From there we could telephone
to Hardwar, replenish our stores and rejoin the river at a place called
Daranagar, some eight miles south of Bijnor, leaving Bhosla and
Jagannath to wait with the boat for the lorry. We decided to take
Karam Chand with us as far as Bijnor so that we would know how
long they would all have to wait.

The bus arrived at eleven-thirty, exactly on time. It was painted
blue and green and it was decorated with highly coloured Himalayan
landscapes and pictures of gods, as stylised as the paintings of roses
and castles on an English canal boat. Its departure was delayed
because of the time taken to load our baggage on to the roof, an
operation which the other passengers, who had been ordered to
disembark in order to make the crossing of the bridge on foot,
watched with undisguised impatience. "They are displeased," said the
bridgekeeper with the equanimity which human beings reserve for the
misfortunes of others, "because many of them are missing their
connections at Bijnor."

It was time to go. Everyone had been paid, including Karam Chand,
who, although he was not entitled to anything because he was on

the pay-roll of the Irrigation Authority, richly deserved to be. Extra baksheesh had been distributed. Karam Chand had been reluctant to take the money but the others seemed happy enough and, for the first time, even Bhosla, that most unforthcoming of men, registered some emotion. For a moment there was even a suspicion of dewy eyes amongst them but he and Jagannath soon recovered from this unmanly display and when we finally left them, squatting in the boat, to cross the bridge they scarcely looked up.

Just as the bus was leaving the bridgemaster whispered something in G.'s ear.

"He is asking you to speak to Prime Minister," G. said. "He says you must ask Mr. Nehru to let him have the bridge for 15,000 rupees next year without putting it up to auction."

I said that what he asked was impossible, and the bridgekeeper turned away disconsolate. I felt I had made a mistake. It is better in India to say that you will do a thing and not do it, rather than say it is impossible. In this way hope is prolonged indefinitely in the breast of the suppliant and one still retains his esteem.

There were fifty-eight passengers in the bus, an excess of only four over the permitted maximum. There was no room in the first class up behind the driver's compartment which was decorated with artificial flowers and had little stained-glass windows set in it above the windscreen, so we took our places in the back of the bus with the second- and third-class passengers wherever we could fit in ourselves. There were Muslim ladies shrouded in the all-enveloping garments called chador. (The place where their faces should have been was a hole covered with netting through which their breath came strongly and unromantically.) There were country men with thin, worn faces and droopy grey moustaches wearing little white fore-and-aft hats, and girls of extraordinary beauty with jewels in their noses. There were wild-looking, barefooted men whose toes were as big as a normal person's thumbs. They wore big, roughly tied headcloths, and they all carried bamboo poles with weighted ends. There were fat, bandy-legged clerks from the town. There were women with babies at their breasts which slept as if they were drugged; and there were small boys who, all the time they were in the bus, wriggled like eels and picked their noses just like English boys. Everyone was half-buried in luggage that was either too fragile or too valuable to go on top of the bus. There was a warm, animal smell of bodies; but it was far less disagreeable than it would have been in England, because the majority of the occupants were addicted to ritual bathing. It mingled with odours compounded of spices, bidis, betel nut and a ghastly smell of kerosene which came from our stove which had been taken into the bus upside down in the frenzy of departure.

The bus ground on, following the leading marks. The wind had got up and from time to time clouds of sand blew through the open windows, blotting out the occupants. After a mile or so we came to a shallow tributary of the Ganges that meandered aimlessly through the wilderness. It was crossed by a flimsy causeway of grass and here we disembarked in order to lighten the load. While we were waiting for the bus to go over, four men came running towards us across the sands, carrying a litter. On it there was a box-like construction with a white cloth over it, edged with royal blue, and decorated at each corner with a small tuft of crimped paper of the sort that Mrs. Beeton used to recommend for enhancing the appearance of lamb chops.

"These men are the Majil le Janihar and they are carrying a body to the river for cremation," G. said.

Soon the bus reached dry land and was thundering through a country of green fields and groves of ancient trees. The driver was trying to make up for lost time, and the passengers became more animated. After one stop we arrived at Bijnor and, leaving our luggage at the Municipal Office which was by the bus stop, we set off at once for the post office. On the way to it we saw two dim, drunken men being drawn up the street in a cycle ricksha. It seemed early in the day to be so far gone.

The post office was an arcaded building with heavily barred windows. Inside it was so dark that for some moments, coming straight from the glare of the street, it was difficult to make out anything at all. It was a large and lofty room and beneath under-exposed portraits of Mr. Nehru as a young man and the Mahatma, numbers of clerks were thumbing despairingly through dog-eared volumes bound in vellum. We booked a call to Hardwar and settled down to wait, but as all the indications were that it would never come through, we left Karam Chand by the telephone and set off to see the town.

It would have required a stronger sense of history than any of us possessed to make much of Bijnor at this moment. Even the invaluable Murray's *Guide* seemed stumped by it. "No ruins," it said after a short preamble in which it identified the town as being the one-time capital of the Rohilla Rajputs, "remain of places identified as being renowned of old ... The Brahmanical threads made here

have acquired a general reputation." But the Brahmanical threads were
not made at Bijnor any more, and the cessation of the manufactory
seemed to have been attended by the demoralisation of the inhabitants
and the indifference of the municipal authorities to their health and
comfort. In the main street clouds of flies hung over heaps of uncol-
lected filth and blanketed the sweetmeats in the open-fronted shops;
sewage brimmed over in the open drains that ran down either side of
the street, or, when it reached a sufficiently high level, spilled through
dark holes into unimaginable depths beneath, leaving the residue to
make its way downstream by gravity which scarcely operated in a
place that was as flat as a pancake. I began to sympathise with the
two drunken men in the ricksha. If one had to live in Bijnor this
was one way to escape from the realities of the place.

Sweetshops apart, the street was remarkable for the large number
of dentist's surgeries with painted signboards over them depicting
gaping pink mouths filled with huge teeth. Inside these establishments
patients were writhing in torment in the chairs and uttering awful
strangled noises. I was anxious to have a closer view of what the
dentists were actually doing to their patients and what restraints they
employed to keep them from bolting down the road; but like professional men everywhere they resented a layman's interest in their
work and huffily drew the curtains in my face.

Also in the main street there was a clockless municipal clock tower,
in red brick, "Erected under the patronage of H. S. Bates, Collector
and Magistrate" in 1926, "Foundation stone laid by Mrs. Bates".
Although it was easy to poke fun at this extraordinary building which
would have been more at home in some sad industrial town in the
north of Britain than in this equally sad place in the heart of Uttar
Pradesh, the nostalgia that had prompted its construct was perfectly
comprehensible. More attractive was the mosque, hidden away
beyond some crumbling alleys, not old but old-looking, with a tank
of water in the forecourt, round which old men with dyed beards
hovered.

We had booked the call to Hardwar at twelve-thirty. It was now
two o'clock. If we did not succeed in getting through within half
an hour the last bus to Chandpur would leave, and our arrangements
would be upset. Originally we had intended to go to Daranagar, on
the left bank and pick up a boat, but according to the clerks in the
municipal office, the boats there drew so much water that they were
unusable at this time of the year. They had advised us to go to
Chandpur and from there to Garhmuktesar, about sixty miles south
of Bijnor. According to them there was no place between Daranagar

and the bridge at Garhmuktesar where there was the remotest chance
of finding a boat, and the map seemed to confirm this.

So far we had travelled thirty-five miles down the river as the crow
flies at a cost of £25, not including the food. At this rate of expenditure
it would cost us £800 to reach Calcutta.

The bus left for Chandpur without us; and it was not until an hour
later that we managed to contact Hardwar. The connection was bad
and the voice of one of the men from Shell came to us as remote
and distant as if over thousands of miles of open ocean. There was
no question of asking after his health. It was simply a matter of
screeching into the mouthpiece the basic information that we had
arrived, and hoping that he understood.

Now we took Karam Chand to the bus stop to send him back to
the boat. It was a funereal journey and when he got there he held on
to the municipal railings and blubbed like a baby.

"He is crying for two reasons," G. said. "He is crying because
he says that you have treated him more kindly than if he was your
own son, and he is crying because he says that the other boatmen
have already gone and when he arrives there he will be alone."

My first impulse was to ask Karam Chand why, if he knew that this
was going to happen, he had not said so before we left the river.
We could have withheld part of their pay and given it to him to hand
over when they reached Hardwar. But I knew that this was not the
kind of question that can be asked in India – it was too logical and
would therefore cause grave offence; besides even if I had asked it
I knew there was absolutely no chance of receiving a coherent reply.
At any rate I did not believe that the boatmen would leave when they
could have a free lift in a lorry. It turned out that I was wrong and
we learned later that, as soon as we had left for Bijnor, they had
departed for Hardwar.

After Wanda had mothered Karam Chand a little he allowed himself to be put in the bus, sniffing and looking tragic. There was a
further interminable wait before it left, and when it did we were
relieved. So much emotion had left us exhausted. It had also left us
with a raging hunger. It was now three-thirty and we had breakfasted
thinly. So far as we could discover there were only two places in
which it was even remotely possible to eat, and both on inspection
proved to be so loathsome that it seemed tantamount to suicide to
patronise either, but there is something about the air of Asia which
engenders an emptiness that is unlike anything one experiences in the
West. Without food one's legs begin to feel like jelly. At this moment
we were all three suffering from these symptoms and, in spite of

the fact that our impulse was to patronise neither restaurant, we entered the Evergreen Hotel.

Evergreen and Hotel in name only, to us it was the quintessence of everything that Bijnor had come to signify. The open-cast kitchen, which faced a road in which clouds of dust were swirling, was full of flies. They were not so immediately apparent as those in the shops. These flies had been rendered comatose by good living. But it was the interior that made the deepest impression. The floor was littered with unwanted food. On the greasy tables the contents of the capless ketchup bottles had long since coagulated, and the air was filled with the restless drone of bluebottles going about their business. Appalled, we sought shelter in an inner, darker room where two local inhabitants, friendly professional men, were lingering over the remains of their meal. It was difficult to imagine the contingency that had driven them to eat in such a place when, as they later admitted, they had homes of their own to go to in the city. This inner room was entirely bare of ornament, apart from two tiers of stone shelves. The only illumination came from a fanlight in the roof. It was more like a mortuary than a place to eat. One of the two diners, both of whom were lawyers, offered us his card. "This is a very dirty restaurant," he remarked cheerfully. "It is better to eat cooked foods."

We gave our order to a small, intelligent-looking boy who answered to the name of Vishnu. After a short interval he re-appeared with some chapatis which he kept clamped to the plate by a grimy thumb. "If you are Vishnu you should be four-handed. You are contaminating the food with your dirty fingers," the lawyer who had given us his card shouted – and to us, "It is useless to remonstrate with such people, they have no idea of hygiene."

Vishnu grinned, "The hands of Vishnu are already filled," he answered pertly, but when he arrived with the tea he removed his fingers from the inside of the teacups before putting them down on the table. The lawyer had a good laugh at this. "That boy," he said, "is a very witty boy. He is saying that although Vishnu has four hands they are filled. This is true. Vishnu has shell in one hand, discus in second hand, club in third hand and lotus in fourth hand. He is clever boy; but he has dirty fingers."

Of all the awful meals that I have ever been called upon to consume, this was one of the worst. Vile, greasy gobbets of unidentifiable meat floated in a loathsome sauce and there were little pots of pale, watery lentil. G.'s vegetable curry was an affront to the senses. Everything had the dankness of left-overs. Our gorges rose and we rejected the meat and the vegetables; but because we were starving and in spite of the thought of Vishnu's fingers, we toyed with the chapatis which were like rubber tobacco pouches and drank luke-warm tea. Even so we knew that we were running into danger. Perhaps Vishnu was not really Vishnu at all, but an embodiment of Kali, The Destroyer.

Outside in the road again we were confronted by a sign over a doctor's establishment. "Consult in all kinds diseases," it read. "1/Phthisis. 2/Catarrh. 3/Fever. 4/Sterility. 5/Medical Certificates. 6/Constipation. 7/All kinds weaknesses. 8/Birth Control."

"If we are staying here we are having all these," G. said gloomily.

Because we had missed the bus to Chandpur we now found our-selves under the necessity of travelling the whole way to Garhmukte-sar Bridge by train. It was an arrangement that would have daunted the most determined traveller. The train left at six-thirty in the evening and arrived, two hours and forty minutes later at a place called Gajraula. The connection for the bridge was at two in the morning. There was no waiting room either at Gajraula or at Garhmuktesar Bridge.

While we were wondering what to do until six-thirty, we were addressed by a stoutish man dressed *à l'anglais* in a tweed jacket and baggy corduroy trousers.

"My name is Srotriya Subodh Shankar," he said, "You are liking Bijnor?"

"It is very interesting."

"It is a quiet place. Now you will come to my house. You have eaten?"

We told him that we had lunched at the Evergreen Hotel.

"Most unwise," he said. "Evergreen Hotel is not a pure hotel. There are no pure hotels in Bijnor. I am Brahman. I am telling you this. It is the truth."

He led us through a maze of alleys flanked by dilapidated houses to his own residence. Most of them were built of small red bricks about two inches thick, the size and shape of gold ingots.

"Those bricks," he said "are the bricks used by the Mughals."

"Then these houses must be very old?"

"No, no, not all are old," he replied. "Some are already falling down and they were rebuilding, using same bricks. You are dis-appointed? That is because you are British. British are only liking old things."

On the way we visited a small, unremarkable temple which con-tained an equally unremarkable black lingam, by which Mr. Shankar set some store. We stood round it for some time looking at it and wondering what to say. Finally, I asked him out of politeness, if it was made of marble.

"Yes, yes," he said, "It is Marmar."

When Mr. Shankar was out of earshot, having misheard him, I asked G. if "Meera" was "Marble".

"Meera* is princess who refused to have intercourse with husband," G. said.

He offered no further explanation and I was not inclined to pursue the matter. I felt depressed. In India even the most mundane inquiries have a habit of ending in this way. There may be two answers, there may be five, a dozen or a hundred; the only thing that is certain is that all will be different. Usually it is because one is misunderstood.

Mr. Shankar's house was well-hidden. We went in through a gateway with a pointed, Islamic arch, up a winding staircase to the first floor and on through a series of dark, shuttered rooms, into which the sun shone in dusty bars of light. Finally he led us into a room on the shady side of the house in which the shutters were thrown open. It was simply furnished. There was a small, modern table and some chairs and the walls were decorated with bazaar prints of gods and goddesses. In one corner there was a crumbling pile of well-used religious books and manuscripts.

After a short interval Mr. Shankar's wife appeared. She was enormously tall for an Indian, close on six foot and she was extremely handsome. She radiated confidence, cheerfulness and sex. She was twenty-eight. Her husband was forty and looked ten years older. They were a pleasant pair. While we ate the delicious spherical sweets called rasgulla, we listened to Mr. Shankar.

"We are Srotriya Brahmans," he said. "Readers of the Srotri-condensation of the Vedas – but I am not reading them. If I was reading them I would have no time for business. I am advocate." Everyone of any substance in Bijnor seemed to be devoted to the Law. On the way to his house we had been fleetingly introduced to several large gentlemen who also followed the profession. "Only my father now is true Srotriya," he went on. "He is praying eleven hours every day. He was landowner, now he has nothing to do but pray."

The United Provinces, now Uttar Pradesh, was the domain of the zamindari, great landlords, many of them absentees. With the coming of Independence the situation was reversed. Now more than eighty per cent of the holdings are in the hands of peasants who own five acres or less each. It is an equitable – and from the point of

* Meera was a Princess who refused to live with her husband, Krishna being her love.

view of increased food production — thoroughly unworkable arrangement.

"I pay six thousand rupees a year in tax," said Mr. Shankar. Without knowing his income it was difficult to know whether to congratulate him or commiserate with him. "We have four servants. My wife goes out very rarely. She has not been to the market for fourteen years; since we were married. All the shopping is done either by myself or one of the servants so, you see, I am a busy man."

He took us out on to a gallery that encircled a small, deep court. On the opposite side of it four handsome children, three boys and a girl, were waiting to be introduced to us. For the meeting they assumed suitably solemn expressions but really they were as lively and full of fun as their mother, and they soon relaxed.

Together we went up to the roof. The sun was going down. It bathed the minarets of the mosque and the roof-tops in a brilliant golden light. The city no longer had the air of doom and decay that had seemed an inseparable part of it. The laughing children, now slyly pinching one another, the mother smiling as enigmatically as La Gioconda and Mr. Shankar who had exchanged the servitude of the Brahman ritual for the equally exacting one of shopping for a household of ten had exorcised it.

But it was a temporary respite, and when this hospitable man had left us at the station, to which he insisted on accompanying us in one of the little pony-carts called tongas, we began, once again, to feel terribly low. Empty, the second-class compartment with its multiplicity of shutters, gratings and fly screens, feebly lit by a single naked bulb, was like a condemned cell — filled with our monstrous possessions the effect was claustrophobic. We felt as if we were buried alive. I was oppressed too, by the fact that we had abandoned the river; to do so, however temporarily, seemed contrary to the spirit of the venture; and we all felt, in varying degrees, unwell.

Wanda was the first to succumb. By the time we reached Gajraula the effects of lunching at the Evergreen Hotel had begun to make themselves felt. There was no point in taking the two a.m. train to Garhmuktesar — there never had been. It would simply mean that we would be marooned on a platform equally lacking in amenity in the small hours of the morning, and I asked the stationmaster at Gajraula if he would allow us to remain in our compartment when the train was shunted into a siding. I expected him to raise all kinds of objections but he, poor man, was so heavily engaged in working two telephones and a signalling apparatus simultaneously, that he was not even able to reply, and I took his silence for assent.

Although the carriages were in a siding the place was as bright as day. With the departure of the engine, the supply of water in the lavatory had been cut off and the nearest arrangements were at the far end of the main platform which, like all Indian platforms, was extremely long.

By now Wanda was really ill with the complaint that had killed off a large proportion of the members of the East India Company. She spent the entire night getting down from the train, dragging herself across the tracks, hauling herself up on to the platform and making the long journey to the other end of the station. Usually, as soon as she returned it was time for her to set off again. At two o'clock in the morning, I was assisting her down the platform when the early train for Garhmuktesar came in, disgorging hundreds of passengers, all like us wrapped in blankets, who made straight for our train uttering excited cries. Cruelly, I abandoned her to her own devices and raced back up the platform. I was just in time to repel half-a-dozen prospective travellers who were so eager to get in that they had got stuck in the doorway.

The next four hours were a nightmare of sound effects; the whistling of locomotives; the hissing of steam; the melancholy, unforgettable cry of the tea sellers as they went from end to end of the platform calling "*Cha Garam! Cha Garam! Garam Cha!*"; the constant slamming of doors; the rattling of door handles and shutters as some late-comers drummed on them, demanding admittance to our compartment. Why our compartment exercised such a fascination when the rest of the train was still half-empty was a mystery. At five we made tea and porridge on the stove. Wanda looked terrible and now G. announced that he, too, was ill.

We took the morning train to Garhmuktesar, and as it rumbled over the Ganges bridge the dawn broke with dark ragged clouds towering against a purple sky. But this was no time to rave about the beauties of nature. We were fast approaching the station. There seemed little point in going on three miles to the town when all we wanted was to find a boat, so we decided to get down at the bridge. There was barely time to shovel our belongings on to the platform before the train was off; whistling plaintively it disappeared round a bend and left us alone on the platform.

The station was nothing more than a halt on the spur which led out to the bridge, sited there, above the flood level, for the convenience of pilgrims who assemble to the number of 200,000 at the full moon in October and November in order to bathe in the river and worship in the temple. It is here, according to the *Mahabharata*, that King Santanu met the Goddess Ganga in human form. There was a ticket office but it was closed and there were no porters. Beyond the spiked iron railings that hemmed the station in there were a number of wretched hovels lying in the low ground between the railway and the embankment of the road bridge a couple of hundred yards downstream. Except for a couple of soldiers, armed with rifles, who were patrolling the approaches to the bridge and who regarded us suspiciously, as well they might, there were no human beings in sight. With our great trunks we might easily have been Chinese saboteurs loaded down with explosives intent on destroying it, who had chosen to arrive at their objective by Indian Railways.

The lack of people was made up for in full measure by the hordes of monkeys which infested the station. No sooner had we arrived than they began to close in on us and our possessions. They were completely unafraid, and when we brandished our sticks they either snarled at us, displaying nasty, sharp teeth, or else turned their inflamed-looking behinds on us in a gesture of contempt.

It was at this moment, marooned in the middle of nowhere, hemmed in by predatory monkeys, while Wanda was trying desperately to squeeze through the railings in order to find a private place, that G. announced that he would have to return to Delhi.

"I am probably having to return owing to pressure of work," he said, "I must telephone my chief."

This was a bit of a shock. G.'s presence was the result of prolonged negotiations with the Government of India at the highest possible level. I had met him more or less by chance when I had visited the office in which he worked, while trying to find out how much water there was likely to be in the Ganges in wintertime. He said he would like to come with us for a fortnight or so.

The following day we had an interview with Mr. Nehru. This was the one at which our friend, the cockney photographer, Donald McCullin, had made his immortal remark to the Prime Minister. "Mr. Nehru," he said, bobbing up from behind a sofa from the shelter of which he had been photographing the great man, "You must find it difficult to control this rough old lot." The Prime Minister had not taken kindly to this remark.

It was a very long interview, and after an hour and a quarter he asked if there was anything he could do to help us. I said that we would like a letter of introduction to all whom it might concern and also, that if possible, we wanted to take an Indian with us as far as Kanpur, preferably one who knew the river.

"I can't understand why you think that going down the Ganges is so difficult," the Prime Minister said. He was tremendously elegant in a suit of brown Indian Homespun. Tucked in one of the buttonholes of his jacket he wore a red rose, in much the same way as a hunt servant wears a hunting horn.

"When I travel I find it very simple," he said roguishly. "The last time I went up to the battle front in Ladakh I went there and back in a day, I used a helicopter. When I was a young man I walked over the top. That's when I felt free, in the mountains."

I stifled the impulse to remind him that he was the Prime Minister of India.

"I'll ask Indira," he said.

He set off down a long corridor in his slippers, shouting for his daughter who in due course appeared.

I explained about G: how he was immured in a Government department without hope of release.

"Are you sure he's up to it?" she said when I told her about him.

"He was in the Navy."

"That doesn't mean anything," she said. "You should know that. Everyone was in something; but if you really want him I'll get him for you."

"He's very keen to come," I said. He was, in fact, the only candidate.

As we were leaving Mr. Nehru showed us a magnificent T'ang horse which the Chinese had given him in happier days. I asked him if it had ever occurred to him to send it back.

"I regard it as one of the perquisites of office," he said with a quizzical look. A few months later he was dead.

Mrs. Gandhi issued her orders with characteristic energy, and down to a certain level they were implemented with zeal and efficiency; but once they had passed out of the ken of her own assistants, and down the ladder, it was noticeable that they began to lose their force until a point was reached on the rungs where nobody had heard of G., and no one knew that Indira had issued her pronouncement. Working away in this no-man's-land my eleventh-hour efforts to secure his release had worn me to a frazzle. The only person who was not affected was G. himself who had awaited the outcome with a log-like calm.

Ever since we had started on our journey down the river I had noticed that G. had become increasingly sad, vague and distant. Nevertheless, faced with this sudden defection, I was both disappointed and furious. I was also alarmed at the prospect of our being left alone in such a place.

"I shouldn't bother to telephone," I said. "You'll go whatever he says."

"That is right," he said with a candour which I couldn't help admiring.

"Well, why the devil did you say you wanted to come in the first place? I had a terrible job to get permission. I had to ask the Prime Minister."

"I didn't know it was going to be like this."

Neither did I.

"You mean you're not tough enough?" I said, taunting him shamefully. "If Wanda can stand it, surely you can?"

"She is your wife. If it is her pleasure to accompany you then she must do so. I am not strong enough."

"When you said that you wanted to come you gave me the impression that you were ready for anything. Are you really proposing to leave us here in the middle of nowhere with Wanda going to the loo every five minutes?"

"Yes," he said. "That is what I am thinking of doing."

As soon as Wanda returned from the other side of the railings I set off with him in search of a boat. I would have preferred to be by myself at this moment, but I badly needed an interpreter. The sudden appearance of a European in such a place, dressed in the costume of the country and demanding a boat, might lead the inhabitants to think that they had to deal with a lunatic. Besides, it was a transaction that had to be carried out with despatch. It was impossible to leave the luggage unattended, even for an instant, as it would be pillaged by the monkeys.

Wanda had promised to stand by it for ten minutes. "I can't promise to stay longer," she said pathetically.

On the bank of the river there was nothing but a few grass huts and some lingams ensconced in little wooden cots so that they could stand in the water without being washed away. It was to this place, 1,760 miles from Calcutta by the steamship route that the India General Steam Navigation Company in the latter part of the nineteenth century had operated the longest inland water transport service undertaken in India. It was difficult to believe it now.

A cold wind blew down the river. Apart from one miserable water-logged rowing boat, the only vessels were some pontoons that were part of a temporary bridge of boats which had been used until the new road bridge was built. The owner of this leaky boat was a disagreeable individual. He wanted 175 rupees, the equivalent of £13, to take us forty miles downstream to a place called Rajghat and twice as much to bring it back again. £40, in all. In the circumstances it was not difficult to refuse, but when I told Wanda she said that if I wanted to go she would come with me.

I persuaded G. to stay with us, at least until we reached civilisation. The nearest place of any consequence was Moradabad, a town to the east of the Ganges. There, when Wanda was fit, we could decide what to do. Whether or not we missed out this part of the river was of secondary importance to keeping her alive.

We settled down to wait for the train and the monkeys stole all the onions, taking advantage of the fact that we were sitting down.

"Lucky I don't like onions," Wanda said faintly.

Soon we became restive waiting for a train which we were not even sure would ever come, and I set off to see if we could get a lift in a lorry. After waiting by the roadside for some time I asked an old man who was passing if there was a bus service. He said there was no bus — "*Bus nahin hai*" — but immediately, as in a play, I heard a droning in the distance. "*Bus ata hai*," he said. "The bus is coming!"

When it appeared it was very full and the driver showed signs of reluctance when I asked him to wait. I ran all the way back to the station. There was still no one there to help us with the luggage, but on the way I recruited a couple of men from the huts in the low ground between the road and the railway. It turned out to be a leper colony — peering out from the dark, miserable interior huts were unfortunate men and women without noses or fingers — but those men who were less badly afflicted, were only too glad to earn a few rupees. But even with their help the work of moving fourteen pieces of luggage, much of it little baskets filled with cooking pots, a distance of a quarter of a mile was painfully slow.

By now the expedition was very spread out. Wanda was in the bushes having been forced to abandon her post defending the light luggage. As soon as she left it swarms of monkeys descended on it. I was half way to the bus with a bedding roll on my head and a leaking paraffin stove in my only free hand. G. was trying to negotiate a flight of steps with another bedding roll and at the same time trying to pretend that he wasn't carrying anything. The two lepers were having difficulty with the tin trunks on the steep flight of steps which led down from the station, and all the time the bus driver was sounding his horn.

"He must be sitting on the bloody thing," Wanda said.

At this moment I would have gladly abandoned the expedition and returned to England.

Chapter Ten

A journey through Uttar Pradesh

There are no points of hygiene to which the attention of a new comer should be more particularly directed than to *moderation* and *simplicity* in his diet. A congestive, and sometimes inflammatory diathesis, with a tendency to general or local plethora, characterises the European and his diseases, for some years at least, after his arrival between the tropics.

Murray's Hand-Book of the Madras Presidency, 1879

Sitting in the bus we saw little of the countryside on the way from Garhmuktesar to Moradabad. In the same way as what are now laughingly called "eye-level grills", the windows were set so low that they seemed to have been intended either for children or for dwarfs, and it was only by crouching down in a furtive attitude and squinting that it was possible to see the villages of brown mud as we flashed past and the fields of young wheat in which isolated palm trees grew, or rather had grown, because most of them were dead and leafless, standing in the plain like giant sticks of asparagus. The bus stopped frequently and every time it did Wanda got out and sought refuge behind the nearest tree or, if the stop was in a village, in places that, according to her, were each more loathsome than the last one. Each time she did so she had to struggle against a tide of beggars, mostly toothless old women, who boarded the bus against the streams of descending passengers, rattling tin cans which contained infinitesimal amounts of paise.

It was a cool, cloudy day. All three of us were in low spirits; nor were our companions of the journey particularly gay. In order to break down the massive reserve of the man sitting opposite me — not because I wanted to communicate with him, but because we were sitting nose to nose — I offered him a cigarette and then, when he accepted it, lit it for him. He expressed no emotion of any kind and got off at the next stop which was the station where we had passed most of the previous night — Gajraula. Gajraula was not only a railway junction: it was also a meeting-place and occasionally a burial-ground for old, broken down buses. They stood forlornly in the dust in the square, like exotic insects that had lost their wings.

By the time we reached Moradabad Wanda was done in. Unable to
stand without help, she sat on one of the trunks while the rest of the
luggage was unloaded from the roof. This was no time to wrangle
with porters and, as a result, a whole horde of them accompanied us
to the station, each happily carrying a single item of luggage.

The waiting-room was high and dim and extraordinarily quiet. It
was furnished with long chairs with extension pieces to the arm-rests
on which generations of sahibs must have put up their legs. Here in the
waiting room we put Wanda to bed on a cane-backed sofa, tucked up
inside her bedding roll, with a temperature of 103. Stubbornly, she
refused to see a doctor. Perhaps she was stupid but, because she was
not English, she equated doctors and cooks as professional men, and
the memory of the treatment she had received at the Evergreen Hotel
was still fresh in her mind. "Besides," she said, "I want to go on with
the journey. And, what is more I want to go on with it tonight."

That evening we took the train to Bareilly in grey rain with Wanda
wrapped in a blanket, like Lazarus newly-risen from the grave. Her
fever had gone down a little, however, and she insisted that she was
fit to continue, which was obviously untrue.

At Bareilly all was wet confusion. The bridge over the tracks was
jammed with people half of whom were endeavouring to catch the
train we had just left, the other half leaving it – both parties were
accompanied by porters carrying huge tin trunks – and all became immovably locked together like a Roman testudo. In this mêlée we lost
Wanda and it took some time to find her because of her red sweater
which rendered her indistinguishable from the porters, but finally she
was discovered propped against a pillar, not caring whether she lived
or died.

"I have been twenty-five times," she announced proudly. She told
me that there was a train to Kachhla Bridge on the Ganges that left the
following morning. I said that it would be madness to attempt to take
it. "I'd rather die on the Ganges than on a railway station," she
said.

At the waiting-rooms we separated. Wanda went to the ladies'
department where I made up her bed for her under the frightened gaze
of a number of Hindu ladies who were already in bed, closely
watched by the attendant, a dissolute old crone, who agreed to supply
her with tea and lemon; G. and I went off to the men's waiting-room.

We had tried, unsuccessfully to get one of the rest-rooms which
had real beds with sheets; but they were all occupied by Indian
sahibs who were already tucked up with their kit neatly stacked

around them, placidly reading. It was a cosy scene and although the regulations which were prominently displayed, stated that these rooms were only to be occupied by bona-fide travellers, there was every sign that they had been there for some time. Station rest-rooms in India are favourite haunts of Members of Parliament and officials who use them as base camps from which they carry on their activities. Things were little better in the men's waiting-room where all the cane sofas, except one, were already occupied; as G. was still not feeling well, I suggested that he should make use of it.

The room was at least twenty-five feet high with small windows at the top which could be opened and shut by hauling on long cords, the sort that invariably break when you pull them. On the wall there was a framed inventory of everything in the waiting-room, both movable and immovable, and a printed tariff of the refreshments which were available in the restaurant together with the weights and measures of each dish and beverage which were listed with meticulous accuracy:

Tea in cup (Readymade 200 cc)	035nP
Tea in pot 285 cc with separate milk and sugar	035nP
1 Dal, 2 Vegetables and Curd, 8 Chapatis (225 gms) or 4 Chapatis (115 gms) plus Rice (225 gms when cooked) or Rice (450 gms when cooked) 1 Papad, Chutney or Pickle or Salad	1 Rs. 15nP
Sandwitches (Eggs 3 pieces) per plate	065nP
Fish if served with Chips or Whaffers	2 Rs. 50nP
Fruit Tipsy Pudding	05nP
Iced Water per glass	0.30nP
Ice per 454 gms	0.09nP
(quantity of less than 454 gms will not be sold)	

Under the list of table d'hôte meals there was a warning notice:

N.B. The above charges are Per Person and Persons found sharing more than one will be charged full rates according to the number of persons partaking.

By the time I had made up my bed on the floor I felt tired and dirty. There was a shower-bath in the washroom and I decided to have one.

It was unfortunate that whoever had painted the towel-rack a strong shade of burnt umber had omitted to put up a wet-paint sign when he had completed his labours. As a result, when I put on the complete change of clothing that I had been happily anticipating for some days, I looked like part of a zebra. Unfortunate though it was, this mishap did have the effect of cheering up the other occupants of the waiting-room, all of whom except myself were already in bed, and there was a lot of deep-throated "ho-ho-hoing". I, too, decided to follow their example and go to bed, partly because of my extraordinary striped appearance and partly because I was reluctant to dine alone in the gloom of the refreshment room on Whaffers and Fruit Tipsy Pudding.

The only reading matter that I had which was easily accessible was an Indian Railway Timetable in which the following notice was prominently displayed:

I WOULD ADVISE THE RAILWAY MANAGEMENT TO TELL THE PUBLIC THAT UNLESS THEY PURCHASED TICKETS TRAINS WOULD BE STOPPED AND THEY WOULD RESUME JOURNEY ONLY IF THE PASSENGERS WILLINGLY PAID THE FARES DUE

MAHATMA GANDHI

It was interesting to speculate on what would have happened if the management had taken the Mahatma's advice, or even been given it. The wording of the pronouncement left it in some doubt as to whether he had actually tendered the advice or was merely threatening to do so. If the management had taken it seriously the entire railway system would have been permanently paralysed.

But I was soon to have access to more interesting literature.

Lying on their couches, facing me where I lay on the floor, snugly tucked up in their bedding rolls, were two Hindu gentlemen of about my own age. Both were reading paper-backed books; occasionally the fatter of the two would utter a chuckle. Finally he could contain himself no longer.

"Excuse me, you are knowing Miss Keeler?"

"No, I don't actually know her I'm afraid," I said.

"But you are knowing Doctor Ward, of course?"

"No; besides, he's dead."

"It is strange that you were not knowing him. It seems that all people were knowing him. Listen to this."

The entire waiting-room was listening happily with the exception of his companion, who was deep in a huge pink paper-back.

"Dukes, Princes and Lords sometimes got their limps impacted or depressed in games or sports and they were all cured by that vateran osteopath. Tender, slim and delicate ladies were relieved of their pains if they suffered from sprain, strain or ruptured muscles. He painted for Royal Family and people crowded to him for their photographs and nude paintings."

"It sounds funny to me," I said. "Besides I'm not a Lord".

"You are not believing this book? It is called true love story."

"Ho-ho-ho! Very funny!" said the man in the next bed apparently to himself.

"Do not take any notice of what he says," said my new acquaintance. "He is very dirty fellow. He is my friend," he added parenthetically. "You have only to see what he is laughing at to know that he is dirty fellow. He is reading book *120 days of Sodom*, in this book there are six hundred perversions."

"How do you know there are six hundred perversions?"

"Because it is my book. I am counting them and now I am lending it to him. He is my friend. But he is dirty chap."

"Ho-ho-ho!" came from the dirty chap in the next bed.

"But now I am showing you this other book. It is serious worrk."

The "worrk" was rather wonkily printed. With rare candour the authors had written on the fly-leaf:

"The whole of the story, which is a wonderful chapter and addition in the political and religious history of ENGLAND, is based on the facts and figures that have been reported in the newspapers and journals of the world. And most of them are fictitious and imaginary and make a good piece of fiction."

"Read it," he said. "Read it aloud." You could have heard a pin drop in the waiting room.

"No," I said firmly. It would have been just like reading to a lot of schoolboys in the "dorm". "You'll be too excited to sleep."

Before attempting to go to sleep myself, I asked my new acquaintance whose job it was to carry out the audit at various bookstalls, if I could obtain this particular book from the one on the station.

"Certainly you cannot obtain this book on station," he said severely. "It is indecent book. It is not suitable book for general public."

I asked him where he had got his copy from.

"I am procuring it from Manager of one bookstall," he said. "He is kindly man. He also is my friend."

The rest of the night resembled an awful dream. It was more like being on a quayside than in a station waiting-room. The whistles of the locomotives when they blasted off were as loud as ships' sirens, and as the trains came in porters carrying goods and chattels marched over me, where I lay on the floor, planting their great feet on my shins as they went. All through the night something, probably a rat — but I was too frightened to look — rustled and writhed under the head of my bedding roll. At about half-past two bathing and clearing of throats began in the wash-house, and from time to time a disgruntled figure would emerge with his dhoti covered with nice fresh paint; even the departure of a singularly beautiful girl wrapped in a sari of blue and gold tissue who for some unexplained reason had spent the night in the men's waiting room was spoiled by her breaking wind as she went through the door. At six-thirty rain began to fall with such violence that it seemed as if it was filling with water. It was a night both to remember and forget.

In the morning Wanda was a little better: the drug was winning. There was a train at nine-forty-five to Kachhla Ghat, and she insisted that we should take it. By this time she could think of nothing else but the clean sandbanks and the solitude of the Ganges, betraying similar feelings to those of a Hindu dying after a long pilgrimage just out of sight of the river. It seemed best to humour her and go on.

The train left from a distant platform, and it was not until we were all aboard that it was discovered that the Janata stove had been left in the waiting room. Although it was only nine-thirty and the train was not due to leave for fifteen minutes, it already had steam up and the air of being about to depart at any moment. Dodging among the trees on the platform, I ran the four hundred yards to the waiting room, which included two flights of stairs. There was no sign of the stove; neither did the attendant show any signs of recognising me as a former client. "*Koi isstove nahin hai,*" he mumbled and turned his back on me. It was obvious that he had already appropriated it to his own use, but there was no time to pursue the matter. The chances of buying a suitable stove at a place like Kachhla Ghat were almost non-existent. If we were to have hot food and drink on the river, I would have to buy one now; but it was now nine-thirty-five.

I raced out of the station and three hundred yards up an un-metalled road full of puddles to the bazaar. Every few yards I tripped over the hem of my baggy white Indian trousers. By rare good fortune the first shop had a Janata stove in the window; but the proprietor of the shop seemed to be in some kind of trance. It was some time before I could convince him that I wanted to buy something. It was now nine-forty.

"Quickly, quickly," I said, in Hindi. "A Janata stove. The train is leaving." "You are in a hurry?" he said, also in Hindi. Presumably because he was asking a question, he made no movement of any kind.

"Quickly, quickly!!"

At last he began to move towards the shop window, but it was difficult to believe that anyone could walk so slowly without actually stopping. It was as if he was swimming through a sea of porridge. Finally, when he had almost reached the window and was stretching out his hand to grasp the stove, did he stop.

"Why do you want Janata stove?" he said, looking over his shoulder. "There are other stoves."

I rushed to the window — nothing in it seemed to have been disturbed for ages — and seized the Janata. It was rusty and covered with dust; but this was no time to bother about trifles like these.

"HOW MUCH IS THIS ARTICLE?" I shrieked.

"Hurry, Hurry! What is hurry? Only Sahibs hurry," he droned. He sounded like a bluebottle. How I hated him at this moment. I could have murdered him, swatted him; but there was no time. Perhaps he didn't understand.

"HOW MUCH?"

"Nine rupees seventy-five," he said. He looked hurt.

I pulled at my robe and all the loose change spilled out of the minute pocket in which I had stowed it. This sort of thing never happened to Lawrence when he wore the costume of the Bedouin. I grovelled on the floor, somehow found the correct money, left the rest where it was and him with it, saying, "Hurry, hurry," to himself, and ran all the way to the station with the stove clasped to my chest, like a lunatic. The station clock showed ten minutes to ten: too late. I arrived on the platform in a state of collapse, with my enormous trousers falling down, only to find that the departure of the train had been delayed for half an hour and the driver had gone off to have a cup of tea.

Three-quarters of an hour later we left Bareilly, the old capital of Rohilkhand. We had not seen the Civil and Military Hotel, the Mosque of Shaikh Ahmad Khandan with a Persian inscription, the three jails, the lunatic asylum, the match factory at Clutterbuckganj, or the tomb of James Thomason, Lieutenant–Governor of the North–Western Provinces and one of the men who made possible the construction of the Ganges Canal, who was appointed Governor of Bengal on the day of his death in 1853. Of whom it has been written:

"Convinced that the secular power must not be used for the spread of Christianity, he still always felt his conscience challenged by the millions of heathen who surrounded him".* I should like to have seen his tomb. But perhaps none of these things existed any more.

* Philip Woodruff: *The Men Who Ruled India*; Vol. 1.

At the moment of departure the clouds rolled away. In a matter of minutes the soaked earth was dry and once again the wind that had risen when the rain ceased began to stir up the dust.

In spite of the brilliant light, the view from the carriage window was not an inspiring one; occasionally the monotony of the landscape was interrupted by a crumbling heap of bricks and a vestigial dome that might once have been part of a palace or a mosque but to which the few books at our disposal made no reference. Even if they had done so I would have been indifferent. I felt that I was on the verge of being struck down by the same disease that had already felled Wanda, and from which she was now slowly beginning to recover. Like the wooden figure of husband and wife that emerge, always singly, from the interior of Swiss barometers, foretelling a change in the weather, it seemed unlikely that for some time to come we should both be on the stage together in good health. Neither was I cheered by the station-master at Budaun, the last halt before the Kachhla Bridge, who assured me that we would not find a boat there to take us downstream.

Kachhla Station, where we were deposited with our luggage, was on the left bank of the Ganges. A strong wind was blowing when we arrived and the air was filled with dust and sand. Here road and railway joined together and crossed the river by girder bridge. The station stood on an embankment high above the river, and the abutment of the bridge was protected by a stone spur on which a pair of adjutant storks, dirty grey-and-white birds with enormous yellow bills and goitrous appendages hanging down over their breasts, stood regarding us gloomily until, put out by our interest, they took off with a heavy beating of wings and disappeared into the murk.

Leaving the others on the platform I set off in search of a boat. Seldom had I felt such an overpowering sense of hopelessness. It was engendered partly by the fact that I was feeling extraordinarily unwell and partly by the conviction that I would not find one. Nevertheless I went down through the village, past some brick buildings which included a dharmsala and the Govind Ballabh Pant Degree College, a surprising institution to find in a place that otherwise seemed to lack almost every amenity, and then by way of a bazaar shaded by trees in which the shops were dilapidated shacks to the bank of the Ganges on which a number of houses stood, some of which had been sliced neatly in two by the flood water. Upstream was the metal bridge on its huge brick piers. There was not a boat to be seen anywhere. Just some pandas half-asleep on their wooden platforms at the water's edge; a strange, wild-looking sadhu talking to himself; some horrid-looking dogs; a couple of crows perched on a long, bent bamboo with a tattered flag on it, making harsh, despairing noises at one another; and, out on the sands downstream, a number of figures congregated around a fire which was making a dark smudge of smoke downwind. The scene had all the melancholy of certain seventeenth-century Dutch landscape paintings.

Although I felt disinclined to do so, I set off to interrogate the people by the fire. By the time I reached them the fire had ceased to smoke, but it was so hot that they had formed a half-circle upwind of it and were extending their hands towards it; for the wind was bitter, although it was past midday. They were all men. It was a measure of my low state that I did not attach any significance to what they were doing there, and it was only when I said, in order to open a conversation, that it was a nice fire and they replied, laughing, "Yes, it's a woman," that I noticed that it was a burning-place. The fore-shore was littered with half-calcined skulls and bones and heaps of baked earth, and the bullock-cart with the unyolked bullocks standing patiently beside it was the one which had brought the wood for the cremation. None of the burning-party betrayed any outward signs of emotion. There were no sanctimonious demonstrations of grief. They were burning a body.

These men confirmed what the stationmaster at Budaun had said, that there was no boat at Kachhla Ghat. However, an old man, Baba Anand Swrup, who had been a carpenter in a school at Allahabad and who, like the old railwayman at Hardwar, had come to end his days as a sadhu by the river, said that a boat had been used when the bridge had been converted to take road traffic as well as trains in 1957, and that as no one had taken it away it must still be some-where in the village.

Eventually, I found the boat upside down in the courtyard of a building that belonged to the Public Works Department. It was a steel boat, rather similar to the one in which we had come down the river from Hardwar, and, although the grass was growing round it, it seemed to be in excellent condition. Unfortunately there was no one to borrow it from. No one in the village knew anything about it at all and no one in Budaun, the nearest town up the line, some seventeen miles away, was sufficiently senior to authorise us to take it; and after spending twenty minutes screaming into the stationmaster's tele-phone, I abandoned the attempt.

Wanda cooked lunch on the platform. It was difficult in such a wind. We ate boiled rice which I picked at gingerly and drank tea, fended off monkeys and starving dogs and, at the same time, listened to rumours brought to us by some students of a great religious gathering which they said was due to take place in two days' time, on 15th December; and of a boat which they said we would find at a place called Soron on the other side of the Ganges. "There may be a lakh* of bathers," they said. "It is a fine and holy sight."

We were delighted to think of seeing 100,000 people bathing, all at the same time, and decided to stay on for the ceremony. It would also give us time to search for the boat.

It was a pity that both these items of information were completely untrue. The gathering of pilgrims was not due to take place until the full moon of the following month and there was no boat at Soron.

Because there was no train to Soron in the immediate future we decided to travel by road. With the aid of the young students who still continued to be very well-disposed towards us we lugged the gear along the platform to the bridge, where, by luck, we secured places on top of an open lorry as high as a house, which was on its way to the town. It was loaded with bagged wheat, and we clung to the sacks like limpets as it howled over the bridge and down the long, straight road, past long lines of bullock carts which were on their way to a sugar refinery. It was a sinister evening. The air was full of dust and both it and the land were a uniform shade of khaki against which the dark mango trees which lined the road stood out in angular relief.

* A lakh: 100,000.

Chapter Eleven

A place in the country

A stranger to the town (Soron) is chiefly struck by the number of substantial and imposing houses and temples, and by the crowds which throng the bazar during the frequent fairs. At these times the shop-keepers do a thriving trade, but out of the season the place is very dead alive and quiet.

District Gazeteer of the United Provinces, Vol. XII

We unloaded our gear from the lorry on the outskirts of Soron, took a ritual photograph of its crew, who were a cheerful lot, and transferred ourselves to two cycle rickshas and an old ekka that was drawn by a pony so emaciated that it seemed scarcely capable of supporting its own weight, let alone the burden it was now called upon to shoulder. In this eccentric convoy we set off for the Dak bungalow which one of the students at Kachhla Station had recommended to us, accompanied by a merchant sailor on leave, who had joined us, unasked, as a sort of running footman.

The bungalow was an ancient structure. It was situated some distance from the old part of the town and was separated from it by an expanse of tobacco fields, from which the ramps of the irrigation wells rose as small, brown, wedge-shaped islands in a sea of green leaf. It was the pattern of all the Dak bungalows we ever stayed in in India; some were larger, some were far dirtier, but basically they were the same. The custodian seemed almost as old as the building itself, and he greeted us with the lack of enthusiasm of one who was accustomed in life to receiving no more than his legal due for any service which he rendered.

The building itself had originally been constructed to house two European officials and their modest entourages, without the necessity of their meeting. The two wings were more or less identical. Each consisted of dim, high-ceilinged rooms in which the furniture was of the simplest kind. The lavatory arrangements were equally so. There was a chamber-pot housed in a massive wooden box, an enamel basin and a number of vessels for pouring water over oneself. This was the domain of the two sweepers, a small boy of ten and his mother who seemed little older than he was. Whenever I emerged from the bungalow the little boy endeavoured to kiss my feet. It was so difficult to dissuade him from this servile behaviour without appearing overbearing, that it was almost better to let him do it.

We spent two days and nights at Soron. It was a pleasant place. Sand lapped against the ancient, northern part of the city of which the only remains are a tomb and the temple of Sita Ramji, situated on a long mound. The old, non-European part was full of crumbling Mughal houses with wooden balconies and dharmsalas with elaborately carved facades behind which there were courtyards with cells opening on to them. In the stone-paved bazaars the principal trade was in beads, receptacles of opaque green glass full of air bubbles in which pilgrims carried away water from the nearby Ganges and the still closer sacred pool, metal sprinklers and baskets for transporting bones. The place was infested with monkeys but here, where they had other interests besides our luggage, we almost grew to like them.

That evening we were visited by the young student who had told us about the Dak bungalow, and with him we set off to visit his grandfather, Pandit Misra, who was eighty years old, but still vigorous. He lived in a fine old house with double green doors surrounded by retainers and numerous progeny. For much of his life he had been an active member of the Freedom Movement and, to put it mildly, a thorn in the side of the British. Altogether he had spent five and a half years in the Central Jail at Agra. His wife had died in 1942 while he was in prison. He was a courtly, tough old man with a handlebar moustache and an imperious manner; dressed in the uniform of the Leaders — a high-collared jacket of village homespun, dhoti and Congress hat. He still owned acres of tobacco, some melon gardens and several houses. Before the expropriation he must have been a landlord of some consequence.

We drank tea and nibbled sweets which he offered us in a high, whitewashed room. Dark beams supported the ceiling; niches in the walls housed painted clay statues of gods and men, and there were photographs which illustrated his stormy career; one with Pandit Govind Ballabh Pant, Chief Minister of the United Provinces, who later became Home Minister in the Central Government, taken in 1932, and another of Subhas Chandra Bose in the uniform of the Freedom Army. "Bose was iron; but Patel was steel," he said.

He spoke of the Non-Violence demonstrations of 1931 when the British sent troops from Etah and ten or twelve demonstrators were killed. ("I forget which.") Age and disillusionment had drawn much of his sting, but not all of it. He was critical of the Congress

Party: "Mad for power and not at all interested in the common man."

At five-fifteen the following morning I set off with G. for the Varaha Muti Mandir, where he wanted to perform a puja. It was a bleak hour, the wind was bitter and sunrise was still almost two hours off. Rigid with cold we sat in the cycle ricksha which creaked through the silent, shuttered bazaar under electric light bulbs which danced madly as the monkeys jumped up and down the wires, making derisive noises at us.

The temple of Varaha Muti, one of many temples at Soron, but the most famous, is situated on the banks of the great pool. The pool, which is a long rectangle, is fed by the Burhiganga, an inconsiderable river which flows in the old bed of the Ganges and is further augmented by water drawn off from the Lower Ganges Canal, for which the municipality pays an annual fee. The water is said to have the peculiar property of dissolving the bones of the dead within three days of their being deposited in it; consequently, it never silts up as it undoubtedly would if they simply piled up on the bottom.

This is not the principal reason for the sanctity of Soron. According to the *Vishnu Purana*, it was at Soron that Hiranyaksha, an obstreperous demon who had pulled the earth down to the bottom of the sea, was slain by Vishnu in his third incarnation as a wild boar, after a battle which lasted a thousand years.

The temple was crowned by a pair of gleaming white spires. Inside it we squatted on our haunches on the stone floor. The cold wind which was blowing outside had followed us into the building. I began to wish that I had worn woollen underpants. From another nearby templet came the loud, intrusive noises of a more modern puja that was being conducted with the aid of loudspeakers.

The walls of the temple were pale blue; the coffered ceiling was ochre and white; the columns which supported the round, scalloped arches were banded in yellow and red. Glass lampshades, the size and shape of pumpkins, hung from the roof. A thin cotton curtain concealed the shrine which was bathed in a pale green light. From behind it came sounds that suggested that someone was doing the washing-up. The entrance to the shrine was surrounded by a carved wooden altar rail on a raised plinth. In his cell to the right the Swami Narayan Giri, with his radio set beside him, sat under a corrugated iron baldacchino, illuminated by a single, naked electric light bulb. Soon, feeling himself the cynosure, he extinguished it and became nothing more than a dark shape.

To the left of his cell there was a well; to the right of it a flight of steps which led to a gallery above. Behind us, in an alcove, a large bell, the gift of a Maharaja of Nepal, hung suspended by massive chains. On our left was what looked like a broken-down wooden bedstead, on which were displayed the photographs of sadhus and swamis dead and gone. Or were they gone? This was Hindu India. Here you could be dead but not gone; equally well you could be gone but not dead.

On the stone floor half a dozen female devotees, some of them very ancient, squatted closely wrapped against the cold with only the painted soles of their feet showing. Two of them were warming themselves over little clay braziers that contained hot coals — I must say I envied them. Apart from ourselves and an old man with a walrus moustache, who wore a long brown riding coat, they constituted the visible congregation. It was rather like a parish church in England. At five-forty, after we had been squatting for ten minutes, G. began to chant the thousand names of Vishnu as a litany in a loud voice. It was obvious that the regular members of the congregation took exception to this, and after a couple of minutes they began a loud, secular, female conversation against which he fought bravely, until it became so intolerable that he had to give up.

At five-forty-five the light went on again in the Swami's cell. He now displayed himself more clearly. He was wrapped in an orange coloured blanket and he was very old-looking, with a short beard, and a sucked-in-looking mouth. His bedding, which was dyed to match, was rolled up neatly beside him. He was surrounded with photographs of whole teams of holy men.

A tiny mouse appeared from inside the shrine and began nibbling at votive offerings by the altar rail. Ten more old women arrived. The hellish draught along the floor was turning my bowels, already far from solid, to water.

G. began to chant again. I asked him what it was.

"It is still *Lalita-sahasara-nama*," he said. "I am devotee of Vishnu in Mother Form."

At six o'clock the Maharajah's bell was given three deafening strokes by the old man with the moustache and, at the same time, a man wearing a pink vest and a dhoti entered the shrine carrying a basket, together with another who had a shaven head. Now the curtain was drawn aside revealing the shrine which was illuminated by coloured lights with Varaha-Lakshmi, the boar god and his wife, dressed in silver tissue with silver head-dresses and wearing swags of pearls and garlands of marigolds.

There was a concerted sounding of gongs and bells; the pujari in the pink vest rang a handbell with one hand while holding a five-branched candlestick in the other; the young man with the shaven head sounded a gong and handbell; the old man with the moustache rang the big bell and at the same time beat on a gong. The din continued for ten minutes during which the women made circular motions in the air with lighted tapers. At the end of it the coloured lights were extinguished; the congregation was sprinkled with water; a sacred flame was circulated at which they warmed their hands; more water — the remains of the god's bath — was ladled out to them in a spoon; and sweets which remained from the offering were distributed. The puja was over. A priest, a distinguished-looking man with grey hair introduced himself. "I am Swami Purushotoma Nand, late Accounts Department, Martin Byrne Limited, Banaras," he said.

When we came out of the temple the wind had died away. Mist was rising from the pool like steam from a thermal bath. Actually the water was freezing. On the bathing steps on the north side where there was a rather comical statue of Tulsi Das, the great poet who translated the Ramayana into Hindi, hardy bathers were winding themselves in their dhotis. On the opposite side where we were standing, five elegant pavilions, built by the Maharaja of Alwar two hundred years before, hung over the water supported on brick platforms and shaded by pipal trees. In them old men closely wrapped in red and green blankets sat mumbling to one another. The pool was lined with temples. All had been built by princes. There was the Raghunath Ji ka Mandir, built by the Maharaja of Jaipur, which had brass doors studded with spikes and, largest of all, at the far end of the tank, the Ganga Ji Ka Mandir with a tall, pyramidical tower, built by the Raja Somadatta of Soron. There were decaying temples whose patronage was lapsing or had lapsed, and there were temples that were no more than heaps of bricks and rubble.

G. now left us to return to Delhi. At this moment both Wanda and myself were feeling so ghastly that the departure of anyone, however well loved, would have had little effect, and after toying with a little boiled rice and some cauliflower we both went to bed.

No sooner had we done so than there was a knock on the door. Wanda answered it in her dressing-gown and announced that it was a party of gentlemen from the town who, hearing of our interest in Soron, had kindly come to escort us to the Temple of Sita Ramji.

In retrospect I do not know how I reached the Temple of Sita Ramji. I could only imagine the agonies that Wanda had suffered, being moved from station to station and bus to bus during the last days. My own were only too real. Legs, arms and stomach all ached and all in different ways. Sensations of nausea alternated with those of violent hunger and were in turn succeeded by an intense lassitude; symptoms, I remembered, of the jaundice which had nearly carried me off in 1942. As in a trance I listened at what seemed a great distance to the exquisite, convoluting English of the spokesman of the party, Mr. Anand Vallabh Upadhyaya, as he described how the temple had been built four thousand years before. I remember feeling that this could not be true but not having the strength to dispute it.

It was not even a beautiful temple. Aurangzeb had knocked it down in a moment of iconoclasm, and a rich merchant had restored it in 1860. There was nothing about it now to raise one's spirits, even temporarily.

I remember making some kind of excuse and tottering back alone to the bungalow and to bed; but not for long. For no sooner had Wanda returned from the temple than another party of visitors arrived at the bungalow, this time half a dozen students. For an hour I listened to Wanda, herself in no fit state to act as hostess, entertaining them in the next room. Finally I grew so ashamed that I dressed and went in to join them. After what she had told them about my condition they were surprised to find me alive, let alone on my feet. They were displeased, and so was she. In penance for my behaviour I allowed myself to be taken on a great circular tour of Soron on foot, during which I was questioned closely about trends in English literature. Because I happened to have a notebook these boys expected me to be acquainted personally with the great writers of the time or, failing that, to know what influenced them to write as they did – questions that many of the writers themselves would have had difficulty in answering.

"What is that building?" I would say pointing to some huge ruin.

"That is fallen-down building," they answered.

We woke very early the following morning. I felt better, (it would have been difficult to have felt worse than I had on the previous afternoon) but Wanda looked done in; this was no sort of convalescence for anyone.

No sooner were we awake than there was a battering on the door. Standing in the ghastly half-light was the sailor. "I wish to introduce you to my son," he said.

It was half past six in the morning. I said that we would meet him later. We had already seen a great deal too much of the father. He had attempted to assume the position not only of interpreter, but of entrepreneur. He had followed me everywhere, even on my walk round Soron. I had been bored to tears by his reminiscences of London and the Liverpool docks. Now he forced his way into the room.

"I am wanting your address in England," he said.

"Why do you want my address in England?"

"I am frequently coming to England. I shall stay with you!"

I said that I was afraid that I couldn't give him my address. At this moment he was the last man I ever wanted to see again. It was cruel, but it was true.

"Why are you not giving me your address?"

"Because I do not wish to."

"Then you are not my friend?"

I took the plunge. "No."

He went off in a huff dragging his son behind him.

I felt a pig.

The train was due to leave at eleven-thirty. A cycle ricksha (now that there were only two of us there was only need of one) and an ekka had been ordered for ten-thirty, but by ten-fifty neither had arrived. To make matters worse the laundry had not come back and no one seemed to know who had it. The situation was further complicated by the arrival of a young student with his favourite school-master who wanted to meet us. We were torn between the need to promote a conversation, anxiety about the laundry and the missing transport, and the very real need to avoid the sweeper who, in spite of having been given a very large tip in order to dissuade him, still attempted to kiss my feet. Confronted with so many things all at once, I felt my reason going.

Eventually, at eleven-o'clock, the school-master sent the student off to find the ricksha and the ekka. The boy returned with the ricksha but without the ekka. The school-master then despatched the ricksha man to find the ekka. We were now without any transport at all. I felt as though we were playing snakes and ladders. Eventually everyone arrived except the laundryman with the laundry – perhaps he was some creature of the sailor's! We set off in search of him in the ricksha, but with maddening slowness: past the huts of the rope-makers and the basket makers, the timber yard, the carpenters' and wheelwrights' shops, the hovels of the depressed classes which lay in sodden ground below the level of the road, past the police station and the Collector's bungalow. Eventually, we found him. He seemed disappointed that we had succeeded in doing so. The clothes were still soaking wet but we were past caring.

Chapter Twelve

From a carriage window

'. . . having done this, 2nd Lt. Newby will proceed to Fatehgarh.'
Old military movement order

For ten miles the train trundled through the plain until it arrived on the outskirts of Kasganj where it halted. Presently, it shunted itself backwards and forwards but without ever reaching the Junction. During this time we were at the mercy of a nosey man with whom we had an irritating conversation.

"How is your health?"

"Rather poor."

"If you are poor what are you doing in first-class compartment?"

"We are travelling down the Ganges."

"Then if you are travelling down Ganges you must be in good health."

"Grr!"

"Why doesn't he ask why we are on a train when we're supposed to be on the Ganges," Wanda said when he retired to the lavatory.

"Fellow is an ass!" said the other occupant of the compartment, a train inspector on leave, who had kindly telegraphed to the Junction from Soron to order lunch for us. It is a common practice in India to telegraph down the line to the next station to order a meal so that it can be put on board when the train arrives.

The confusion of the Junction was indescribable. It was as if this was the last train out of a city in which the occupants were about to be put to the sword. Fighting his way to our compartment through a mass of humanity came a small boy with our lunch balanced on a tin tray. Something had gone wrong with the arrangements. It was not the fish we had ordered but very greasy goat. Worse still, the boy stayed on the train to collect the plates. (He got off two stations further on.) In order not to hurt his feelings we dropped most of the lunch down the lavatory, which was not as easy as it sounds.

All through the long afternoon the train rumbled through the country between the Burhiganga and the Kali Nadi. The Ganges was

between ten and twenty miles away to the north. For most of the way
the line ran parallel to one of the branches of the Ganges Canal but it
was only visible once when the line crossed over it. The distance from
Soron to Fatehgarh, which was our destination, was not more than
seventy miles, but the train, stopping as it did at every station, took
six hours to cover them.

For most of the way the only other occupant of the compartment
was a delightfully silent Muslim gentleman who sat on his bedding roll
with his legs drawn up; occasionally he smiled, first at us, then to himself and then banged his knees together as if enjoying some private
joke.

Looking out of the window I was overawed, as I had been twenty-
two years before, by the immensity of the Indian Plain. Then I had
been a very junior officer (I was always a junior officer throughout
my military career), on my way to join the Indian regiment to which
I had been posted, and it was at Kasganj Junction that I found myself
alone for the first time since leaving Scotland on a cold day in January
three months previously.

On the way to Kasganj I met a Lieutenant from the Gurkhas. He
spoke several Indian languages with facility. How I envied him.

At Kasganj I left him to take the train to Fategarh, my final destination. "You're going to have trouble with that servant of yours,"
he said, as the train pulled out. There was no time to ask him why.

Now, once again, I was on the train to Fatehgarh. It was the same
time of day more or less; only the season was different. Now it was
December; then it had been the end of March. Then I had looked out
on a monotonous and desiccated landscape that sizzled under a brassy
sky. Now it was the cold season and in the fields men and women,
bent double, were weeding the newly-sprouting wheat and barley
under a sky that was as drab and dusty as an army blanket. All the
crops were low and green and the absence of sunlight intensified their
greenness. Only the rice harvest was finished and those fields that until
recently had been the greenest of all were now rectangles of brown
stubble, separated from one another by low banks of earth. In the
whole landscape there was not a hedge to be seen. The horizon seemed
illimitable; only when there were trees on the rim of it was it possible
to guess whether it was a mile or twenty miles distant.

In the irrigation channels which cut straight through the plain,
pairs of men were using the swinging basket, as they had always done,
to lift the water into the fields, a bamboo basket suspended by four
cords. Sometimes the difference in level was too much for them to

manage by themselves – about six feet was the limit to which they could raise it with a single throw; more than that and there would have to be two or three pairs of men, each with a basket, standing one above the other, lifting the water from one scooped-out basin to the next until it reached the top and could flow down into the fields by its own gravity where two or more men turned it into the different beds. In this way a team of eight men with two baskets can irrigate an acre a day, but it is very hard work.

There were wells at which the bullock-drivers urged their beasts up and down the ramps, backing them up and then sitting on the rope as they went down to keep it taut until the leather bucket appeared dripping over the well-head; then a second man took it and poured it into a hollow in the platform from which it ran down glistening into the channels from which yet a third man distributed it over the fields. And in the sandy places there were Persian wheels with earthenware pots attached to them, alternately ascending, overturning and descending, worked by blindfolded bullocks doomed to circle the well as long as water was needed.

The train chugged on, past brilliant fields of mustard and deep green garden crops; past shrines and small white temples and, more rarely, a mosque. On the dusty roads wretched-looking ponies drew ekkas loaded with six or even eight persons, together with their belongings. It went on and on past groves of mangoes, clipped-looking toddy palms, plantations of yellow flowering pulse, nim, acacia and shisham trees; villages of houses that were dun-coloured rectangles of dried mud, windowless and roofed with sagging thatch; villages surrounded by piles of dung and stacks of twisted grass; villages shaded by ancient trees festooned with the funnel-shaped nests of the tailor birds now empty and with red flags hanging limply, high among the greenery.

At Patiali, a decayed town that was once on the banks of the Ganges, but was now eighteen miles from it, we were joined by some sort of official. Before getting into the train he bellowed "Why has your station not got it? Every other station has it!" at the station-master who cringed before him in an awful way. It was sad to see how Indians of no consequence had transferred their subservience from ourselves to their own countrymen. I wondered what it could be that his station lacked. At four o'clock the quiet man put on a crocheted prayer cap, spread a mat on the floor of the compartment and prayed with his back to the engine, facing Mecca. At Dariaganj hordes of beggar children, long-haired and happy, left their encampment on the outskirts and raced towards the train.

The day was nearly over now. The crows were going home, cawing mournfully. The people in the fields were beginning to straighten their backs. At Kaimganj people boarded the train carrying young trees, sugar cane, bundles on the ends of sticks, brass pots, baskets containing hens and long bamboo poles with murderous iron axe-heads attached to them; men from the country who had invested in shoes of European design limped past — the more sensible carried them in their hands; spotted dogs lay comatose in the dust; Muslim girls in tight trousers squatted drinking from a tap with their head coverings thrown back.

Dusk fell. The sky changed from khaki to muddy grey; the bullock-carts were squeaking their way home now; but the drawers of water were still working their beasts at the wells; all but lingering lovers had gone from the fields; little yellow fires were burning in the rice stubble; in the clearings among the trees by the villages long, horizontal ribbons of smoke from the cooking fires on which the evening meal was being prepared hung motionless in the air; high-pitched, mournful whistles came from the engine of the train. How sad India was at this moment; like a person afflicted with melancholia. In a few more minutes it was quite dark.

Chapter Thirteen

Remembrance of things past

The word *Fath* is spelled in eleven different ways – *Futeh, Futh, Futhe, Futick, Futi, Futte, Futteh, Futtih, Futtoo, Futtun, Futty*, all modes being absolutely wrong.

Murray's Hand-Book of the Madras Presidency
Preface to the edition of 1859

The winter rains normally fall about January, and when they are over a raw and dusty west wind sets in, sometimes bringing clouds which result in mischievous hailstorms. This wind continues almost without intermission throughout the summer, growing hotter as the year advances, until in April it has developed into the fiery *loo*. During May and June, which are the hottest months, the mean temperature for the twenty-four hours is usually well over 90°, though the atmosphere is occasionally cooled by the slight showers that sometimes accompany a dust storm. With the breaking of the monsoon at the end of June or in early July, the temperature falls, the hot west wind ceases to blow, and the intense dryness of the summer air is changed to a close and oppressive dampness which continues until the rains cease in September. In the trans–Gangetic lowlands, in the rains ... the whole country is flooded, the villages rising out of the water like islands in a muddy sea.

Climate of the upland portion of Farrukhabad
District Gazeteer of United Provinces, Vol. IX, p. 18

The railway station at Fatehgarh was as it had been when I had last arrived there: in the hands of the Military. A splendid, moustached Rajput jemadar crashed to attention on the platform as if he had been expecting us – which was impossible as nobody was – and directed us to the office of the Railway Transport Officer where there were further great clashings of boots and leapings to attention. As a civilian I found this rather agreeable. No one seemed to think it strange that an Englishman and his wife should suddenly emerge from the darkness in the middle of Uttar Pradesh together with a lot of luggage. Eventually I got through on a military line to the Commandant after speaking with his wife, with whom I had a difficult conversation in Hindi. The Colonel was at the Regimental Cinema but every so often a mysterious, parrot-like voice chipped in saying, "Duty Clerk, Duty Clerk, this is Duty Clerk." I was back in the Army all right. I told him who I was and read him the letter of introduction that had been written for me by our friend the Major–General who was Master of the Ordnance. In a happy trance we allowed ourselves to be relieved of our luggage and set off for the Mess in a cycle ricksha. Last time I had travelled in a tonga (a pony-drawn cart).

I tried to recall what it had been like on that hot, somnolent Sunday afternoon in March 1941; but apart from the fact that I had not been able to find anyone to report to at the Mess, and that the temperature had been 106°, I could remember nothing. Now it was dark and cold and there was mist in the air through which the lights on the edge of the parade ground shone nebulously.

After what seemed a long journey we passed what I recognised as the bungalow in which I had once lived. It was in darkness. Now we turned into the neatly hedged drive flanked by pots of petunias and nasturtiums disposed at regular intervals, and drew up at the Mess under the porte-cochère that was still flanked by the guns which the 5th Battalion had captured in the Burma War of 1885, and on which the bougainvillaea still grew. Roaming sentries in great coats and jungle hats, just like Wanda's, armed with rifles and fixed bayonets, regarded us suspiciously. It was difficult to remember that so far as India was concerned there was still a war on.

We were shown into guest-rooms which had not been there in 1941. There were chintz curtains at the windows and English prints on the walls. In some miraculous way our luggage had already arrived. A mess servant appeared wearing the uniform blue, yellow and orange cummerband and pagri with a silver regimental badge pinned to it, and began unpacking. He asked me where we wanted to dine, there or in the mess. Given the choice I said in the mess. It seemed odd to be asked. When I had been in it last women were not allowed except on special occasions. Perhaps the Indians had relaxed the rule.

There had been little change. Apart from the introduction of running water and the new set of guest-rooms, the Mess was the same, a single-storied building of red brick with a deep, arcaded verandah where we used to leave our beautifully polished Sam Browne belts, our topis, or our elegantly squashed caps, according to the time of the day; but no one wore belts and topis any more. There were the same long cane-backed chairs and the same reed blinds which used to be lowered in the heat of the day when the loo, the awful wind, was blowing. The heads of horned game still hung on the walls but now, in addition, there was a large glass case containing a lion, shot by Brigadier Gurdial Singh in 1947, with little piles of moth-balls on its paws, ears and head, and there were cases of swords captured from the Japanese.

The ante-room was brighter than I remembered it. It had been given several coats of paint; but there were the same lost-looking second-lieutenants sitting in armchairs reading old magazines who, as I had done, had already discovered that, apart from the Mess, Fatehgarh lacked amenity; only now they were all Indians. Beer was still served in silver goblets, but Indian whisky and gin were cheaper than Indian beer; and there were still the same shouts for the Abdar, the Mess Butler, to come and replenish them, but it was a different Abdar who answered the summons. The stern old man with the lugubrious expression whom I remembered, Mohammed Ishaq, had been gathered to his forefathers in 1950. Most of the furniture was the same. The copy of the despatch from Henry Havelock, partly written in Greek and taken into the beleaguered Residency at Lucknow, was still in its accustomed place by the fireplace; as were the colours of the 11th and 16th Native Infantry. But there were some new portraits: of Sepoy Ansari, tortured to death by the Japanese and posthumously awarded the George Cross; of Sepoy Kamal Ram who had won the V.C. in Italy at the Gari River, and of General Kariappa, the C.-in-C., who was a member of the regiment. There was a Japanese flag captured by the 2/7th in the Arakan, a framed letter from a Sepoy in a German prison camp asking that six rupees a month should be deducted from his pay and given to the Red Cross; and a silver model of the hill on which the 1st and 3rd Battalions had fought against the Pakistanis in the Jumna and Kashmir operations.

That night we sat at the table almost as long as a cricket pitch which an officer of the regiment had bought from the Bulgarian Embassy, at which seven kings had dined on a single night, and which still showed the cigar-burns supposed to have been made by Edward VII who was one of them. Behind me were the colours that were taken by the loyal remnant of the Regiment into the Residency at Lucknow, the only place in the Empire, as I had been taught, where the Union Jack was permitted to fly day and night. Tennyson's words were still engraved there in the Mess; "And ever upon the topmost roof our banner of England blew." It was a strange sentiment to find still enshrined in the mess of an Indian regiment of Infantry.

This had been the scene of my first humiliation and, far worse for him than for me, the humiliation of my newly acquired servant who said he was a Christian. At dinner it was the custom for each officer to be attended by his own bearer, wearing the splendid regalia of the regiment. On the first night on which I had dined in, as soon as I had taken my seat I was conscious that something had gone wrong with the domestic arrangements. There was a great deal of whispering among the servants which I was certain was not customary — I myself hardly dared to open my mouth — and, strangest of all, my own, whom I had been told to despatch to the mess earlier, did not appear. I put it down to the fact that he lacked the proper uniform to appear in public, as indeed I did myself.

Later, in the ante-room, the Commandant had button-holed me. "That bearer of yours, where the devil did you get him?" he said.

I told him.

"The fellow's a — " (I never heard what he was. It sounded something like "urrrr"). "He's an untouchable; not only that, he comes from a criminal tribe. Not your fault, of course. You couldn't be expected to know but it sticks out a mile." He went into various technical details about how in future, I could recognise an "urrrr". "There was practically a mutiny among the servants at table to-night," he went on, "He's going back on the first train tomorrow morning. You're in number one bungalow, I believe. The two chaps there have both got excellent bearers. You can share theirs for the moment. I've already spoken to them. They're quite happy about it."

Looking at the Commandant I had been quite sure that anyone would be only too happy to do anything that he suggested.

The billiards room was the same as it had been with its two-tiered seats, for those who were not playing, against the walls. Here Wanda, wearing pink trousers, was taught to play slosh, a variant of pool, by the junior officers who were delighted at the interruption of what had promised to be another tedious evening. The choice of dining in the mess or in the guest room had been intended for me alone, not for Wanda; but the officers had been too polite to say so when she appeared. The heads of sloth bear, crocodiles, stag, serow, burial, oorial, ibex, markhor and a swamp deer shot by the Khan of Sherpur in the 1920s looked down on her blind-eyed — the place was a shambles of game — Here, too, I had played slosh during the long, hot evenings, but never with women in pink trousers.

The next morning I went into the garden and down the long path to the belvedere on the high bank above the Ganges. It was here that the table had been laid on dinner nights in the hot weather and it was here, when my turn came, that I had proposed the health of the

King-Emperor and it had been drunk in port and madeira with the temperature in the high eighties, while the river, shrunken and green at this season of the year, had flowed sluggishly past; and it was here during dinner that the band had played selections from Gilbert and Sullivan. Now the roses were in flower as they had never been in that hot summer, and the flowers that the gardener called kissmiss; and the wind which stirred the leaves of the giant nim trees was a cooler one than I had ever known.

My memories of Fatehgarh were not altogether happy ones. Stupidly, I had let it become known that I was not interested in what I described as "peace-time soldiering" and that my ambition was to go to the "real war". It was stupid of me because I knew nothing that would make me anything other than a liability to an Indian regiment in the field.

My ambition to go to the wars soon reached the ears of one of my superiors, a new and irascible man, and I found myself in charge of the Regimental Accounts, trying desperately in the long afternoons in the semi-darkness of my bungalow when everyone else was asleep and the temperature whirred up to 120°, to restore to its proper place 25 paise which I had inadvertently transferred to the Regimental Lead Fund.*

I might have remained at Fatehgarh indefinitely if an officer had not arrived back from the regular battalion in the Western Desert. He was a pleasant regular Captain, with a large, blonde moustache, rather like a Saxon Thane in appearance; or rather what the illustrations in the Nursery History of England had long since convinced me that Saxon Thanes had looked like. As the only officer in Fatehgarh who had had experience of modern warfare, I regarded him with awe. Fortunately for me he shared my dislike for my superior.

"There's a regulation," he said one evening when we were tippling on his verandah, "that if you pass the Lower Standard Urdu Examination, you have to be sent overseas. It's the only way you'll ever get out of here."

I had already made some progress in the language and had reached the point when I could give a short, declamatory lecture – I could answer no questions – on that most useless of weapons, the Boys Anti-Tank Rifle. "This is a powerful gun," I used to say, falsely, but with no apparent conviction. My little lecture was my only accomplishment.

* A fund the money for which came from the sale of the lead dug out of the banks behind the targets of the firing range.

Now I engaged a Munshi, an elderly teacher to get me through the
Lower Standard Examination and spent the afternoons working away
with him at the limited syllabus which was required for this modest
test. These lessons were a blessing in disguise. I found it impossible
to have them and at the same time do the Regimental Accounts which
were still beyond me anyway, so I secretly employed a clerk in the
Regimental Office to do them for me. Everyone was happier as a
result.

I also acquired a bearer, one of those whom I had been sharing with
the two regular officers in whose bungalow I had been living since
I came to Fatehgarh. When they went overseas I had him to myself.

Amir was an impressive-looking man. He was tall and thin and had
a long slender beard which was turning grey, but which he dyed
saffron. In addition to Hindi and Urdu he spoke both Arabic and
Persian, the latter excellently. He had no time for any officer who
could not address him in one or other of these tongues. He also spoke
some English, but would only employ it when speaking with visitors
and Memsahibs. Under his stern influence I made rapid strides with
the language.

Amir lived in a hut in the compound with two tent-like figures
whom I sometimes saw at a distance, who were his wives. The hut
was more like an upended match-box than a dwelling, and I often
wondered what happened when they were all three inside together.
Did they remain standing up, like match-sticks? He had children but
I never saw them; presumably they were housed elsewhere. Amir was
an excellent cook, one of the best Indian cooks I have ever encountered, and as one of the few diversions open to the unmarried
officers was to entertain each other to dinner in turn in their various
bungalows, I enjoyed a popularity that was really his. He also waited
on me in the Mess, the most splendid-looking of all the servants. The
rest disliked him because they thought him arrogant. He was. He
cashed my cheques; furnished me with loose change; mixed my drinks
and when things went well took the credit which was due to the
other servants with whom I had been saddled: the gardener, the water-
carrier, the sweeper and the night-watchman who used to sleep on
the front steps of my bungalow as soundly as I did on the verandah,
leaning on his stave with his lighted lantern beside him. According
to himself Amir protected me from tradesmen and similar thieves but,
as he exacted a commission on everything that was sold to me from
outside, I think that the result was precisely the same as it would have
been if he had not been there at all and I had transacted the business
myself. He kept an account book which he presented to me for

inspection from time to time. Even I could tell, from the very precision with which it was drawn up, that it was falsified, but it would have required a financial genius to prove it.

Amir was never ruffled, and when summoned he would appear silently wearing the grave, impressive expression that was habitual to him and say "Huzoor?" with a slight hint of inquiry in his voice, his head tilted very slightly backwards in a proud way that was good to see in a country in which the prevailing attitude was, and still is, an abject one, as unfathomable as his account books. I paid him 35 rupees (£2 12s. 6d.) a month which was slightly in excess of what was customary, but it seemed worth it to retain the services of such a distinguished-looking servant and one of so many parts. He even, on one occasion, acted the part of procureur. It was characteristic that he did not initate the idea but when he himself was approached with it, he carried it through with an efficiency that was almost in-human.

For unmarried officers Fatehgarh was an awful place. There was no club and no swimming pool where assignations could be made, and even if there had been there was no one with whom one could make an assignation. We were oppressed by the lusts of the flesh and there was no way of assuaging them. By the look of the young officers I saw on my first night in the mess, this was still true twenty-two years later. At that time there were still some regimental wives in residence, but for the most part they were the property of officers of field rank. Social intercourse was difficult enough with them; any other kind was unthinkable.

It was not a subject that could easily be put out of mind. It was omnipresent in a country in which the population had increased by more than fifty million in ten years. To me it was a source of wonder that the decrepit buildings of which the villages and cities were largely composed, did not collapse as a result of the vibrations set up by these multitudinous acts of creation, just as the walls of Jericho had fallen down at the blast of trumpets. Even the continous round of Hindu Festivals to which, as a keen young officer, I was not only invited but expected to go, and which the men celebrated with such gusto, were mostly of an unequivocally sexual nature; and the games of squash in the open courts which were like an oven in the late afternoons and the long route marches, both of which, because they were "exercise", were reputed to act as bromides, were to me, at least, stimulants rather than deterrents.

The torments pursued one even to the breakfast table. Prominent amongst the little correspondence that got though to us at this stage of the war were large, plain envelopes containing catalogues sent to us by Indian purveyors of contraceptives and aphrodisiacs, together with self-measurement forms which unfolded to a remarkable length. Printed on bright pink and green paper, colours chosen perhaps because of their inflammatory qualities, they were remarkable for their spelling, the wealth of detail and for the novel apparatus which they listed, much of which was new to us. One piece, the "French Tickler", had a small plume of feathers on its business end while another, when fully charged, extended a pair of miniature fingers in an obscene parody of the Victory sign. So far as I know no one ever sent for any of this equipment; not for any prudish reasons but simply because at Fatehgarh it would have been as much use as a pair of snow-shoes.

It was therefore with excitement that I accepted an invitation from Harry and Charlie to visit the stews at Farrukhabad, the old city to which Fatehgarh was a mere military appendage, which lay upstream on the banks of the Ganges. I was not only pleased to be invited; I was honoured. Although they were only a couple of years older than I was, they were both regular soldiers; separated from me by great gulfs of seniority and experience. That they should ask me to accompany them was a mark of favour since, up to this moment, though they had not been unkind to me, neither had they been particularly companionable.

Although Farrukhabad was only three miles from Fatehgarh I had never visited it. One-time capital of the Bangash Nawabs who had lost and regained it innumerable times, it was surrounded by crumbling mud walls and equally crumbling bastions set in them. It had had a violent history and as late as 1803, by which time it had been ceded to the East India Company, life in the city was terribly insecure: "Murders were so frequent in Farrukhabad that people dared not venture there after sunset; and the workmen who came out to the cantonments always retired to their houses during daylight,"* an Irish Lord wrote.

The city was out of bounds; possibly because there had been an outbreak of cholera. Because Harry and Charlie had both served on the Frontier and both spoke Pashtu, the language of the Pathans, and because what they were proposing to do was against the regulations, they had decided that they would visit the brothel in the guise of Pathan horse-copers. Because I spoke no Pashtu it was decided that

* George Annesley, Viscount Valentia, second Earl of Mountnorris: *Voyages and Travels to India, Ceylon, the Red Sea, Abyssinia and Egypt in the years* 1802, 1803, 1804, 1805 and 1806; London 1809.

I should accompany them in the same guise but as a mute. I made no demur; as a second lieutenant this seemed the proper role for me. It was an absurd scheme and in retrospect I am certain that I was more excited at the prospect of being dressed as a Pathan and entering a forbidden city, than I was in visiting a brothel — the few brothels which I had visited had been not only disappointing but disproportionately expensive to the pleasure I had experienced inside.

Amir was in charge of the entire operation. It was he who selected the brothel — we assumed that there must be more than one for a book in the Regimental Library listed 167 prostitutes together with 231 female beggars in gainful employ at Farrukhabad. Admittedly this information was extracted from the census of 1901 but it seemed inconceivable with the general increase in the population that the figure could be any less forty years later. It was Amir who selected the girls, and haggled with their keeper; got hold of the Pathan clothing — the shalvar trousers, the lugris (embroidered waistcoats), the headcloths and the chaplis, the stout, open-toed Pathan sandals. The chaplis had had to be specially made for me because I had such large feet and their non-arrival until the last minute had imperilled the venture. "You can't possibly go in shoes. You'll look like a babu," Charlie said. And it was Amir who dressed us, oiling and adjusting our hair which was fortunately of a modish rather than a military length (one of the good things allowed us by the Regiment), and looping it over our ears in some semblance of the tsanrai, the characteristic curl; it was he who stained our visible extremities brown with some vegetable juice which he obtained from the baazar. When he had finished with us we looked and smelled splendid, but the disguise would not have deceived a child.

It had originally been intended that we should travel on horse-back to Farrukhabad, in our capacity as horse-brokers; but the idea had to be abandoned as there was no one whom we could trust to look after the horses when we reached our destination, so we travelled by tonga instead. As we entered the city under what was left of one of the lesser of the ten gates of the city, two corpses were being hurried out through it borne on stretchers, with footmen carrying torches running alongside them. "There is sickness in the city," said the tonga driver. In order that he would not know where we came from, we had travelled on bicycles as far as the cross-roads by the maidan and we had picked up the tonga there which Amir had ordered for us. I experienced a pleasurable feeling of excitement. This is what I had always thought India would be like before I came to it; not reading contraceptive catalogues over a mock-English breakfast.

It was hot in the city and there were strange smells compounded of sewage, bidis, dung and spices; smells that one hardly ever smelt in the cantonment and never all at once. In the bazaars it was as bright as day under the lights which shone out from the open shop-fronts and we were glad when the tonga turned off the main road into a dark and narrow lane and drew up outside a tall, old house with elaborately carved wooden balconies on the upper floors. As we got down the door opened and we were led into a dimly-lit room on the ground floor. We were expected.

The girls were already waiting, together with an old crone. They were very young, and they knelt before us on cushions in an attitude of submission which I personally found displeasing. All three were heavily weighed down with silver and jewellery but very little else — pendant earrings, neck-chains, waist-chains, nose-studs, and anklets with silver bells on them. They were a delightful golden colour and had huge, oval eyes, sulky mauve mouths and pencilled eyebrows which extended sharply upwards and gave them an odd, bird-like look. I could see little to choose between them, which was fortunate for me because it would have been difficult to express a preference in my guise as mute.

There were few preliminaries, but while we were drinking tea and nibbling listlessly at sweets, the old woman brought in a small boy of eight or nine for our inspection. He was a disagreeable-looking little boy; but in the profession which had been chosen for him it would have been difficult for him to be anything else. Presumably the keeper of the brothel, who all the time remained invisible, had been told to expect a party of Pathans and had prepared accordingly. Personally, I suspected that this was Amir's idea of a practical joke — or was it? And why only one? Were we supposed to draw lots for him or make use of him in alphabetical order, or in order of seniority? At least there were three girls. I was glad when Charlie rejected his services on our behalf and he was led away. Now we were alone; the old woman had not returned. There were heavy, exotic scents. Was this the myrrh and frankincense that I had read about in the Bible, at last, or was it musk?

"All I hope," said Harry, "is that I don't get a dose."

I was glad that he was nervous. I was too. I had enjoyed the dressing-up and the journey through the city in the tonga but I was not so sure about the next part; especially as it seemed that we were all to perform together among the cushions on the same piece of threadbare carpet — didn't they trust Pathans? And I, too, was extremely reluctant to "get a dose"; and when we were undressed we all three looked so extraordinary with our faces and necks and legs and arms stained with vegetable juice in alarming contrast to our white bodies — no one had thought of staining them — that the girls had set up a great wailing, and it had taken the old woman several minutes to reassure them.

On the way back in the tonga we discussed our experiences. They had been brief enough, but like survivors of a battle that was just finished, we were too close to the engagement to sort out truth from fiction. We all agreed that they must have been double-jointed; otherwise it would have been impossible for them to assume some of the postures which they had. Mine had made me feel like an octogenarian. We had all three found them efficient, but it was obvious that they had not enjoyed dealing with three multi-coloured savages. Both Charlie and Harry said that they found conversation difficult and they thought me lucky to be cast in a role in which speech was not required. Personally, I could not see that there had been anything to talk about; besides the din made by all those pounds of bells and bangles had been terrific.

The elation which we at first felt on quitting the brothel soon gave way to a deep, post-coital melancholy and the fear which Harry continued to voice that he might have already "got a dose". How I wished at this moment that I had sent for some of the more rudimentary apparatus listed in the catalogues; but when we got back to the bungalow and were all three soaking in our hip baths trying to get the stain off, Amir was most indignant when we told him of our apprehensions. He took it as a slight on his organising ability.

"Huzoor," he said. "There will be no trouble. Certainly they are not virgins, but then you are still too young to have need of virgins. Virgins are for old men. These girls have only just come from the country. They are fresh. They have only just begun."

A few weeks later I was told that I had passed the Lower Standard Urdu Examination and had been posted to the Battalion in the Middle East.

When I returned to the Mess from the garden a Major was waiting for me. He was dressed in workmanlike trousers of jungle green. No one wore the huge starched shorts I remembered any more.

"It's a strange thing," he said in an off-hand way which didn't deceive me, "but we can't seem to find your name in the Visitors' Book. You did say you arrived in March, 1941, didn't you? Well, it isn't there. You don't seem to have signed out when you left either."

He was right; somehow I had failed to sign the book. Perhaps it was because I was never asked to do so. I had arrived on a Sunday when nobody was about which might have accounted for the omission; but it was strange that I had also omitted to sign it when I left. The names of all the other officers who had joined at about the same time as myself were there; as was that of a friend of mine, an officer in the Garhwal Rifles, who had spent a weekend as my guest. Their names apart the whole thing might have been a dream. Perhaps I had never been at Fatehgarh. Later the Major appeared again.

"You were here," he said. "We found you in 'Records'."

"I'm sorry," he went on, "but we have to be careful. With things as they are at the moment with the Chinese, this is a prohibited area for civilians. Properly speaking you should have permission from higher up to be here at all. I doubt if you would ever get it. Naturally, we are delighted that you are here. So far as we're concerned you are still a member of the Regiment and always will be, but you understand now why we can't take you down to the lines. We can show you nothing of a military nature."

I was touched; but nevertheless I offered to leave.

"No, no!" he said. "It would be bad; bad for the honour of the Regiment."

I walked through the Civil Lines, past vast, old bungalows, some of them built before the Mutiny in 1857. The largest of all was the bungalow that had belonged to the Collector, the chief administrative officer of the District, who was always a senior member of the Indian Civil Service. It had a thatched roof more than forty feet high. Sometimes the Collector used to dine with us as the principal guest on Band Nights. Now the place was a Degree College. In the six months I was at Fatehgarh I had never seen it. I had never even visited the Civil Lines. The gulf between civil and military was complete.

I walked to the church of All Souls on the Maidan. It was a red stone, Victorian Gothic building with a tall spire. It had been built as a memorial to the men, women and children, the survivors of the siege of the Fort, who had been mowed down with grapeshot and sabred on the parade ground in July 1857. The money to build it had been raised by a punitive tax on those citizens of the place who were thought to have supported or condoned the Mutiny. I had never liked it. Even at that time, with the British still in India, it enshrined the memory of something that after so long seemed better forgotten. After the massacre the bodies had been thrown into a well over which a cross of hideous design had been erected. Now the outer wall of the churchyard facing the road was being whitewashed in anticipation of the visit of an Indian General who would pass that way. Even the tree trunks had been decorated with alternate bands of brick red and white paint.

Inside the church rotting punkahs, the long rectangular fans which swung backwards and forwards, which the punkah-wallah used to operate by pulling a cord, hung down over the varnished pews. The altar was gone, but the place was still kept clean by a family of Christians who lived in a hut in the corner of the churchyard and only one or two of the stained-glass panes in the east window were broken. The place exhaled an indescribable air of melancholy.

Beyond the church a battalion with a band of pipes and drums was practising the General Salute, raising great clouds of dust from the Maidan that had been baked by the suns of more than two hundred summers. In the distance the more elegant spire of the old East India Company church, now an office, rose into the dusty sky. In the cemetery of the East India Company inside the mud-walled fort on the banks of the Ganges, the ground between the tombs was being systematically weeded by a fatigue party in readiness for the inspection. The broken columns, Doric temples, obelisks and pyramids from which most of the plaques had long since gone, produced a nostalgia that was more supportable than that of the memorial church.

It was to this fort, on the night of the 17 – 18th June 1857, that Colonel Smith, the Commander of the Tenth Native Infantry, withdrew with the remaining Europeans, Christian Indians and one sepoy, Kalai Khan of the Tenth Native Infantry, on the arrival of the mutinous regiments from Oudh which had crossed the Ganges to win over the Tenth to their cause. There were 120 of them of whom only a quarter were capable of bearing arms, the rest being women and children. 115 men, women and children had already left in boats a fortnight previously to go down the Ganges to Allahabad or Kanpur. Part of this band of refugees had accepted the offer of Hardeo Bakhsh, a landowner, to take refuge in his castle at Dharampur on the Ramganga, a tributary of the Ganges, but sixty-five elected to go on. They reached Nawabganj north of Kanpur, where they were seized and executed.

After withdrawing to the fort, Colonel Smith had more than a week to prepare for the inevitable siege. Fighting had broken out between the Oudh mutineers and the Tenth who, all along, had refused to murder their officers, being content with the District

Treasure which had fallen into their hands. The treasure was the object of the pitched battle which now took place in which the Tenth were practically annihilated. There was a further delay in the assault imposed on the troops from Oudh by the astrologers who stated that the propitious date for the attack was 25th June.

In the fort there was no shortage of food or water, but the defenders were terribly thin on the ground and only three of the twelve bastions could be properly manned. Unfortunately, too, there were more gun-carriages than guns as the fort had been used as a gun-carriage factory; worst of all, much of the small arms ammunition was blank.

On 25th June the rebels began to bombard the fort, as the astrologers said they should, using two light guns; but the defenders proved resolute. The wife of a Sergeant Ahern who had himself been killed took her post in one of the bastions and proved herself a good shot, as did the Chaplain; but Mr Thornhill, the Judge, shot and wounded himself by mistake. Considering the number of assaults that were made by the mutineers and the number of shots that were fired, casualties among the defenders were light.

On the seventh morning, after several abortive attempts, the besiegers succeeded in exploding a mine under one of the curtain walls. The ingredients of this mine had been supplied by the Nawab of Farrukhabad as had much of the other warlike material, including scaling ladders. By the ninth day they had begun to mine the principal bastion which was commanded by Colonel Smith. The situation was hopeless. On the tenth morning while it was still dark, the defenders abandoned the fort, letting themselves down from the walls on to the river bank, and set off downstream in three boats with the same intention as the earlier party had had of reaching Kanpur or Allahabad. Of this voyage there were only four survivors, and when the British re-entered Fatehgarh the following January they began to take a vengeance for what had been done which fell on guilty and innocent alike.

Chapter Fourteen

Slow boat to Kanpur

The following morning, 18th December, we left Fatehgarh in a
rowing boat bound for Kanpur, about ninety miles downstream. The
boat and the three boatmen who went with it had been found for
us by the Assistant Engineer of the Public Works Department, but
it was the Major who had struck a bargain with them on our behalf
and who had made them put their thumbprints to the written agree-
ment at an impressive little ceremony which had taken place outside
the Mess. "Just in case they give any trouble," as he said with what
I thought was unnecessary ferocity. To me they looked a mild trio.
They agreed to take us to Kanpur for seventy-five rupees, plus an
extra twenty-five rupees for the hire of the boat and an advance of
ten rupees with which to buy food for the journey. This time there
was to be no doubt that the boatmen were to do their own cooking.

They were supposed to appear at seven-thirty, but no one seriously
thought that they would do; and it was not until eight-forty-five that
the boat was sighted slowly drifting round the bend in the river from
Farrukhabad.

Unofficial guests or not, we were given an impressive send-off.
Together with the Major we went down through the garden and
across the quarter of a mile of sands to the water's edge, heading
a procession of gardeners, mess servants, regimental policemen
and the Mess Sergeant, all of whom, with the exception of the latter
who acted the part of Earl-Marshal, were carrying luggage and
provisions.

The boat was a miniature version of a Thames lighter. It was about
twenty feet long and it had a beam of about eight feet. Except for
a small open well-deck forward which was intended for the oarsmen
to sit in it was completely decked in. The oars looked ill-balanced
to me and too flimsy to survive the journey to Kanpur. They were
bamboo and the blades were made from old pieces of packing case.

We said good-bye with some emotion. Then the boatmen pushed
off from the shore and we watched the Major and his little party
straggling back across the sands towards the Mess. I wondered if I
would ever see them or Fatehgarh again. It seemed unlikely.

It was a beautiful morning. Mist still hung over the water and downstream with the early sun shining through it the river was the colour of honey. On the high, crumbling bank, temples and old bungalows gleamed white amongst the ancient trees. To the right was the little combe at the foot of which the Ganges had first laid its spell on me. I had gone there alone the previous afternoon expecting to find the trees cut down, the shrine gone, Arcadia vanished. In fact, nothing had changed. The great piece of carved stone, with its frieze of figures, held as long as the stone endured in the lifelike attitudes with which they had been endowed by some unknown sculptor, was still embedded in the heart of the noble and mysterious tree; fresh marigolds were scattered on the plinth from which the black lingam rose; and there was still no one there.

But, this morning, the foreshore was animated: men were planting melons in the silt; others were carrying bundles of grass on their heads and red earthenware pots suspended on poles across their shoulders. There were fishermen carrying bag-shaped nets strung on bamboos, and others carrying the cone-shaped baskets which were used for trapping fish on the river bottom; and there were women walking upstream, talking gaily to one another, drying their saris which fluttered like brilliant flags in the breeze. The water in the river was a cloudy green; and as it took us down it churned ceaselessly.

By ten-thirty the sun was hot on our faces. For the first time since we had left Hardwar there were flies. They had come down with the boat from Farrukhabad and had found things so much to their liking that they had decided to stay on. There were so many that it was useless to try and swat them; instead we whirled our arms around our heads like dervishes in an effort to get rid of them. They were interested only in the passengers; they left the boatmen alone.

Invisible, some ten miles to the east of the Ganges and closing rapidly with it, was the Ramganga, a river infinitely more fickle and unpredictable than the Ganges itself, now in the final stretches of its course from the borders of Nepal to its junction with the main stream. The country between the two rivers was a wedge of flat land riddled with connecting channels which the Ganges and the Ramganga made for themselves at each successive inundation and then abandoned, leaving the cultivable silt covered with a layer of sand. Because of this there were no towns or even villages of any consequence on their banks. Even the fort at Dharampur in which Hardeo Bakhsh had sheltered the fugitives from Fatehgarh had long since been washed away.

The three boatmen were Hindu Kahars from the left bank of the Ganges near Farrukhabad, a caste which had always engaged in fishing, the cultivation of water-nuts and the land. Until they had fallen into disuse its members had also been carriers of palankeens. The eldest of three, and the one to whom the boat belonged, Lalta Prasad, was a tiny, timid-looking man with cropped, grizzled hair and an equally grizzled moustache. He was the father of Jagdish, the youngest boatman, who was not more than seventeen; otherwise he was an almost identical copy of his father who looked well over fifty but said he was forty. The third boatman, Ram Baba, was thirty according to his own computation, but looked younger. He was a wiry man with a toothbrush moustache. He looked rather like a guardsman.

Although these last two, Ram Baba and Jagdish, were now sitting on the bench in the oarsmen's well, up in the bows, with their oars attached to the thole pins by rotten cords all ready to row, they were not doing much to assist the boat's progress. For most of the time they sat in a trance state, smoking the bidis which we had given them, only arousing themselves when "old" Lalta Prasad, who was crouched over the steering oar in the stern, made some sharp remark, and then only to pull a single stroke sufficient to keep the boat on its course. All the motive power was provided by the current which was taking us down at not more than a couple of miles an hour.

I did not want to suggest that they should start rowing, although all my inclinations were to do so. "We will bring them to Kanpur on the evening of the third day," they had told the Major. How they were going to do so was a mystery. At this rate it seemed unlikely that we would reach it in a week.

All that morning and throughout the short afternoon we drifted down past fields of winter wheat and beds of melons and wastes in which nothing grew; under steep banks or which small clumps of mud houses stood amongst equally isolated clumps of trees. Some of these houses were so close to the bank that it seemed certain that they would fall into the river when the next rains came; only the trees under which small schoolboys clustered writing laboriously on slates suggested that these settlements might be old ones. It was difficult to tell. These mud houses were ageless.

During the whole of this day we only saw two boats, a pair of snub-nosed, clinker-built ferry boats, loaded with men and bicycles. In some of the reaches the stream was between three and four hundred yards wide; in others the navigable channel shrank to forty feet. Apart

from an occasional rip or a deep place over which the water seethed
and bubbled as if there was a hot spring beneath it, the river made
no sound. It moved on inexorably as a single, integrated mass, more
like a glacier than a river.

This was the day Wanda dropped the windshield of the stove over
the side, and together with Jagdish and Ram Baba I spend ten minutes
up to my neck in water, alternately feeling for it with my toes and
diving in the faint hope of finding it. It was hopeless; the current
was so strong and the water so cold and cloudy with silt that we
had to abandon the search. Without the windshield the stove would
not work and I spent the next hour making another from an old tin,
with nothing but a blunt tin-opener and a penknife.

Lalta Prasad and his crew showed no signs of stopping. "We do
not eat until the evening comes," Lalta Prasad said. So we lunched
without them, on sardines and bananas and tea, all of which they
refused.

"They make me feel as if I was having an orgy," Wanda said.

All that day they only stopped once and then only to allow Lalta
Prasad to go ashore to steal some dung which he saw piled up in a
field.

"It is always cold on the river when night comes," he said, "and
then it is too late to find fuel."

By five-thirty we were just short of the village of Singhirampur,
which was about eleven miles south-east of Fatehgarh on the right
bank of the river. Considering that we had travelled more or less
with the aid of the current alone, it was surprising that we had got
as far as this. For whenever Lalta Prasad had prevailed on Jagdish
and Ram Baba to pull a few strokes, the rotten old piece of grass
rope which secured Jagdish's oar to the thole pin promptly broke,
or rather it severed itself on a sharp piece of metal with which the
gunwale was reinforced at this point, and it took such a long time
for him to knot it together, that when he had done so Lalta Prasad
always forgot to give the order for them to start rowing again, and
we drifted on as before. Yet when I suggested to him that he should
do something about this sharp projection he simply said, "It has
always been so", and that was that.

The sun was sinking as we floated down towards Singhirampur. It
was a calm evening. The only sounds were the melancholy cawings
of crows in the distant trees, and the voices of some men who were
clustered together on the foreshore close to the fire on which a body
was burning. It was a grisly spot by normal western standards; but

we were becoming inured to such sights. Whitened skulls stood in the water and, on the foreshore, the lines of black ash left by the falling river were dotted with the heads of marigolds. On the bank scavenger birds waited, more or less patiently, for the mangy dogs to have done with two imperfectly burned corpses which were stranded close by. It was too much even for the burning party, and one man got to his feet and began to wallop the dogs with a bamboo pole. Reluctantly they slunk away and, dropping one by one into the river, began to swim across it in line ahead. When they reached the other side they stood close together for a bit like a party of revellers wondering where to go next, and then loped off into the sands to the eastward.

The sun went down behind Singhirampur. Ahead now was a small village, partly shielded from view by tall grasses. From it came the sound of children playing a game. We had looked forward to spending the night in a village, but we already knew enough about the habits of boatmen on the Ganges to know that this would not happen. The current took the boat out in a wide sweep away from the village towards the sands and it was here, on the edge of them, where the current was sluggish and the water was covered with a thick and horrible froth that, perversely, they decided that we should make our camp.

I asked Lalta Prasad why we could not stop on the other bank where the water was deeper and cleaner and there were some amenities; and where we might even be able to do a little shopping. "Sahib," he said. "We do not know these people."

"But this is a holy place. It is a great place for bathing. The book says so."

"Holy it may be," he said, stoutly, "but we for our part, will remain here."

I found this mistrust of people whom one had never seen depressing; but it was useless to argue — besides he was most probably right. We did prevail on him, however, to take the boat further downstream to a place where the water had a little less body to it.

The sky turned to deep bronze. Downstream the river, seemed to stretch away for ever. Fish rose. A large brown bird like a heron with shining white wings, flew upriver with slow wing beats. Ram Baba said it was an *Andha Bagla* — a Paddybird. From the village, doubly inviting now that we knew we would never get there, came the deep, warm sounds of animals lowing in the byres, an occasional angry voice, and the cries of small children. The boatmen lit a hot little fire of dung on the shore and began to cook chapatis and dal.

In the boat Wanda was cooking a chicken. The river began to smell strongly of green, damp things.

By seven o'clock the moon was down. The men were already in bed, half-buried in the sand around the ashes of the fire. Here, there was so little fuel that it was impossible to find enough for a purely social blaze-up. We drank rum mixed with the juice of fresh limes and thick, boiled river water, and ate delicious curried chicken and biscuits with jam. We were happy and would not have changed our situation with anyone in the world. At eight o'clock we made up beds on the deck and, with infinite difficulty, crawled into them. It was horribly early to go to bed, but there was nothing else to do. By this time it was pitch dark and no light or sound came from the village.

Both of us had dreaded the long night ahead of us. In the event the horror of it exceeded our wildest imaginings. We had hoped that the rum punch which we had concocted would make us sleep soundly. The opposite was the case. We had had enough to produce a certain sense of excitement but not sufficient to put us out. It was damnably cold and we lay on the deck strapped into our bedding rolls side by side like embalmed consorts in a pair of sarcophagi. When we did doze off we both woke at three o'clock, the time at which, with Karam Chand, we had grown accustomed to some drama occurring; but this time nothing happened.

The hours that followed were an exquisite torment. Even the false dawn, heralded by the crowing of cocks in the village, was welcome but no one stirred. The boatmen slept on, heaps of rags and tattered blankets around the dead fire. We were parched with thirst and the sound of the river bubbling under the boat only accentuated the feeling.

Finally, I decided to make some tea. The stove was just out of reach; I had forgotten to fill the kettle with water and, worst of all, I had mislaid the matches. I got up and began looking for them.

"Don't make such a noise," Wanda said severely. "I am trying to sleep."

"I'm looking for the matches. Have you got them?"

"You want me to get up and look for them?"

"I want to know if you've got them!"

From these unpromising beginnings, while I blundered about the deck and hung over the side trying to scoop up a reasonably clear kettleful of Ganges water, there developed a row which culminated, for the second time on the journey, in Wanda threatening to return to her country and her people. It was a threat that through all the years that we had been married had never lost its original savour, and the proximity of the railway made it one that it was perfectly possible for her to carry out.

Slowly life came back to the river with the trumpeting of Sarus Cranes and hideous sounds from the village as the inhabitants cleared their throats. Our own differences seemed petty when we considered the splendours of the morning sky which was now a brilliant, if rather powerful red.

The boatmen cooked some dal, and at half past seven we set off. In the river a Gangetic dolphin (*Platanista gangetica*) rose from the bottom where it had been wallowing and frolicked about the boat, blowing like a steam engine. It was a baby one, about four feet long, jet black, with a round head and a long, narrow spoon-shaped snout. Big flocks of white egrets flew overhead and black and white avocets with long, turned-up bills made high-pitched squeaky noises on the shore, where a disconsolate little party of men clustered about their boat which had foundered during the night. In answer to Lalta Prasad's shouted enquiry as to what had brought about this mishap, they answered that it was a very old boat and the bottom had fallen out of it.

By ten o'clock it was really warm. Ahead a long straight reach of river and the tree-shaded bank faded away mysteriously in the haze. One or two white-clad figures performing their pujas at the water's edge only accentuated the feeling of isolation from the grey northern world from which we had come. As we went past a sadhu saluted us and then submerged himself in the river completely, as if to wash away the memory of what he had seen.

For ten miles the stream hugged the high right bank taking us down at a uniform two miles an hour until at midday we came abreast of the village of Gori, where clerks dressed in white shirts with large orange fountain pens in their breast pockets and with huge bicycles, waited more or less patiently for the ferryman on the opposite shore who showed no signs of coming for them. Now, once more, the current took us into the wilderness of sand in mid-river, its only inhabitants some sad-looking shag or cormorants, which were perched on a great, bleached tree-trunk that was slowly rolling down towards the sea. Eating tomato sandwiches and drinking tea to keep up our spirits, we floated on under a vast sky covered with clouds that were like spun-glass, watched closely by the boatmen who were probably looking at a tomato sandwich for the first time in their lives. No one could accuse them of being garrulous, but if we smiled at them they generally smiled back and one could ask little else except that they should propel the boat rather than simply sit in it, which was the one thing that they resolutely refused to do.

After an hour or so the current began to take us westwards again round a big bend, and here we met some fishermen who were sitting on a sandbank drying their nets. These nets were twenty or thirty feet long and the bottoms were weighted with iron.

"We call them iron nets," Lalta Prasad said. "I know these men. They are from Arwal, on the Kuda Nala between the Ramganga and Ganga."

"But have they any fish?" I said. Although we consorted with fishermen constantly, so far we had not succeeded in eating any fish.

"They have no fish," he said.

"Why have they no fish?"

"Because they are not fishing."

In mid-afternoon we came down towards Chandarpur, a small place on the right bank. On a bluff above the river, an ancient mosque stood in a grove of trees. Black birds weaved in and out among its three, tall minarets. It was an enchanting place.

The enchantment was diminished by the presence of a party of fourteen men who were attending the burning of a body on the foreshore. They were a cheerful lot, the Hindu equivalent of a works outing to Southend. As we went past they suddenly lost interest in the whole lugubrious business. Laughing they pushed some unburnt limbs into the river and doused the fire with river water, enveloping themselves in clouds of steam.

While Lalta Prasad and Ram Baba were ashore stealing dung, an immense, amorphous thing rose to the surface attended by tremendous gurglings and rumblings. It was like some monster born of primaeval slime. It remained on the surface for only a few moments; then it sank from view and did not appear again. I asked Lalta Prasad's son, Jagdish, what it was.

"It is the Gaunch," he said. The way he said it invested the creature with the awful quality of a Bandersnatch.

South of Chandapur the bank was eaten through by ravines to the sides of which clung small villages of mud huts. This was Hindoostan as European artists saw it in the early nineteenth century, and it was as if one was seeing it through their eyes. Banyan trees grew on the bank. Their long branches hung down over the river like bell-ropes, and, in their shade, the water was the colour of greengages. Small boys were fishing, perched in nooks in the bank or else clinging precariously to the bared roots of the great trees. Above them, on top of the bank, emaciated men wearing big head-cloths trotted along carrying bamboo poles with bundles slung at either end. Four men were carrying a white-shrouded corpse on a stretcher, followed by a number of mourners, one of whom was carrying a pot with a fire burning in it. There were castor-oil plantations, palm trees and fields of bushy-topped millet plants; and there was a small red stone temple with dozens of subsidiary spires which had figures of animals carved on them.

The current was sluggish and I implored the boatmen to row — first in Hindi, then English — "Oh, why don't you row, you bastards!" and they did — but only a few strokes.

At four o'clock Kusumkhor was abeam, a village so battered by the elements that it was difficult to tell where the earth ended and the buildings began. The houses clung precariously to the edge of the cliff by the skin of their teeth, like a mountaineer in difficulties. On the beach below boys were playing cricket in the deep sand, using pieces of driftwood as bats and a ball made of old rags.

Just below Kusumkhor, at the end of a long spit of sand, the Ramganga joined the Ganges. I was surprised to find it here. According to the map it should not have been. Perhaps it was not the Ramganga, even though the boatmen said it was. No one was interested except myself and in a few years' time it would all be different anyway.

Whichever river or combination of rivers it was it gave a much-needed impetus to our boat and we swept down close to the left bank at twice the speed at which we had been travelling previously. A mile below the junction we landed to look for wood. Although the boatmen had enough dung to cook with we were not prepared to endure another fireless night. Unlike Karam Chand and his men, they seemed indifferent to the pleasures of a good warm blaze.

Across the water, where the sun was setting like a huge blood orange, ripples of heat undulated over the flats. Beyond them were some strange-looking mounds, bare except for a few moth-eaten palm trees. Upstream mist was beginning to spread over Kusumkhor, and soon it obliterated it completely.

We were not particularly successful in finding wood. Most of it was thorn and unbreakable, and what driftwood there was had lodged itself in inaccessible places halfway up the bank, which was here almost vertical. In trying to reach a particularly tempting piece that was just out of his reach, Jagdish fell into the river with a satisfying splash.

By the time he had been cleaned up and fitted out with dry clothes it was getting late; already Lalta Prasad was mumbling about robbers. With these inadequate supplies of firewood which ensured us another fireless night, we set off across the stream, over which small square-tailed birds were dipping and twisting, to an immense sandbank to which the boatmen had taken a fancy.

While they lugged their few belongings ashore, we set off together ostensibly to look for driftwood, but really so that we could be by ourselves for a little. This was the time of day we both liked best; when the sun was down, the land to the west was dark against the sky and the river was like molten metal. Besides ourselves the only human being in this wilderness was a man who was urging a heavily-laden donkey towards the distant shore, anxious not to be benighted in such a place. There was no wood to be found but on the shores of a brackish lagoon that had been left by the falling river we picked up a flattish, mud-coated object as hard and as heavy as iron, eighteen inches long and a foot wide, which we bore back to the boatmen, homing on the bright little beacon of the fire which they had already kindled using the precious wood and round which they had built a circular wall of dung cakes.

"That," they said, "is the head of the Gaunch," and took no further interest in it.*

We lit the lanterns and made punch, giving a shot of it to each of the boatmen, who accepted it indifferently. They were good men but they lacked the camaraderie of the camp fire which we had enjoyed with Karam Chand and his crew. By this time they had cooked and eaten their meal, and there was no camp fire worthy of the name to encourage camaraderie, anyway.

Much later we ate the warmed-up remains of the curried chicken of the previous night, together with rice, dal and half a large bottle of something called Kalvert's Royal Sliced Mango Chutney, which was so delicious that it practically constituted a separate course in itself. The chicken was a bit rubbery; with the sort of fowls available in India it was easy to see why the inhabitants had invented curry.

The moon began to set. It was reflected in the river in a series of little golden pools each of which wobbled like a jelly. Soon it disappeared into the mist which enveloped Kusumkhor and a light but bitter wind began to blow from the north.

It is a common belief of those who have not camped in lonely places that they are eerily quiet. But the noise in this great solitude,

* Probably *Carcharias gangeticus* — A fresh water shark, also found in the Euphrates.

miles from the nearest habitation, the gurglings of the river, the continual rumble of collapsing banks, the awful, insane ululations of packs of jackals, the trumpeting of cranes and the sound of other unidentifiable birds beating their wings on the water, which resembled the noise made by a goods train chugging through a flooded cutting, was deafening. It was worse than the streets of Rome. Only when dawn – or what seemed to us, exhausted by our efforts to find sleep, a slow-motion film of a dawn – came seeping through slats of dark cloud was there a moment of peace.

This was the morning of the third day. Since leaving Fatehgarh we had covered not more than thirty miles, about a third of the way to Kanpur. Lalta Prasad had said that the entire journey would take three days. At this rate we would be lucky if we did it in nine.

Teal and pochard and bar-headed geese roared overhead while upstream, the cranes came back to life and began beating their wings after their brief repose. Close to us on the sand one of the odious-looking Pharoah's chickens strutted. "Waiting for us to die," Wanda said.

It was now possible to see the water which we had been using for our tea-making and rum-drinking the previous night – the water which everyone from Mr. Nehru to the old sadhu at Hardwar had told us no harm could come from. We looked at it with awe.

"If we can survive that we can survive anything," Wanda said.

"It should be all right; we boiled it."

"It's like boiling arsenic," she said.

At eight, reluctantly, the sun broke through the clouds and equally reluctantly the boatmen shoved off. The current took us and as we went down Wanda made porridge on the stove, while Ram Baba and Jagdish hung head downwards over a makeshift clay fireplace which they had constructed in the well forward, cooking chapatis.

As it grew warmer we peeled off layer after loathsome layer of clothing. Ahead of us there was a mirage in which a boat floated in mid-air upside down. Twenty minutes later we were close to it; by now it was the right way up. It was a clinker-built country boat, perhaps thirty feet long, with an upturned bow and a square stern. The small deck house was thatched with reeds. It had a crew of two men; one was steering, the other was on the bank towing the boat upstream, plodding along bent double with the line over his shoulder attached to a piece of bamboo which he pressed against his chest. The mast to which the tow line was made fast, was prevented from collapsing by a number of guys and backstays.

In the space of an hour we saw four more boats. The river was becoming populous. There were camels on the bank now, swaying down in the direction of Kanauj. A turtle rose to the surface; four elegant little cranes picked their way through the shallows and we passed three men who were skinning a bullock on the bank, surrounded by waiting dogs and vultures. At one o'clock we were abreast of the ferry at Kanauj.

Here in 1540, close to the ferry, on the left bank of the river, the army of the Emperor Humayun, paralysed by inactivity and weakened by desertions, was utterly defeated by the Afghan, Sher Khan who had assumed the royal title. After the defeat – there was hardly any action – Humayun fled across the river to Kanauj on an elephant, and narrowly escaped drowning while doing so. In 1528 his father, Babar, had forced the crossing of the Ganges in the opposite direction, and there defeated the always-revolting Afghans. The dynasty founded by Sher Khan, an able man, lasted fifteen years. In 1555 Humayun returned and overthrew Sher Khan's grandson, the ineffective Shah Sur, and in the following year Humayun was succeeded by his son, Akbar.

Although Murray's *Guide* said that there was little of interest at Kanauj and what we had been told at Fatehgarh corroborated it, we had looked forward to going there and finding out for ourselves. After all, it had been the capital of Northern India. The *Gazetteer* made it sound interesting: "The iconoclastic fury of Mahmud of Ghazni swept away all the Hindu religious edifices of dates anterior to the tenth century ... Surrounding groups of ruins and mounds of masonry debris show where stood the towers, the palaces and the temples of the past. Old tiles, old coins, and pieces of broken sculpture encounter the ploughshare in its course through the neighbouring fields. The removal of the ancient bricks with which these fields are strewn has hitherto proved a task of despair ..."

To visit the city, which at this time of year was completely isolated from the Ganges, would mean leaving the boat and our belongings and setting off on a long walk. We decided to go on; which was fortunate as we were already a considerable way downstream from the landing-place. "After all we can always go back," Wanda said falsely; her interest in Kanauj was less strong than my own, since what she really wanted was to get to Kanpur where we both hoped to receive some letters from home – so far we had received none at all. Although I pretended to agree with her, I knew that we would never return to Kanauj, and we didn't.

Although he had not understood our conversation, Lalta Prasad had heard the word "Kanpur" mentioned several times, and he took the opportunity of voicing the fears of himself and his crew.

"It will take us six days to reach Kanpur," he said, piteously. "And it will take us twelve more days to return, using the tow rope. In this way most of the money which you are to pay us will be consumed."

"If you had better oars and better rope to secure them we might already be at Kanpur," I said, unkindly.

"They were always thus and as for the ropes they are cut by the iron thing," he answered gloomily. He was a man of a markedly fatalistic temperament; but it was difficult not to sympathise with him. He and his crew were living on a handful of dal and a few chapatis twice a day. Finally it was agreed that they should put us ashore the following morning when we reached a place on the right bank called Araul where there was a railway station. At once Lalta Prasad adjusted "the iron thing" and from this moment onwards both Ram Baba and Jagdish began to apply themselves to the oars with diligence.

All through that day we took turns at the oars. By the afternoon we were in a stretch of the river which bore an uncanny resemblance to the one we had passed through coming down to Kusumkhor, and at precisely the same time. Where there had been a mosque on the right bank with minarets at Chandarpur, here there was a ruin — whether it was a mosque or a temple it was impossible to say. It was certainly ruinous. There were the same shady banks and further down there was a large village on a bluff, from which the houses descended in steps in nalas on either side of it. Women stood in the doorways, silently watching us go by; cows stood equally immobile in the shadow of the mud walls, as if pasted to them adding to the illusion that this was a film that we had seen before and one that had momentarily stopped; but as we turned the bend it began again. Here, on the other side, the scene was more lively: on the upper ramparts dogs were fighting one another energetically and a woman was laying into them with a stick, while down in the river, where some fishing boats were moored, equally energetic girls were walloping away at their washing, shouting to one another with coarse, cheerful voices.

Here we went aground, and to the amusement of the laundry girls got out and pushed the boat, with Wanda sitting majestically on the deck like a Queen on a punctured carnival float that was being removed from a procession. It was strange how few women we had so far seen on the banks of the river. Mother Ganges seemed to be for men.

The cliffs grew taller. At the foot of them huge chunks of Mughal brickwork lay in the river. The cliffs were reddish-brown and they were so sheer that they looked as if they had been sliced with a knife. They were also riddled with holes in which blue rock-pigeons had their nests, from which came sleepy, afternoon noises. Then Jagdish clapped his hands and they exploded out into the sunlight in slatey clouds shot with the green, purple and magenta of their neck feathers.

A mile or so further down we came to Gangaganj, also on the right bank at a place where the cliff receded from the river and the land could be seen running back green with young wheat and patches of sugar cane, groves of mangoes and clumps of palms. It was in this pleasant countryside that Mian Almas Ali, Governor of Kanauj under the rulers of Oudh in the last decade of the eighteenth century, had established a military post and, here on the high ground by the river, he had constructed a garden enclosure.

It was a strange spot. Below it, two columns of brick and stone lay in the water, embraced by the branches of a great tree from which bright yellow flowers sprouted. The enclosure itself was surrounded by a high, partially broken wall of thin bricks with an entrance gate facing downriver under a crumbling arch. Inside it there was a Hindu temple with a tall spire on which there was a gilded figure of Hanuman, the monkey god, and in a far corner under some old trees there was a delicate, octagonal pavilion with a bulbous, fluted dome. It made a pleasantly frivolous contrast to the forbidding monolith which rose above it. By it a couple of pallid cows were nibbling the scanty grass and a sadhu sat in the shade of a pipal tree.

The temple itself was dark and airless and smelt of bats. There was a green stone lingam with a snake carved on it and in niches round the shrine there were stone figures of Hanuman, Rama and twenty other gods. While we looked at them we ourselves were being watched by a rat as big as a cat which waited calmly for us to go away. I liked the garden of Almas Ali, but the temple was a disagreeable place.

Now we entered an archipelago of sandbanks. On the shore mist was gathering in the combes and on the cliffs and all around us sand was crashing into the river.

After many heart-searchings the boatmen chose an inlet in one of the sandbanks as the place where they would make the camp. It was not a bad place, except that the water in the bay was rather dirty for making tea with.

We had a splendid dinner in which filthy tinned bacon was effectively disguised with smashed-up cauliflowers, potatoes and chillies and the last of the chutney, and went to bed. We had finished the rum, and there was nothing else to do. It was the twentieth of December; and although we were not certain what day of the week it was, we consoled ourselves with the thought that if we had been in London there would still probably have been four shopping days to Christmas.

We set off at eight the following morning and half an hour later arrived at the ferry at Araul. There was little to see — some high brown cliffs topped with trees, a ruined building and men planting melons on the shore. It was an appropriate place to end an unexciting voyage.

Lalta Prasad went off to fetch a bullock-cart from the village and when he returned with the great, creaking vehicle, we presented him and the others with some blankets and various small things and offered to pay them there and then.

"No," he said, "I and Ram Baba will accompany you to the railway station. Jagdish will remain with the boat."

Having loaded the bullock-cart, and said good-bye to Jagdish who was grumpy at being left behind, we set off perched on top with the boatmen lurching along behind the cart towards the cliff, and there entered a deep, shady combe which led steeply up through it in the direction of the village. On the bank there was a shrine to Siva garlanded with marigolds, and in a niche in the cliff looking like a mummified corpse, there was a sadhu with mud-encrusted hair.

The cart lurched up into the village: past women and children who were kneading dung-cakes and slapping them on the walls of the houses to dry; past old men sunning themselves in doorways; past loud-voice bullock drivers at the wells and children who came racing out of school to join the boatmen behind the cart — Lalta Prasad who was carrying the Janata which had leaked over everything and Ram Baba who stopped every few minutes to pick the bedding rolls out of the dust when they fell off the cart.

Finally we reached a road made of bricks, which the driver of the cart said was a *pakka* (real) road; the one through the village, he said, was *kachcha* (bad). The *pakka* road was more shattering than the *kachcha* one, but after a couple of hundred yards we reached the Grand Trunk Road, and drove up to the railway station. As we arrived two wretched-looking malefactors, roped and handcuffed, were led out to a waiting lorry by a horde of policemen, rammed into it with what seemed unnecessary violence and driven away in the direction of Kanpur.

Without being asked to do so, the boatmen lugged our baggage on to the platform. I was interested to see that they would not allow

us to engage in manual labour in public. Although it was now some-
what reduced by judicious repacking we still seemed to have an
awful lot of luggage: two tin trunks, two bedding rolls, two canvas
bags — one with the library in it — a can of kerosene, two baskets —
one containing the stove, the other vegetables — a huge water-bottle
which we had never used, a bag full of cameras, and most useless
of all, a typewriter. When they had done this I wrote several letters
of recommendation, paid them seventy rupees and gave two to the
driver of the bullock-cart who was quite overcome. Lalta Prasad and
Ram Baba were delighted, too, as well they might be, leaving us
half way to our destination and being paid in full, and they parted
from us with some emotion. On the whole we had been fortunate
with our travelling companions; at least none of them had been real
villains.

There was very little of interest in Araul Mankapur; the village
stretched for a couple of hundred yards along the Grand Trunk
Road which itself stretched from Calcutta to the North-West Frontier
and was here fourteen feet wide.* There was a fly-blown bazaar and
on the northern outskirts of the town, where the workshops of the
artisans were situated, women were chipping mill-stones from lumps
of rock, and men were repairing cycle rickshas and replacing with
practical metal strapping the trellised back-rest between the awning
poles of the ekkas which had been woven from cord since time immemorial. At a quarter to twelve the Kanpur train came in.

The outskirts of Kanpur when we reached them were as unlovely
as those of any other city. There was a wilderness of brickfields and
kilns with forests of rusty iron chimneys rising from them. There was
the office of the Animal Husbandry Department, followed by the
Institute of Cancer Research, a huge modern Hindu temple, the Eye
Hospital and the Labour Exchange, which seemed a long way out of
the town, and a glimpse of the Grand Trunk Road with two elephants
plodding up it. There was a Muslim burial ground with washing
drying in it and a large hoarding advertising a cough cure which
showed the sufferer apparently being strangled. Nearer the centre,
high walls blocked out the view of everything except some sinister-
looking factories, and the barrel-roofed dwellings of the railway
workers by the marshalling yards at Kanpur Anwagunj. A few
minutes more, in which we were too busy getting our gear together
to look out of the window, and we arrived at Kanpur.

* The Grand Trunk Road was planned as a highway for armies in the sixteenth century
  by the Afghan Emperor Sher Khan. It was completed under the administration of
  Lord William Bentinck, Commander in Chief, 1833–5.

Chapter Fifteen

Christmas at Kanpur

The Retiring-Room at Kanpur Station in which we spent the night was not an agreeable place, and it was one which the austerity of the river had left us ill-prepared to endure. The bathroom was as damp and cheerless as a grotto, and the sheets and pillow-cases on the beds were those of the previous occupants. It was only by a display of bloody-minded intransigence that the attendant, in whom craftiness and gormlessness were equally compounded, could be persuaded to change them for freshly-laundered ones, and when they did arrive they were as damp as the others had been dirty. In India it is possible to win every battle but the last one.

All through the night armies of mice careered about the floor, taps dripped in the adjacent bathroom and at five o'clock the neighbours began to make snuffling noises.

"If people don't stop getting up before dawn," said Wanda, "I shall die."

As soon as the day was more advanced we set off for the Kanpur Club in search of more comfortable accommodation at the suggestion of the Railway Transport Officer whose office on the platform was a haven of military efficiency.

The Kanpur Club was situated in the Cantonment which lay to the south-east of the city between the Ganges and the Grand Trunk Road.

The place was much as I remembered it from 1941. Well-trained servants padded about and, although it was too cold for swimming in the pool from behind the neatly-trimmed hedges came the cries of "Oh, good shot!" and "Well played!" of Sahibs and Memsahibs, most of them Indian, at tennis.

The Secretary's Office was to be a scene of humiliation. He, too, was an Indian.

"We are travelling down the Ganges. Could we possibly stay at the Club for a few days?"

"There is no accommodation at the Club."

"Can we apply for temporary membership?"

"You have to be proposed by a member."

"We don't know any members."

"In that case it is not possible for you to do so."

"We have a letter of introduction from Mr. Nehru."

"The Prime Minister is not a member of the Kanpur Club."

We crept out of the building, boarded the waiting ricksha and were pedalled away.

More kindly, because he did it without seeing us, the Resident Magistrate gave up permission to stay in the Circuit House which was in the northern part of the Cantonment and had once housed the Lieutenant-Governor. It stood isolated among closely sheared lawns and huge trees in which vultures squatted and it was very grand, as befitted the temporary residence of Judges on whom, just as in Britain, the weight of dispensing justice hangs heavily, particularly at night. There was a vast dining-room with a lost-looking table in the middle of it and an equally large drawing-room with lines of chairs disposed as if some now long-dispersed company had decided, in a moment of frivolity, to play musical chairs after dinner. Everything was highly polished and although it was undeniably melancholy, it was, and this was important to us in the reduced state in which we found ourselves, extraordinarily cheap. Bed, breakfast, afternoon tea, and innumerable buckets of boiling hot water brought to the bathroom twice a day by the water carrier, cost six rupees for the pair of us, which was nine shillings.

While Wanda was unpacking I set off with the butler, who insisted on accompanying me, for the Sati Chaura Ghat.

The Ghat was a delightful place, approached by a sunken lane shaded by trees. On the bank there was a hexagonal temple dedicated to the worship of Siva, and at the foot of the steps which led down to the water distinguished-looking Brahmans were performing their Pujas. There was nothing to differentiate this ghat from other ghats I had already seen, except for a white cross behind an iron railing on which was written "In Memoriam, June 27th, 1857".

It was here during the Mutiny that the survivors of the siege had been massacred by the Nana Sahib's troops as they boarded the boats which were to take them down to Allahabad.

On the way down to it the butler had been garrulous but he must have identified me as a person of no consequence, for on the way back to the Circuit House, and throughout our stay, he never spoke again unless spoken to.

The Cantonment was not a cheerful spot. A germ-laden copy of

Murray's *Handbook for the Bengal Presidency*, 1882, which we had bought in the bazaar the previous evening, stated flatly that "there were no buildings worth visiting" in the city either. "The sole interest attaching to the place being from the frightful massacres which took place here during the Mutiny of 1857", it proceeded to describe the events which led up to them in fifteen columns of print, at the same time referring in the most critical manner to the "spirit of insane confidence" displayed by the General in command, Sir Hugh Wheeler, for allowing, among other errors of judgement, "a detachment of the 84th to pass on to Lakhnau".

We also had with us two Murray's *Guides to India*, that of 1933 and 1962, both of which had had different editors, and it was interesting to trace the changes that had been brought about by time. In the 1933 edition the massacre was described as "cowardly" and General Wheeler as "a gallant veteran" who "most unselfishly despatched 80 men of the 32nd under Capt. Lowe, to Lucknow, and 50 men of the 84th on the following day, although he was well aware that, in case of attack, his own position was not defensible." In the 1962 edition Kanpur was said to have "Mournful associations for those of British birth"; the massacre was neither "frightful" nor "cowardly" but "subsequent" and there was no description of it or the Mutiny at all.

It was a Sunday. Lunch was not served at the Circuit House except by special arrangement and we had made none. We were deterred from going to eat in the city by the distance that separated us from it and by the absence at this hour of any transport. Instead we sat half-asleep in the thin sunshine on hard, upright chairs, drinking beer which tasted of glycerine, trying unsuccessfully to combat the melancholia which hung over us like a pall. It was brought on by the far-awayness of our friends and family, the imminence of Christmas and the knowledge that we were almost certain to spend it alone together in the Circuit House.

In a desperate attempt to exorcise these suicidal feelings we walked mile after mile, in the ghastly atmosphere of Sunday-afternoon Aldershot: through deserted military lines; past trees with white-washed trunks; past the house of the Lieutenant-Colonel to whom our friend, the General in Delhi, had given us a letter of introduction (luckily for him he was on leave); past old, pre-Mutiny bungalows with white-columned porches and steep-pitched tiled roofs and contemporary ones not yet finished, whose owners picnicked proudly outside them in tents; past what had once been the Church of Scotland, which was now the U.S. Baptist Church where some elderly, sad-looking Anglo-Indians were clustered under the porch. Eventually we arrived at the Memorial Church which was close to the place where General Wheeler had constructed his entrenchment, and where he and the Garrison had resisted the mutineers.

Brickwork pillars, many of them overthrown, indicated the former whereabouts of some of the key points in the defence — "the Main Guard", "the Provision Godown", "the Redan 3 Feet Deep" and so on. It was difficult to imagine a place less adapted than this in which to endure a siege, for it was as flat as a pancake.

The Church was the colour of tinned salmon and it had a large water tank on top of it. It was said to have been designed as a garrison church for Malta, but someone had put the plans in the wrong pigeon-hole and it had been erected in Kanpur instead.

In the garden there was a stone memorial screen and a sickly-looking angel executed in white marble by an Italian, Baron Maro-chetti, who was a protégé of Queen Victoria and the Prince Consort. Until the Partition of India it had stood in the Memorial Garden in the City above the Well into which the bodies of the massacred had been flung. In 1947 it had been saved from a mob which was intent on destroying it by the gallant efforts of a number of Indian Christians and re-erected here. At the same time the Memorial Gardens became the Municipal Gardens.

"Neither screen nor statue can be considered quite satisfactory," Murray's *Guide* said in 1933, but by 1962 there had been an inexplicable reversal of taste and the statue was then described as "beautiful". The Christians had been right to save it.

When we returned to the Circuit House we found Karam Chand waiting for us.

"I have taken two months' leave from my job," he announced, "and I am going to accompany you both to Calcutta. I am devoted to you," he said.

As we flopped down on our beds, which he had already made inside-out, he knelt down to undo my shoe-laces.

It was difficult to know what to do with him. With his boat he had been an asset; without it he was something of a liability. Even if we succeeded in hiring a boat it would already have its own boatmen, and Karam Chand's presence in it would only be a source of friction. Besides, I did not like this metamorphosis which he seemed intent on effecting from waterman to body servant. After all, it was on me that the brunt of his attentions fell: nor, so far as I could see, did we need a Cantinflas. We were not going round the world in eighty days. There was no need of a brilliant improviser. There was a certain inevitability about our journey; provided that we did not succumb to some disease or capsize and drown, the current would surely take us to our destination.

The most important thing was to save Karam Chand from loss of face when he returned to his employment, as we persuaded him he must.

There were the inevitable tears. I wrote a long and eulogistic letter to his employer, the Irrigation Engineer, and after giving Karam Chand a good dinner we furnished him with a railway ticket and some money for the journey. Once again the brave, rather pathetic little figure rode out of our lives.

We spent six days at Kanpur. It was for longer than we intended; but we hung on there stubbornly: waiting for mail from England which never arrived — there had been none at Fatehgarh either; trying to find a motor boat to take us to Allahabad; and simply because it was Christmas week and we had a faint, irrational hope that we would find more jollification there than we would on the river on Christmas Day.

It was the nights which proved the most insupportable. The Circuit House was a good one and a half miles from the town; but when we came to travel to it by the long, dark military avenues, it seemed more. There was the choice of going on foot or summoning a bicycle ricksha, for taxis were rare in the city. The nights were cold and foggy, and travelling in an open ricksha we used to arrive rigid with cold in the Mall, which was the fashionable street. In the Mall in Christmas week, the expensive grocers' shops were crowded with well-hipped Indians buying expensive English cakes and biscuits, "Escotch" at seven pounds a bottle and Christmas cards, showing robins, groaning stagecoaches, Shepherds, Mangers, Wise Men and Santa Claus — even orthodox Hindus took Christmas seriously here. The more modern restaurants were like their counterparts elsewhere in India. They had a depressing, thirtyish décor of a sort which I had hitherto associated with countries behind the Iron Curtain; after eating an ill-chosen dinner in one or other of them we generally walked back burping and blowing-off in the dark to the Circuit House but in a slightly less suicidal frame of mind.

More agreeable were the narrow lanes of the "native" city, off the Chandi Chowk, north of the Ganges Canal and the railway station. They were flanked by decrepit brick tenements and tall, dark warehouses filled with sanitary ware. Here, too, was the street of the gold and silver merchants, in which fine, chunky leg bangles and armlets of good workmanship were displayed in glass-topped cases or else extracted from huge old-fashioned safes that looked as if they had been looted from an embassy, and sold by weight. Here the atmosphere was friendly and there was an air of excitement and animation that was lacking in the European part. As we were the only Europeans there at such a late hour we were always given an enthusiastic welcome by the merchants who sat outside their brilliantly-lit premises.

"Gom here! Gom here!" they cried flapping fat, pallid hands in our direction in a gesture of dismissal. "Go away! Go away!" they said to less important customers than ourselves, making violent gestures of welcome, so that they might devote themselves to us. It was all rather confusing.

Here, too, in the open-fronted restaurants one could also eat better and more daringly than in the Mall, No ill came to us dining in these exotic places; by this time our stomachs were as tough as a pair of old boots. But to us Kanpur seemed a formless city. Perhaps because it was isolated from the Ganges and the bathing ghats by enormous wool and cotton mills and tanneries, muncipal gardens and offices, the jail, police lines, court houses and the old cemetery.

The cemetery dated back to the time of the East India Company. With its crumbling temples, obelisks, truncated pyramids and columns symbolically broken it was like the ruins of ancient Rome in microcosm. But the small boys playing cricket among the tombs, saying "Ullo, Ullo, 'ow are you", "Very well thank you", the nim and banyan trees whose leaves dappled their cricket pitch with shadows and the great anaemic-looking cows nuzzling the outer wall left one in no doubt that this was a long way from the Imperial City.

It was a relief to find a cemetery at Kanpur in which the occupants had died in ways other than by massacre, but life in the days of the Company had still been woefully short. On one slate tombstone alone was inscribed the following:

> Louise, who departed this life at Cawnpore on the 8th April
> 1832, aged 7 years and 4 months.
> Adele, who departed this life at Cawnpore on the 9th of June
> 1836, aged 4 months and 20 days.
> and of
> Louise, their mother, who departed this life at Nudjuffughur
> on the 17th of July 1836, aged 31 years, 3 months and 11 days
> and of

Wm. Vincent Esq. of Nudjuffghur
and to the memory of
Sophie, his second wife, who departed this life on the
9th of February, 1845, aged 36 years, 1 month and 19 days
and of their 4 children
Marie-Helene, Eugene, Marie-Lise and Maria, who departed
this life respectively, on the 14th of June, 1841, the 19th
January, 1844, the 7th of June, 1844, and the 4th February, 1845.

It would be wrong to suggest that our stay in Kanpur was wholly depressing. We made a number of friends. Our search for a motor-boat led us to visit a firm of auctioneers that was situated in the Mall and which was the property of an old-established Goanese family which had deep roots in the city, one of whose ancestors, Manuel Xavier Noronha, had been instrumental in saving the lives of some eighty Europeans during the Mutiny. Without them our Christmas would have been gloomy indeed.

The business was conducted by two brothers, Mr. William and Mr. Stanley, both men of indefatigable enthusiasm and even the premises themselves were of a kind that are encountered with increasing rarity anywhere, and then only as an artfully contrived "front" for a merchant bank that has been taken over by a larger organisation, or a wine merchant whose principal source of income is a product of the barley rather than the grape. The place was a Dickensian labyrinth, filled with retainers all of whom appeared to be omniscient in their particular field.

The only criticism that could be levelled at the brothers was that they assumed that their friends would be as pleased to see us as they were themselves. On the occasion of our first meeting Stanley telephoned to an Englishman and his wife, when it was already well after midday — in India not necessarily the breach of etiquette that it would have been in Europe — suggesting that they should invite us to lunch. The lunch was excellent but although we made every effort to be affable our involuntary hosts were enveloped in an almost palpable cloak of wariness. It was obvious that they regarded us as a pair of bohemian scroungers — who could blame them when, in effect, that was what we were — and we never met them again or any other members of the British colony at Kanpur for that matter, except a bank official who volunteered, while cashing a travellers' cheque, that our arrival had been widely discussed.

In contrast to the chilliness displayed by our compatriots was Christmas dinner with Mr. William, his wife Mary and the rest of the Noronha family. It was preceded by quantities of drink to which we had grown unaccustomed. Afterwards we lay about listlessly among stuffed tigers and other trophies of the chase shot by Mr. William who, in spite of advancing years and increasing deafness, was a noted and passionate hunter, ourselves feeling rather like things that had just been returned from the taxidermist.

Later we attempted to telephone our children in England. As a conversation it was not a success. Neither of the parties could hear a word that the other was saying, but the operator at Kanpur who had been roused by our bellowings came to our aid and passed on small snippets of information.

"Now they are saying that it is snowing ... Now that they are receiving many letters but they are not reading them because they are not able to do so. Please write more distinctly ..." and so on.

In the evening we went to the cinema. The film was a gruesome musical comedy set amongst almond blossom in Kashmir. Soon we were fast asleep. It had been a long day.

It had begun at midnight on Christmas Eve with Mass at the Roman Catholic Church in the Cantonment. When we arrived the service had already been in full blast for half an hour and when we left at one in the morning the congregation, which by this time was asleep on its feet, was still being harangued by the Indian priest who showed no signs of coming to an end of his peroration. Even Wanda was impressed. "They would not stand for that in my country," she said. "Many would not stand at all."

"Why?" I said. I was not really interested. By this time I was a bit fed up with her church. Everything in it seemed to go on for such a long time, and here both the preliminary addresses and the sermon had been given in Hindi and English.

"They would not be able to. They would be drunk."

At eleven o'clock on Christmas Day we went to "my" church. I had insisted on Wanda coming too, principally to have my own back on her for what she had inflicted on me.

The Memorial Church at Kanpur was nothing like the Memorial Church at Fatehgarh. There was nothing dilapidated about it. Everything had the appearance of being constantly polished and burnished, from the varnished pews to the brass plaque in memory of General Sir Mowbray Thompson, K.C.I.E., late of the 53rd Native Infantry, the last survivor of the Massacre who died in 1917.

The congregation consisted of some twenty of the British Colony and a number of Anglo-Indians who made brave efforts to look their best; but although we sang lustily and smiled benignly when we thought anyone was looking in our direction, it was no passport to the British colony and although, as the bank official had told Wanda previously when he had cashed her cheque, everyone knew who we were and where we had come from, we walked out of the church without anyone saying a word to us.

"If they behaved like this with the Indians then they deserved to be massacred," Wanda said.

It was an unseasonable thought, but it was difficult not to agree with it.

However, as we plodded out of the churchyard past the waiting cars, towards a cycle ricksha which happened to be free, cheerful cries came to us across the road from the Indian Officers Club which was immediately opposite the entrance. It was our friend, the young Flying Officer from the Railway Transport Office at Kanpur Station who had already shown his kindness to us in a number of ways, inviting us to have a drink with him and some of his fellow officers on the lawn. They were a friendly lot and we went on our way to eat our Christmas dinner with the Noronhas, heartened and refreshed.

The Flying Officer had a friend who was also a fellow-officer in the Air Force. The two of them had conceived a passion for two girls, the daughters of a distinguished professor who inhabited a bungalow a few hundred yards from the officer's club. In a country in which it is still the rule, even amongst members of the middle class, for the young to defer to the wishes of their parents in such matters, the difficulties that they were encountering were more or less insuperable. But the girls were as enthusiastic as they were, and both parties were employing all the machinery of assignation, long outmoded in the West.

The following evening we had dinner with the two boys.

"We can see them quite clearly through our binoculars," one said.

"In the evening they stand at the window and burn matches and we burn them also," said the other. "Now some officers are complaining to the Mess Havildar because there are no matches in the mess."

"What jolly fine girls they are!"

"When they go out they have a maid-servant who is always with them."

"But she is well-disposed towards us and now we have given her a letter."

"Two letters; one for each of them."

"What beautiful girls!"

Inflamed, they suggested that we should accompany them on what they described as a "recce" of the premises. In Red Indian file we crept across an expanse of Parade Ground, that was as exposed as General Wheeler's entrenchment had ever been, towards the bungalow.

We were all standing goggling at it when suddenly dogs began to bark, the front door was flung open and we were illuminated in a shaft of light from the interior. Silhouetted in the doorway was a menacing figure who might have been the owner, his wife or the maid who was acting as duenna. We did not stop to find out but beat a disorderly retreat to the road.

"You see. Nothing will come of it," said one of the lovers gloomily. "It is all too difficult".

Chapter Sixteen

The Ganges at Prayag

Prayaga is the land between the Ganges and the Jumna, up to a certain distance from the confluence. *Pra* having the sense of extensiveness and excellence; *yaga* being *yajna*, a sacrifice or offering. Yajna was one of the gods destroyed by the monster Vira-bhadra at Daksha's sacrifice on the banks of the Ganges near Hardwar.

Divers Potan kings have sought to build here a castle, but none could doe it till Acabar layd the foundation and proceeded with the worke. It stands on a point or angle having the river Gemini on the south side falling into Ganges. It hath been fortie yeeres abuilding.

William Finch: *Purchas His Pilgrimes*, 1625

On 27th December, we left Kanpur for Allahabad by train. We had spent a lot of time down by the river at the principal ghat, negotiating with the boatmen who were there in considerable numbers, for a rowing-boat. The trouble was the distance. By the Grand Trunk Road, which was pretty nearly straight, it was 119 miles. By boat following the convolutions of the river in its low state, perhaps a third as much again; but no one seemed to know exactly. "The journey may be accomplished in eight days, perhaps ten, and it will take twice as long again to return," one of the more optimistic boatmen said. "I am ready to accompany you with four men," and named a sum which was not excessive, but was beyond our means. Our efforts to obtain a motor-boat had been equally fruitless. The only one we could find belonged to the Resident Magistrate who showed no signs of being willing either to hire or to lend it to us, in spite of the Prime Minister's letter which Wanda had now sheathed in plastic material in order to save it from falling to pieces, so often had it been read. We were reluctant to ask him, as he had obliged us by allowing us to stay at the Circuit House.

The train left at six-thirty a.m. At this hour the outskirts of Kanpur were as cheerful as those of Leeds on a winter's morning. It was fearfully cold and pools of water in the waste ground looked as if they were frozen solid, as did the persons who squatted by them in the keen wind, performing their early morning duties as is customary in India among the rank and file, except in the centre of cities, in the open air. As soon as we boarded the train we unstrapped our bedding rolls, which were full of old boots and shoes and sand, as well as blankets, and forced our way into them with all our clothes on.

While Wanda slept, I sat shivering with my legs drawn up thinking of the undignified altercation I had just had with the taxi-driver who had demanded four times his proper fare — a typical traveller in India, at one moment elevated by the splendour of the country; the next cast down by its miseries. The only thing that was consistently agreeable was the river; life on it was sometimes hard, but it was always supportable, and in some strange way it produced feelings that were a combination of elation and contentment which neither of us experienced anywhere else.

Our friend at Delhi, the Major-General, had given us an introduction to one of his officers at Allahabad who was at the station to meet us. He seemed surprised and relieved to find that we were not a pair of bearded savants, for this was the impression he had somehow gained. With him we set off for the Fort which is at the confluence of the Jumna and the Ganges.

Allahabad, although it does not appear to be so from the map, is as formless in its way as Kanpur, and its ancient outlines are more blurred than they would otherwise be by the additions made to it by the British in the course of the last hundred and fifty years or so: the civil and military cantonments (the original civil cantonments were destroyed in the Mutiny), several clubs, a government press, a racecourse, a gun-powder factory, a Masonic Lodge, a jail, a workhouse, a university, a Christian village, a memorial hall with a tower 147 feet high, a high court, parade grounds, rifle ranges, several Christian missions with missionaries engaged in an unequal struggle to convert the heathen, several hospitals and a railway settlement the majority of whose inhabitants were Eurasians situated along the train line which separated the old city from the European quarter.

But it is at Prayag, the place where the Ganges, the Jumna and a third river which is now invisible to the vulgar gaze, the Sarasvati, meet and mingle that Allahabad is known and venerated by Hindus; perhaps the most venerated place of pilgrimage in all India and, on certain days of the Mela, the great fair, the scene of what is almost certainly the greatest assemblage of people gathered together in a confined space for a single purpose anywhere on earth. Every year at the winter solstice, which generally occurs on 14th January, between three-quarters of a million and a million people bathe at the Sangam, the confluence of the three rivers. (On 3rd February 1954, during the Kumbh Mela which has a special significance and only occurs at intervals of twelve years, it was estimated that five million were present.) The place is Tirtharaj, the king among places of worship, which enables human beings who bathe and worship there to cross the ocean of existence and attain salvation.

Akbar's great fort at Allahabad lies to the east of the city just above the confluence.

Until the early part of the nineteenth century the splendour of its exterior was only surpassed by the beauty of the buildings within it – the palace of the Mughal governors, the zenana which was embellished with delicately carved columns, and the residences which overlooked the Jumna. It also contained the pillar of King Asoka which was raised in the neighbourhood of Prayag in the second century B.C., and what was perhaps the oldest existing remnant of old Prayag, the Patalpuri temple, in whose outer court stood the undying banyan tree which Akbar, with a generosity which was rare among the Muslims of his time, allowed to remain there after his occupation of the city. But according to the pandas, or pragwals as they are known at Allahabad, Akbar's attitude was not dictated by Imperial magnanimity; it was simply that Akbar himself had been a Hindu. The pragwals say that he was an ascetic in his previous appearance on earth who drowned himself at Prayag not in order to attain immortality but to be reincarnated as a Mughal Emperor.

We had found both the pillar and the temple slightly disappointing. Apart from being highly polished and covered with inscriptions which included the Edicts of King Asoka, the column was not an object of intrinsic beauty, and its situation, standing as it did in the middle of a nineteenth-century military encampment, was an unseemly one for such a hoary work of antiquity; while the subterranean temple into which a grey and ghastly light filtered through openings in the roof made in 1906, in which the undying banyan is represented in a niche by a bit of an old pipal tree, with its meretricious images of gods and disagreeable custodians, was more like the subway leading from South Kensington Underground Station to the Science Museum than a holy place.

However, from the Officers' quarters on the walls of the fort it was possible to look down on the Jumna. Here, in this last reach before it joined the Ganges and at this season, it was half a mile wide, slow moving, deep and blue in the sunlight. Although it looked cleaner than the Ganges it was really much dirtier and, according to the medical officer in charge of the Mela who had just analysed it, it was, unlike the Ganges, heavily laden with coli.

Now, at midday, the river was dotted with white-canopied boats, filled with pilgrims who were returning upstream from bathing at the confluence, and as they passed the chanting of the women was punctuated by the regular sound of the oars as they turned in the rowlocks. On the narrow strip of foreshore at the foot of the wall long lines of men and women were going home on foot, each with a brass pot of water taken from the confluence. Across the river the rice fields were a brilliant green. It was a calm and pleasant scene.

The next day we hired a rowing-boat at the ghat by the big bridge over the Jumna to take us down to a place called Jhusi on the left bank of the Ganges opposite the confluence. There was nothing romantic about hiring a rowing-boat at Allahabad. Centuries of dealing with pilgrims had made the boatmen excessively venal. Worst of all, it was one of those nightmare days which confront all travellers abroad from time to time, on which I suddenly found myself temporarily unable to utter the simplest phrase in the language of the country. Although still able to understand what was said to me, I was forced to fall back on a Hindi conversation manual which was full of expressions which, if they were not actually outmoded, were no longer in general use, such as, "He received twenty stripes," and "Should an enemy attack you in front and rear at the same time, what will you do?"

Hiring a boat was a long tedious business. It exhausted the first boatman with whom I haggled, and he suddenly announced that he did not, in fact, possess a boat at all, saying elegantly:

"*Apko kasht pahunchka kar mujhe khed hai.*" ("I am so sorry to have troubled you.")

The second displayed more stamina.

"*Kam-se-kam kya dam hai?*" ("What is the lowest price?") I said, thumbing the book.

"Sahib, I will take you to the Sangam for ten rupees."

"*Oh, chale, jao, nahim to man tumko Police ke kavale karunga!*" ("Go away, or I will hand you over to the Police!") I replied after an unavailing search through sections headed WALKING, CYCLING, MOTOR-

ING, THE TRAMWAY, TRAVELLING ("I intend to go to Persia." "Where is the Ladies' Compartment?")

An empty threat as there was not a policeman in sight.

"Then I will take you to the Sangam for nine rupees – and the Memsahib, too."

"That's generous of him," Wanda said, when this was communicated to her. "What did he think I was going to do, run along the bank barking?"

"*Yak adhik huwa.*" ("That's too much.")

"For seven rupees I will take you to the Sangam. What is seven rupees to you who have come so far to bathe in Ganga?"

"*Main tumko itna labh hone, nahin dunga.*" ("I cannot give you so much profit.")

"Six rupees."

"*Main itne paise nahin dunga,*" ("I will not give so much"), I said after an interval in which I got bogged down in EATING AND DRINKING which was full of odd expressions such as "I have done eating", "Cook it!"

"I cannot go to the Sangam for less than six rupees."

I was running out of ammunition.

I hesitated over "He will be hanged tomorrow," under JUDICIAL, and "He will be transported for life," under MILITARY, wondering how anyone could be prevailed upon to join the Army in peace time; and finally found what I had wanted under CARRIAGES.

"*Main tumko do rupaya kaede ke mutabik deta hun.*" ("I will pay two rupees according to the tariff.")

"Sahib," he said, "I will take you to the Sangam for two rupees and the Memsahib, too." He seemed as pleased as I was that the tedious business was at an end.

But I was determined to have the last word. I found what I wanted, again under CARRIAGES.

"*Tumko adhik nahin milega.*" ("You shall not have any more."), I said. With all my *tum*ming, I was as bad as the Bridgemaster at Sukarthal.

"That's all right, Sahib," he said in excellent English.

We drifted down past the Fort; past the sally-port from which Muslim princesses had once emerged fleetingly to bathe; past the enclosure in which grew another banyan which, if it was only accessible (it is in the forbidden military part), would also become an object of pilgrimage and veneration; past the walls with their great rusty-looking cut stones, each with its mark on it, made by the stone mason who had cut it, glowing in the sunshine. From the river the

Fort was a noble sight. Finally, after what seemed an age, we passed the south-eastern bastion and for the first time saw the sandbank.

Although it was only the 28th December, the seventh day of the Hindu month of Pausa, and the great bathing day, Makara Sankranti, was not for another seventeen days, corrugated iron sheds, tents, grass huts and bamboo towers were already beginning to sprout from it and over them on long poles the flags and pennants and strange signs of the pragwals and the sadhus, the former at the southern end of the bank, the latter further up towards the Izzot railway bridge, fluttered in the wind. Invisible behind the Bund of Akbar, the great embankment constructed to keep the Ganges out of the flat country north of the Fort, another even larger encampment was being set up which extended upstream as far as Daraganj where the special Prayag pilgrim railway station was.

From the southern extremity of the bank a long horn of sand extended far out into the Jumna. Somewhere by the tip of it was the Sangam, the meeting-place of the three rivers.

One moment we were in the blue, slow-moving Jumna. The next a flood of water the colour of milky coffee cut across it, rocking the boat and tossing the Jumna back on itself in a last shimmer of blue and white.

But it was only for a moment. Then the Ganges swallowed the Jumna; it was as if that river had never existed and it went on, apparently undiluted, on its course to the east, taking us with it. At the same time it engulfed the Sarasvati of which there was no visible sign anyway.

All the way up the sandbank as far as the Izzot bridge people were bathing in the Ganges. In places the bank was fifteen feet high and some bold spirits were bathing at the foot of it in the pale yellow froth which the silt made when it crumbled around them in the water; and they bathed less hazardously at the Triveni ghat where the pragwals sat under umbrellas and from the boats and platforms at the Sangam itself, which was the most pleasant place of all. The right bank of the Jumna was dark with them opposite the confluence and from this multitude there rose a whirring sound like a nest of winged insects that had been disturbed.

The boatman landed us on the left shore of the Ganges at a place where there was a little nest of skulls at the water's edge. They were the skulls of children and grown-ups and they all stood by some strange chance the right way up, some in the water, others half buried in the sand which was soft and hot underfoot, with their great eye sockets staring at us reproachfully.

We set off towards the distant river bank which was wobbling in the midday heat, passing a place where some men were planting melons on little pillars of sand in deep pits, until we came to a muddy backwater which separated the sandbank from the shore in which some washerwomen were working. While we were wondering how to cross this obstacle, a camel came down to the water and lurched through it. We took off our white cotton trousers, slung them over our shoulders and followed the camel, through the stinking mud which reached to our knees while the washerwomen shrieked with laughter and pointed out an easier way which we had not seen.

Behind them the river bank was a high, steep cliff in the side of which banyan trees grew, extending long, exposed roots down towards the shore. The face of this cliff was honeycombed with caves which could be reached by a series of crumbling staircases. The floors of the caves were littered with the remains of fires of the sadhus who usually lived in them but who were now in the camp on the other side of the river. The roofs of the dark passages which linked them were festooned with thick clusters of bats and the smell of their excrement was like rotten chocolate.

On top of the cliff there was an old fort. This was the site of old Jhusi, the ancient city of Pratisthan, the seat of King Trilochanapala, the son of one of the last Parihar kings of Kanauj who had been expelled from it by the other Rajput princes who had been disgusted at the feeble resistance he had put up when Mahmud of Ghazni had taken and sacked the city in 1018.

Here all alone on a platform sat a Vishnuvite sadhu. He was looking out across the river to the Mela grounds.

A little way inland, in an enclosure in which lentils and mustard plants were growing, was a huge well. Its mouth was eighteen feet across, and it was at least forty feet deep. While we were looking down into it a young man appeared and without being asked lowered a bucket into it and drew up some water for us. It was delicious.

"It is the Samundra Kup," he said, "the Well of the Ocean," and showed us a notice in English which read:

There is a big well in the city of Pratisthanpur and a man becomes rid of sin by seeing it or drinking water from it. He will obtain the fruit of having walked round the whole earth by walking round this well on the full and new moon days and on the occurrence of the solar and lunar eclipses. He derives much merit by a bath in it and by giving charity there he will enjoy all the pleasures of heaven. There is no doubt about that.

A little way downstream on a hill surrounded by a low wall was the white-washed tomb of the Muslim saint Saiyid Sadr-ul-haq Taqi-ud-din Muhammad Abul Akbar — otherwise known as Sheikh Taqi — who died at Jhusi in 1384. It was covered with a faded piece of green silk, and flanked by three other tombs over which flew a red banner. Old Jhusi with its solitary sadhu, its coarse but friendly washerwomen, its ancient tombs and trees and its brilliant fields of rice extending to the water's edge, had a rare and simple air. It was a place to return to.

In the evening we walked back over the Ganges across the forty spans of the Izzot railway bridge. Upstream to the north long strings of camels and bullock carts were crossing the bridge of boats which carried the Grand Trunk Road in the direction of the city. The river tore down under it, tugging at the caissons. From them small boys were diving into the water and being swept, miraculously, into the shallows where still smaller children who were making unhappy mooing noises were bathing with their mothers. The dust hung heavily over the approaches to the bridge and the smoke rose straight into the air from the fires at the burning ghats, where even at this late hour wood for the cremations was still being weighed out on the scales. Inland a green sea of fields lapped at the wooded banks and stretched away northwards into the distance. When the rains came there would be a forty-foot rise in the level of the Ganges and they would be submerged under twenty feet of water. Downstream the two rivers and the white boats on them were flooded in an intense golden light; beyond the Jumna mist was already forming in the rice fields; swifts swooped about the walls of the Fort which threw a dark oblong shadow across the sandbank on which camp fires were now beginning to burgeon. As the sandbank had dried out and its surface had become hard it had cracked. Now it was covered with thousands of deep fissures. By day armies of men were engaged in filling them in. Seen from the height of the bridge it resembled a huge jig-saw.

Under one of the last of the forty spans of the bridge a lunatic was sitting out in the stream on a pillar of silt fifteen feet high. This pillar, which was precariously supported by one of the buttresses of the bridge, was on the point of collapsing into the water. The lunatic was gesticulating violently and singing at the top of his voice. He seemed perfectly happy. How he had got there in the first place was a mystery; how he was to get back alive was equally incomprehensible. No one except ourselves took the slightest notice of him. This was India. He would work out his own salvation. As he sat there a train rumbled overhead and the vibration caused more chunks to fall off his perch, reducing still more his chances of survival.

Chapter Seventeen

The way to Mirzapur

We left Allahabad on the last day of the year to travel down the river to Mirzapur. It was only fifty-five miles by train but more like ninety by the river.

At first it had seemed impossible to find a boat. With the Mela getting under way this was the only season of the year when the boatmen could count on making any money, and those we spoke to were reluctant to take us. There was said to be a rather well-off sadhu who possessed a motor-boat, but it seemed so improbable that we were not surprised when both he and his craft failed to materialise. It was only when we finally decided that we would have to go by train that the Manager of the Mela, an exceptionally calm and efficient man who was also an Assistant Magistrate, managed to find two men who would take us to Mirzapur for ninety rupees. They were Mallahs, a caste whose members by tradition always worked as boatmen when not engaged in crime.

Their boat was the smallest we had so far used. It was also the most elegant. It was a typical Allahabad boat of the sort used for conveying well-hipped pilgrims down the Jumna to the Sangam. It had white cushions for the passengers to sit on and a canopy stretched over iron hoops to protect them from the sun. It was eighteen feet long, had a beam of three feet six, and drew about six inches of water unladen. Its hull was built from tin sheeting fastened on to a wooden frame and it was painted light blue and white with a yellow and black band round the gunwales. It stood very high out of the water and with its square stern it was rather like a miniature junk; but a junk built for an Edwardian gentleman. Even the two boatmen, Bag Nath and Hira Lal, with their rather droopy moustaches, had a faintly Edwardian air about them, although Bag Nath had to some extent modernised himself with a crew-cut. By the time the trunks and the bedding rolls were stowed aboard there was very little room for the four of us.

We set off from the landing-place by the Fort in the early afternoon and shot down into the Ganges. It was full of rips and whirlpools, bubbling and erupting.

We went down at a terrific rate. This was what we had imagined in our ignorance that travelling on the Ganges would be like all the time, when we had first arrived at Hardwar and seen the water rushing down past the Dharmsala of Der Ismael Khan on its way to the Ganges Canal. Behind us the Fort was already sinking into the distance; to the left was Old Jhusi, with its ramparts half-hidden by its arcadian groves of trees and with its solitary flag flying over the tomb of Sheikh Taqi. The right bank was thirty feet high, and as the level of the river fell day by day, it had left a succession of horizontal scours on the face of it. Along these little paths which were rather like sheep runs men were plodding upstream towing twenty-foot boats up the last couple of miles to Allahabad, bent double with the pieces of bamboo clasped to their chests to which the ropes were attached.

Navigation was difficult; with so much luggage there was only room in the boat for one person to row at a time and the baggage was badly stowed anyway. Having asked to row I found it impossible in this strong current to stop the boat turning round so that at times we found ourselves descending the river stern first. There was nothing wrong with the oars; although they were only made from a couple of bamboo poles with two pieces of packing case for blades, they were beautifully balanced. It would not have mattered if the river had not been so full of fish traps. They were open-ended triangles and quadrilaterals of staked nets, some of them more than two hundred yards long; and with the stream running at some six knots it would be difficult to get out of one of these enclosures if we once got into it. Finally Bag Nath, the man with the crew-cut, became sufficiently apprehensive to put a steering oar over the stern and thenceforward the boat was more or less under control.

According to Bag Nath and Hira Lal these traps were for catching Hilsa, a fish which I had always thought only lived in estuaries, which they said were "*bahut achchha*", very good fish, and for some time they expatiated on how delicious they were. It was little consolation to us who had so far not tasted one single fish while on the Ganges.

At this late hour of the afternoon, there were no fishermen to be seen, and the site of their operations was deserted; and when finally we did meet some fishermen who were lying on a sandbank and the boatmen asked them for fish, they simply laughed and said, as all the other fishermen we had so far met had said, that all the fish had gone to Calcutta, and made expressive gestures with their hands, indicative of nothingness.

But it was good to be back on the river. The sun shone on it from

a cloudless sky and there was a gentle breeze from the north which
only fell away towards evening. And the river was as it had always
been, except that it was more powerful, and there were many more
boats either being tracked up the bank or else running down under
sails that were like old bedsheets, with almost more holes than material
in them. Some of the boats were going down together in pairs with
one square sail set on a yard that was lashed to the masts of both
vessels, and below, on deck, the crews shared an equally communal
tobacco pipe between them. There were jackals on the bank and
corpses in the river, very white, with their legs extended and one of
them had a crow walking up and down it, like a captain pacing the
bridge, but these macabre details were as nothing compared with the
splendour of the yellow river swirling down under the huge sky eight
hundred and eighty miles west-north-west of the Bay of Bengal.

Just before sunset we entered one of those reaches in which there
was nothing in sight but sand and the banks receded on either side
until they were a feint line in the distance.

Here we came down abreast of some country boats belonging to
the Ganga and Brahmaputra Water Transport Board. The crews had
been building bandals in the river to close the offtakes from the main
channel. Bandals are an ingenious and simple arrangement for con-
centrating the flow of water into the main stream so that it can scour
the bottom and keep it deep and open. They are also a very ancient
arrangement. A series of parallel lines of bamboos are driven into
the bed of the river just above the mouth of a large backwater, each
succeeding one a little further downstream at an angle of about thirty
degrees to the current. Each bandal is about fifty feet long and the
bamboo piles of which they are composed are a foot apart. Each of
these uprights is supported by another pole which is driven in at an
angle on the downstream side and lashed to the top of it. Bamboo
mats are then placed on the upstream side of the obstruction and tied
to it so that they hang down into the river to a depth of three feet
below the surface. As the flow of current into the backwater is held
up by the mats, it creates a slack behind the bandals in which the
river sheds its silt, eventually forming a shoal, sealing it off completely.

The sun set in a low haze and the sky above it turned a dull
orange; but high overhead it still continued to radiate long streamers
of purple light eastwards against the dark blue sky in which the
evening star shone brilliantly and alone. It was an improbable effect,
but it soon faded away and then it was dark.

Above us the bandal builders crouched on the bank and looked down into the boat while the four of us strove by the light of a couple of lanterns to get the food trunk out of the bottom of the boat in which it had firmly embedded itself. It was like trying to get a coffin out of a grave. Even when we finally succeeded in lifting it they still watched on, entranced. It made rum drinking even more difficult than usual. We were looking forward to a good drink and we intended to give one to the boatmen too, as it was New Year's Eve; but it was impossible before such an audience. Later, when their interest was exhausted, we drank rum together and ate a chicken and potatoes laced with chillies; and at nine o'clock we all went to bed, stretched out under the canopy on the makeshift deck, the first time since we had been on the river that we had slept with a roof over our heads.

There seemed little point in trying to stay awake until twelve o'clock in order to see the New Year in. We had had our little celebration. Besides we were in India where it was not even New Year's Eve which according to the reformed Indian Calendar, falls on the 30th Phalguna, our 20th March, and is called Mahavisuva (Year-Ending Day). Even if we wanted to think of our loved ones, Indian Standard Time was five and a half hours ahead of Greenwich Mean Time which would mean thinking about them and engaging in celebrations at half past five in the morning. And far out from shore in the Ganges it seemed ever more absurd. On the Ganges one year, a century or even a thousand years was much as another; the only difference was in the seasons – and here on the sands in the middle of it they were only indicated by the level of the water and the power of the sun and the rain.

At five o'clock awful spitting noises from the bank announced the beginning of another day, and Bag Nath and Hira Lal changed their sleeping position from one lying alongside one another head to toe to a more intimate arrangement in which they were head to head and back to back, a difficult operation which they accomplished with awful groanings and thrashing of limbs. We were both wide awake now and it seemed that the dawn would never come. When it did, we staggered up the bank with our soap-boxes and towels and found that it had been worth waiting for. The moon was still up in the west and the freezing wind which poured over the sands gave them a clear, clean look, as if the world had been suddenly reborn. Big skeins of geese were going overhead. These feelings of rebirth were not shared by the bandal builders who sat huddled together in the mouth of their grass hut with their teeth chattering. The river was like ice, so cold that it seemed impossible that one could ever heat it sufficiently to make tea, and when the water finally did boil and we were just about to put the tea in the pot, the boatmen suddenly pushed off without any warning and we were on our way.

At eight we passed Sirsa away on the right bank, but all we saw of it were a few temples, and we never saw the place where another river, the Tons, entered the Ganges at all. The Ganges now embarked on a series of vast bends first to the north and then to the south; augmented by the Tons it was bigger than ever, in some places more than five hundred yards wide. Turtles shaped like carving dishes surfaced close to the boat and big fish rose which the boatmen called Sur. Apart from an occasional ferry we saw scarcely any boats at all. In some places the banks were low and green with fields of rice and barley sloping gently up from the shore. Instead of being built of mud as they had been previously, the village houses were mostly of brick. The farms were substantial two-storied places with tiled roofs like farms in the Lombard plain, but here they were surrounded by acacia, nim and pipal trees and interspersed by dense, tall grass and plantations of bamboos which sometimes sprouted up through the tops of the trees like flag-poles. In other places the banks rose above the river in steep cliffs that were so corroded by the weather, that it was difficult to know whether they were earth or stone. At a place called Lachagir the cliffs were full of caves which the boatmen said were inhabited by sadhus; and close to them on the shore, there was a brick well-shaft from which the surrounding earth had been washed away so that it stood alone like a tower. Above it, on top of the cliff, there was a ruined fort. Once this had been a port of call for steamers of the India General Steam Navigation Company. "Here," wrote the author of the *District Gazeteer*, mysteriously, "according to tradition stood the lac palace of Dur-Yodhana,* in which the Pandava brethren, had the plot succeeded, were to be burned to death."

All through the day we took an hour each in turn at the oars, and as it grew hotter the sweat poured off us while Wanda fed us sweets and fruit and bidis as the spirit moved her.

---

* Dur-Yodhana was one of the sons of the Princess of Gandhara and a leader in the war of the Maha-Bharata. After a pregnancy of two years she gave birth to a piece of flesh which, when it was divided into a hundred and one portions and placed in a hundred and one jars, produced a hundred sons and one daughter. The Pandavas were their cousins, of whom Dur-Yodhana was violently jealous, particularly of Bhima, who eventually smashed Dur-Yodhana's thigh with a club and then kicked him on the head, putting him out of action.

At one o'clock we were at the bottom of the first big bends of the river and here we anchored in shoal water in the middle and did what we had longed to do, jumped into it. While the boatmen performed their pujas, sprinkling the boat and themselves with water, we washed ourselves in privacy, hidden under the stern. Afterwards in the time it took us to eat a tin of sardines, some bread and marmalade and a couple of papayas they cooked themselves some chapatis and then we were off again. These men were more like fugitives than boatmen.

Immediately afterwards we saw two crocodiles lying out on a sandbank. One was very large, disguised as a gnarled old tree trunk; the other was smaller with a snout as finely pointed as an expensive American fountain pen. The big one disappeared immediately, the other waited until we were abreast of it before it slid into the water.

"I wouldn't have bathed if I had known there were coccodriles,"* Wanda said.

A whole school of dolphins escorted us into the next reach to the north. On the left, on the long peninsula formed by the big bend made by the river, fields of rice, wheat and mustard extended to the water's edge. There were huge mango trees and tall, plumed grass in which the wind sighed, with the sound of a distant sea. The women walking on the shore, having washed and dried their saris, let them flutter behind them in the strong wind that was blowing from the north. But it was only here where the river watered the fields that this country, the north-western part of the district of Mirzapur, had such an air of fertility. Inland, north of the Grand Trunk Road from Allahabad to Banaras, there were waterless saline wastes in which nothing could grow and which looked, according to the *Gazetteer*, as if they were covered with hoar-frost. This country was called Bhadohi and once it had been part of the domain of a mysterious and civilised race called Bhars which had been finally submerged in the Aryan invasion of the Ganges Valley. The remains of their water tanks, always aligned in a different direction from that which was customary among the Hindus, and some dilapidated forts are to be seen in this region still.

To the right, on the outward bend of the river, there were steep cliffs which glowed as if they were red hot in the afternoon sun. All this reach of the river was full of birds which, apart from the morning and evening flights of geese and duck, had been strangely absent since we left Allahabad. Flocks of lapwings scurried along the shore leaving their footprints in the mud and calling apprehensively to one another;

* From the Italian *coccodrillo*.

dark brown crag martins dipped about the cliffs and in the shallows spoonbills were raking the bottom with their long black and yellow bills. There were other kinds too, but it required more knowledge than either of us possessed to identify them. The boatmen were not much help. Every time I asked them about some particular species all they said was "*chota chiriya*" which meant "little bird", at the same time flapping their arms and making chee-cheeing noises.

We were now in the district of Mirzapur and the boatmen said that we would arrive at the city the following afternoon. Gradually we crawled up to the top of the last long bend towards the north. It was a hard slog in the teeth of the wind and I was glad that I had learned to scull and knew how to "feather", an accomplishment which the boatmen regarded with a certain amount of awe. By the time we succeeded in turning it the sun was setting. Here, on the edge of a mudbank, a bandal boat was moored and Hira Lal, who was at the helm, steered us in towards it. Obviously he intended to spend the night there.

Apart from the proximity of the bandal boat, it was a horrible place, especially for us. It lacked every amenity: a bank on which to stand while washing; cover for even the simplest needs and, what was worse, it was necessary to plough through a couple of hundred yards of mud in order to reach any kind of shore. I said that we would continue. I was reluctant to go against the boatmen, for I knew that they liked to camp with people they knew and trusted, but this was too much. Nevertheless I knew that it was a mistake to go against the custom of the country, but this was something that I and my countrymen had never learned, and, it seemed, never would. They were very displeased.

Soon it was quite dark and we had to feel our way down through the shoals using an oar as a sounding pole. Now when I suggested that they should stop, both boatmen ignored me and Hira Lal who was at the oars redoubled his efforts.

"You shouldn't have told them to go on," Wanda said. I could have murdered her.

They went on and on for more than an hour. There was thick mist over the river now and it was as cold as hell. Every few minutes we went aground. Finally I had to beg them to stop and when they did it was at a place which was also separated from the shore by an expanse of stinking mud. It was exactly the same sort of place that they had wanted to camp at originally, only this time there was a village on the bank above the beach, and like all the other boatmen they detested villages.

"This is a bad place," they said, reproachfully.

We made camp and cooked our various foods by the light of the kerosene lanterns without speaking to one another. The village on the bank above us was as silent and dark as the tomb; not even a dog barked in it. Finally, under the influence of hot rum and lime the boatmen thawed; but all they would say was that this was a bad place. It was impossible not to agree with them.

On the other side of the river a wedding was being celebrated and the sound of trumpets and drums floated across to us clearly. A month previously we would have asked the boatmen to take us across to it, but we had had enough for one day. While we were washing up, five men came down the bank from the village and lit an enormous brushwood fire. They carried on a conversation for five minutes and then disappeared as abruptly as they had come without looking in our direction at all. What on earth were they up to? Was this their way of having an evening out?

The previous night we had slept with the side curtains brailed up. Here, because none of us wanted to be in full view of the village and because it was draughty, we lowered them. It was a mistake. Soon the atmosphere was like a Turkish bath, with the smells of dung, chillies, paraffin and dirty blankets thrown in for good measure. Worst of all, both of us found ourselves under the necessity of going ashore, not once but several times during the night. Inside, under the canopy, the boat was not only smelly but black as pitch and these repeated journeys were nightmare ones. First we stepped on the supine bodies of the boatmen who seemed impervious to these needs but who, each time we trod on them started up with the intention of defending themselves. Then we lowered ourselves down into the cold clammy mud which reached half-way to our knees.

It was no use wearing shoes because when we returned to the boat they would have been so muddy that there would have been nowhere to put them; and it was equally difficult with bare feet as the boat had so much freeboard that it was impossible to hang over the side to wash them without falling in, unless one was a giant. The only solution was to bring back a kettle of water, stick one's feet under the canopy and pour it over them. It was a ridiculous arrangement for, as Wanda said when she returned after one of these sorties with her teeth chattering and with long grey stockings of mud on her legs which one kettleful of water was insufficient to remove, "If it wasn't for the boatmen we could do it from the boat – and they are fast asleep."

The boatmen were so anxious to leave that when we woke the

next morning we found ourselves in midstream and already under
way. It was only a quarter to six and the sky over the village was
just beginning to grow red. There seemed little point in getting up,
so we lit the stove and stayed in our bedding rolls.

There was no wind and the water was like oil. Over it terns and
swallows were flying low and from the mudflats clouds of ringed
plovers rose and wheeled uttering melancholy whistling sounds,
alarmed by the boatmen who were chanting their pujas. The sun
rose at a quarter to seven and with it went the mysterious beauty of
the early morning. We stopped on a sandbank to wash. The sand was
covered with delicate white shells which were like tiny translucent
fingernails and little conical ones with horizontal rings round
them.

There were villages on the left bank now. At a place called Ferojpur,
where there was a landing place with a big flight of stone steps, women
with baskets on their heads were carrying sand up from three high-
sterned country boats. There were others down at the water's edge
washing pots in the river whose clothes were so discoloured that
they were almost indistinguishable from the bank behind them.

Now to the north and south, the bank receded again and the river
became immensely wide. To the north there was sand as far as one
could see from the level of the boat; to the south was an outcrop
of the Vindhyan hills, a rather barren-looking sandstone escarpment
on which grew a few solitary bushy-topped trees. We were about
eight miles to the east of Mirzapur.

The river took us down to a place on the right bank where there
was a village on a cliff and a small island off-shore piled high with
slabs of stone on the top of which there were a couple of columns
about seven feet long, one still standing, the other on its side.

"This is Bindhachal, and here is the Mandir of Vindhya-Vasini
Devi, Mahayama Durga, and we are going to do a puja," Bag Nath
said, as he steered the boat in past the island towards the shore where
there was an impressive-looking ghat. He was not asking us. It was
a statement.

The ghat looked as if it had been subjected to an artillery bombard-
ment. Massive masonry buttresses had been overthrown by the flood
waters and lay in the river. The water, which must have risen to an
extraordinary height, had swept over the top of the embankment
which was equally solidly constructed, tearing stones from their
foundations and hurling them about in disorder. Nevertheless it was
a cheerful place. Hordes of small children were swimming in the
river, elderly holy men dozed in the sun, and half a dozen barbers

at the water's edge were shaving the heads of those who were about to set off for the temple of Mahayama Durga.

While the boatmen were away we ate a tin of sardines which had something wrong with it. The sardines were not actually rotten but they had a very curious taste. By the time we had discussed them and savoured them rather like a couple of amateurs discussing a bottle of claret (but how infinitely less disgusting it is to discuss a wine that has gone off than a sardine) and because we were hungry, we had eaten the lot. I was sufficiently apprehensive about these sardines to record the fact that we had eaten them in a notebook, so that if we did get ptomaine poisoning there would be some information for a doctor to go on if we were already unconscious; and when the boatmen returned from their puja, which they did in a surprisingly short time, with shaven top-knots, glowing red tilak marks on their foreheads, smelling of sweet oil and with garlands of marigolds round their necks, and suggested that we, too, might like to visit the Goddess of Destruction, it seemed appropriate to do so.

The temple was in the centre of the village, and was approached by a narrow lane. The shops surrounding it displayed heaps of brilliant coloured powders for making the tilak mark and others for reddening the soles of the feet, ingenuous clay statues and cheap cotton scarves. The way into it was through an open-sided court slightly raised above the road and approached by steps. It was filled with pandas; drums and bells sounded.

Vindhya-Vasini-Devi was undoubtedly very old. The way to her shrine was through a low entrance. She was enclosed in a brass or gilded cage, and the walls were of silver carved in low relief. There was a feeling of terrible constriction in this narrow cell. She had a tiny shrunken black head with the staring eyes of a madwoman, the whites of which were made from silver plates. Her beak-like nose had a jewelled ring inserted in one nostril; white flowers hung down like hair from her head and without them she would have been bald. Her little black foot rested on a black rat and round her neck there were swags of marigolds. She was a horrid-looking little thing. We stood barefooted in a slush compounded of Ganges water, mud, squashed flowers and gouts of red liquid which might have been blood but probably wasn't. But not for long. There were crowds of prospective worshippers behind us and we were only there on sufferance; soon the pressure became intolerable and we popped out into the covered court like a couple of corks.

Vindhya-Vasini-Devi had another name. She was also known as Bhagwan Bhowani, the Black Mother; and it was to her, until

Sleeman* destroyed them, that the Thugs used to come from all over
India, usually in the Autumn after the rains, to offer her a share of
what they had taken from their victims after strangling them with
the ruhmal, the square knotted cloth. And when they themselves
were finally hunted down they died on the gallows with the trium-
phant cry on their lips "*Jai Vindhyachal*," after adjusting the nooses
round their own necks which they did with practised hands.

Having come so far it seemed a pity to go back and we pressed
on at the head of a considerable procession until we reached the main
road: to the left just beyond the village there was a river bed crossed
by a castellated and loopholed bridge, in the middle of which stood
a mad-looking sadhu ringing a bell; to the right there was a temple
by the side of the road in which the body of the god was hidden
behind a red cloth; its face was a huge amorphous thing of clay and
there was only the faintest indication of a mouth. Although it was
impressive it was nothing compared with that of Vindhya-Vasini and
after seeing it we went back to the ghat where we found the boatmen
fast asleep. They looked as if they were dead, an illusion that was
enhanced by the garlands of marigolds which they wore, and we woke
them with difficulty. Their efforts of the last couple of days and the
emotional excitement of the puja had knocked the stuffing out of
them. Drooping over the oars, half asleep, they paddled the boat
down the last few miles to Mirzapur.

Here, on the western outskirts of the city, the river bank was more
substantial than the constructions which stood on it. The ancient
houses of the merchants, who until the middle of the last century
had conducted their business with conspicuous success, now hung
precariously over the river in an extremity of decay. In one place
what must have been a noble flight of stone steps had led down to
the water but under the assault of the river, it had collapsed and
now it was nothing more than a great heap of cut stones on which
laundrymen were beating their client's clothes to pieces.

---

* Sir William Sleeman (1788–1856), Indian official and major-general. Superintended
suppression of Thuggi and dacoity, 1835–41. Author of *Rambles and Recollections of
an Indian Official, A Vocabulary of Thug Language* and other works.
    A map made by Sleeman in 1838 of part of the Kingdom of Oudh with the "assis-
tance" of twenty eminent Thugs who between them had murderd five thousand
persons — one of them called Buhran had strangled 931 — shows 274 Bele, the murder
and burial places used by the Thugs. In each one of them there were hundreds of
murdered persons — as exhumation proved. They were as equally and closely spaced
along the roads as if they had been bus stops. It has been conservatively estimated
that, until Sleeman began their suppression, the Thugs were disposing of thirty
thousand travellers a year.

In half an hour we reached the bridge of boats on which a one-way system operated, controlled by bells. It was packed with bullock-carts which came thundering down on to it through a steep and narrow cutting in an endless stream on their way back to the country districts north of the river. Upstream of it half a dozen vessels were unloading bricks which emaciated-looking men were carrying away up the bank on their heads, and we nosed our own boat in amongst them until it grounded. The journey was over and we had nowhere to go. "Sahib," Hira Lal said. "We will take you further down the river to Kashi (Banaras). We can do this and still return in time for the Mela."

It was a temptation. We knew no one at Mirzapur. Admittedly someone in the High Commissioner's Office in New Delhi had given us the name of the Manager of a carpet factory at Mirzapur who, he said, had a bungalow in which customers sometimes stayed, but we had no idea how to get in touch with him, nor were we confident that he would be pleased if we suddenly appeared unannounced and asked if we could use his firm's bungalow. But, having finally got to Mirzapur, it seemed silly to pass it by.

With little hope of finding one and feeling slightly ridiculous, I set off up the bank in search of a telephone. A little way inland I came to some old buildings picturesquely situated in a grove of trees. This place had once been an indigo factory and some of the vats in which the preparation had been made were still there. Now it was the office of a carpet manufactory and the manager, a kindly, middle-aged Indian, at once sent some of his men to help with the luggage.

While they toiled up the bank with it I sat in the boat writing letters of recommendation for the boatmen. Then I paid them the ninety rupees which had been agreed upon plus an extra ten rupees as a present. We were sorry to leave them and they, who so far had shown no emotion of any kind, did so now. The last we saw of them was rigging a bamboo mast to tow the boat upstream.

Chapter Eighteen

The fort at Chunar

She tho' short her duty was with man
With ample virtues filled her narrow span.
Why shed we then unprofitable tears
For one so old in works tho' green in years.

Epitaph to the beloved wife of Key Sergeant J. Fleming who died
23 December, 1833 at the Chunar Fortress.

We spent the next three days with Geoffrey and Jennefer Seager at
the carpet factory at Khamaria on the north side of the Ganges where
they had an enormous bungalow. It was a bungalow of the old sort
with thick walls, a steep pitched roof and a wide, colonnaded porch,
on which tailors and dressmakers and hairdressers were usually to be
found at work, for the Seagers' household was an extensive one and
its needs were insatiable. We were given the bachelor quarters. They
contained a bathroom with a sunken bath and here on the first night
we wallowed together in the hot water which the water carrier produced in huge quantities. It was our first hot bath for twenty-eight
days. Afterwards we drank hot rum punch, sitting by a big fire and
dined off roast duck and Christmas pudding. Then we went to bed
taking piles of English newspapers with us and read the weather
reports from London to one another with relish.

Mirzapur was not a particularly ancient town (it is supposed to have
been founded in the time of Shah Jahan) but it had an air of decay
about it which belied its age. Until the 1780s it had been a place of
importance as a centre of the silk industry which, at that time, was
conducted by members of the Sannyasi sect who lived in Banaras.
They sold silk at Mirzapur to other Sannyasis who came from the
Deccan in order to buy it. This trade was practically crippled in 1781
when a customs house was opened at Banaras which imposed a
punitive tax on raw silk in transit. Although this was later reduced,
the business never really recovered. There was also a great trade in
cotton coming to the town from Central India by way of the Deccan

road from Nagpur which terminated at Mirzapur, from where it was
sent down the river by country boat to Calcutta.

With the opening up of the Ganges to steam navigation its prosperity increased still further. In 1828 the East India Company decided
to find out if it was practicable for a paddle steamer to make the
passage from Calcutta upstream as far as Allahabad, and in September
they despatched the paddle steamer, *Hoogly*, upriver.

In a normal year the river would have been in full flood, but in
1828 it not only failed to reach its maximum height: but began to
subside earlier than usual. It was a risky journey, but twenty-three
days later *Hoogly* anchored at Allahabad after a surprisingly uneventful
voyage without suffering any serious grounding, a voyage of 787
miles which up to this time had taken three months.

At this time one of the four Principal Assistants to the Chief
Examiner of the East India Company in London was Thomas Love
Peacock, the author of *Headlong Hall* and *Nightmare Abbey*. It was his
business to deal with problems connected with steam navigation and
one with which he was probably better fitted for than any of the
others, as he had for a short time been in the Navy as secretary to
a Rear Admiral, an employment which he had found distasteful.

It was as a result of his advice to the court of Directors that it
was decided to go ahead with plans for a steamer fleet on the Ganges.

The first of these vessels, the *Lord William Bentinck*, had an alarming
trial voyage in October 1832. With the Directors of the East India
Company on board it collided on the Thames with a collier, but
otherwise it was successful. It was taken to pieces, packed away in
an East Indiaman and sent off. In April 1834, it was launched on the
Hooghly, and in the Autumn of that year it went up to Allahabad
and back in thirty-eight days. The first regular service had begun.

Although Mirzapur's prosperity increased as a result it only lasted
twenty years. In 1859 the East India Railway from Calcutta reached
Kanpur. Its opening coincided with that of the first tanneries and
cotton mills there. In 1864 it was extended as far as the right bank
of the Jumna at Allahabad. With the coming of steamships Mirzapur
had supplanted Allahabad as a centre of trade; now it was itself supplanted by Kanpur as the principal market for goods in Upper India.

Nevertheless even today Mirzapur is not moribund. There is still
a flourishing carpet industry; the brass pots of Mirzapur are noted
throughout India and the noise made in beating out the sort called
phul and ornamenting those which are cast with repoussé work is
deafening. The sandstone of the Vindhyan hills behind the town is
famous and all the stone buildings of Banaras are constructed with

it. It is difficult to know what the town hall at Mirzapur is constructed of, but it looks like milk chocolate.

The region immediately to the west of Mirzapur where the Vindhyan hills approach most closely to the bank of the Ganges is remarkable for the number of temples devoted to the worship of Kali or Durga, Siva's wife in her most hideous and destructive form. Not far from it on a little plateau which is a sort of outrider of the main range there is the temple of Ashta-bhuja Devi, the eight-armed Devi, which is approached by a long flight of steps. On the top there are a number of unimpressive buildings guarded by some toothless old women who look not unlike Kali themselves. In one of them, partly underground, and in darkness lives the goddess Patal Kali. It was only by using up half a box of matches that we were able to enjoy her black ape-like face, red lips and round silver eyes, doubled up in this hole together with a couple of educated Hindu gentlemen from Mirzapur who, like almost every other educated gentleman we had so far met, happened to be advocates. Patal Kali was a nasty-looking bit of work. I wondered whether they worshipped her; but I could think of no way of asking them without appearing excessively ill-mannered.

Below the hill, under the mango trees, there were ruins and some carvings of strange-looking bearded figures. Presumably they were the mysterious Bhars, for this was the site of Pampapura, one of their cities.

To the east of it in a lonely valley leading into the hills there is another temple devoted to Maha-Kali, approached by a rough path. On either side of it extremely hairy sadhus were sitting under trees and the hairiest of all was concealed in a cave on the right of the road.

"I am cold, I am cold," he said as we trudged past. It was not surprising as he was an old man, and apart from a lot of hair he was wearing nothing but a loin-cloth and some ashes.

The temple of Maha-Kali was in a courtyard which had a cloistered walk round it, in the middle of which there was a well. By the well-head there was another sadhu who seemed to be even more uncomfortable than the one we had just seen squatting in his cave. He was on his knees and he had one hand held above his head. He appeared to be in some kind of trance. For his own sake I hoped he was.

It was not a good time to visit this temple. Another old crone appeared and told us that the goddess was asleep. We gave her money and instantly she agreed to allow us to have a quick look at her.

Maha-Kali was behind a curtain. She was lying on a sort of catafalque covered with black velvet which was ornamented with swags of black cord. Her tiny body was covered with a large white sheet and all that could be seen of her was a bird-like head and a gaping mouth. It seemed dangerous to break in on her in this fashion, so we went away.

Together with Geoffrey and Jennefer we went downriver, twenty miles or so, to the fort of Chunar where a steep-sided sandstone rock half a mile long and a hundred and seventy feet high at its northern end jutted out into the Ganges, deflecting it from its course. On the summit of this rock, which was shaped like a foot and reputed to be the footstep of a giant on his way from the Himalayas to Cape Comorin was the fort. It had first become important during the incessant struggles between the Pathans and the Mughals in the sixteenth century. Babar had visited it in 1529 and the countryside round about is to this day peppered with the tombs of members of his army who, having been consumed by wild beasts with which the area was infested, were accorded the status of martyrs, presumably to cheer up their dependants. The Afghan Sher Khan Sur, later the Emperor Sher Khan, got possession of it in 1530 by the simple expedient of marrying the wife of the governor who had just died. In 1536 he was besieged there by Humayun who took it after a six months' siege but lost it to Sher Khan, who reoccupied it as soon as the Emperor continued his advance southwards; it remained in his hands and those of his descendants until 1575 when it was taken by Akbar. Later it fell into the hands of the Nawab Wazir of Oudh. It was stormed by the British after several attempts in 1765 and seven years later, after having been exchanged for the fort at Allahabad, it was finally ceded to the East India Company. Warren Hastings fled there by night from Banaras in August 1781 after the revolt of Raja Chait Singh, and in 1791 it became the headquarters of the European "Invalid" battalion, in which men who had signed on in India for twenty-one years or for life and were unfit for service in the field resided. The last Invalid died in 1903. From 1815 onwards it was a state prison; in 1890 the garrison was withdrawn; some time later it became a reformatory for boys.

The way up to the fort was by a long gentle ramp on the west side of the rock past the European Cemetery. Above it the walls rose sheer. Many of the smooth stones of which it was built were marked with triangles and figures that looked like stylised egg-timers, the signs of the stone-cutters or the wall-builders who had put them there. Beyond the gate was the lower ward of the fort, and facing it another ramp and another gateway, probably built in the early nineteenth century, which consisted of two pillars each ornamented with immense stone balls and an archway decorated with balls and fetters, reminiscent of the macabre embellishments used by George Dance in his design for Newgate Prison. The word "Welcome" was cut in the stone. "Welcome" was as inappropriate here as it would be on a doormat outside the office of an Inspector of Taxes. Beyond this gateway the ramp led uphill to the left. It was so steep that one after another we fell flat on our faces, which was no doubt the intention of the military architect who designed it. At the top of it there was a low sandstone building, the outside of which was decorated with a series of arches. The inside was vaulted but contained nothing of interest at all. To the left of this building there were old deserted quarters built within the walls with high, timbered ceilings; room after room echoing and empty.

After weeks in the plains it was like being in a helicopter. Two hundred feet below the Ganges swirled round the base of the rock. A ferry was setting off across the current towards the north bank. Away to the right, where the sandbanks shimmered in the sun, country boats were running down before the wind under big red sails; upstream towards Mirzapur the banks sloped gently inland, green with crops, and from the river the outworks of the fort rose in a series of wards and terraces reinforced by bastions, with a staircase running up through them by which British soldiers had gone down to the river seventy years before. To the south there was a further complex of buildings.

Here in the upper ward, there was an immense well. It was nearly thirty feet across, and was said to be a hundred and twenty feet deep. The upper part was lined with courses of masonry, the lower part was scooped out of the solid rock. From the upper ward a staircase full of rubble led down through the rock and emerged in a fissure, open to the sky and half blocked by pipal trees growing on the lip of it, which penetrated into the side of the well some fifteen feet above the water. This tunnel was full of bats. They were not in dozens or even in hundreds. They were in thousands, and as we went down into it they came flocking up, as I remembered people coming towards me on a staircase in the Underground once when, as a small boy, I had taken a wrong turning. Only now they came very fast, and with a horrible flaccid beating of wings, pouring over our heads up towards the sun and leaving behind them the vile rotten-chocolate smell of their excrement.

To the south of this well there were rows of ruined barrack-like buildings, many of them roofless, and little courtyards open to the sky which were cut off from one another by iron fences topped with spearheads. Beyond them, on a hill was the vast sandstone bungalow that had once belonged to Warren Hastings with room after room, partly European, partly oriental, one of them a forest of pillars, all decaying or decayed. Behind the bungalow there was a weird maze of narrow alleys, everywhere hemmed in by spiked railings and chevaux de frise which led to a house whose upper storey was collapsing into the ground floor rooms. At the angles of the garden wall there were two stone gazebos built like blockhouses with loopholes instead of windows. One of them looked down on to a huge whale-shaped building that had once been the powder-magazine, built in 1780.

This southern part of the fort, with its deserted courts with the long rank grass growing in them, its extraordinary buildings and long alleys blocked with spiked railings, had a nightmare quality that one associated with the paintings of Chirico or the prison engravings of Piranesi. We were glad to leave it.

Chapter Nineteen

A stay at Banaras

A well-known French physician, Dr. D. Herelle ... observed some of the floating corpses of men dead of dysentery and cholera, and was surprised to find that only a few feet below the bodies where one would expect to find millions of these dysentery and cholera germs, there were no germs at all. He then grew germs from patients having the disease, and to these cultures added water from the Ganges. When he incubated the mixture for a period, much to his surprise, the germs were completely destroyed.

Sri Swami Sivananda: Mother Ganges

Many scores, every year, of pilgrims from all parts of India, come hither expressly to end their days and secure their salvation. They purchase two large Kedgeree pots between which they tie themselves and when empty, these support their weight in the water. Thus equipped, they paddle into the stream, then fill the pots with the water which surrounds them and thus sink into eternity.

Reginald Heber, Lord Bishop of Calcutta:
Narrative of A Journey Through the Upper Provinces of
India from Calcutta to Bombay, 1824–1825

The principal hotel at Banaras was not a gay place, but then gaiety is not a characteristic of Indian hotels however well-appointed they may be. Most of the guests were elderly Americans and Europeans who had been brought there for a couple of days on their way round the world. They now sat on the verandah, huddled over the picturesque charcoal stoves, although it was warmer inside, shivering and wondering if the soda water which had been added to their enormously expensive whiskies was safe to drink — their dream of the splendours of the Orient rapidly dissipating. What was worse the hotel was full up, except for an "annexe", but this was not time to be choosey and we took it unseen.

After dinner which was quite good, a large rat appeared in the bar.

"Waiter!" said a strong-minded Englishwoman. "There's a rat under my seat." (By now everyone else was standing on chairs.)

"Yes, it lives there," he said, and went on his way.

The "annexe" was a filthy bungalow some distance from the main building. In the morning a gruesome-looking bearer brought us tea in a cracked teapot. Our one ambition was to get away and while Wanda paid the bill I ordered a taxi. At once a huge black American car of the '30s, the sort of thing used by gangsters to block the road, appeared. Everything was loaded aboard it before we discovered that it was not a taxi but a hire car. The bill for the short journey to the Tourist Bungalow was enormous, but we were too exhausted by the row we had had at the hotel about the loathsome accommodation we had been given to dispute it.

"Robbers!", said Wanda gloomily, as it drove away.

The Tourist Bungalow in which we spent the next few days was more modest than the hotel but more agreeable. It was built round three sides of a pleasant lawn bedded out with chrysanthemums and dahlias, although the view from the bedroom towards the Cantonment station over a stagnant pool of water and across a wasteland in which donkeys rolled on their backs in the dust was not so good.

Early the following morning when it was just growing light, we set off for the Ganges on foot. By this time it had become so much a part of our lives that we could not bear to be separated from it for long. We were like lemmings obeying an irresistible impulse.

We could have travelled by cycle ricksha, for even at a quarter to six, a nasty hour at Banaras in mid-winter, a number of drivers were sitting in their machines on the waste land outside the bungalow, swaddled in blankets and gloomily smoking bidis; but the previous evening we had met a young Indian student from the Hindu University at Malviyanagar who had given such a harrowing account of the way in which the cycle ricksha business was conducted that we decided to give up using them in future and travel by other means. According to him, there were at least four thousand licensed cycle rickshas in the city and three times the number of drivers, most of whom were labourers from the country who were attracted to the job by the prospect of high earnings. Scarcely any of them owned his own ricksha. Most of the machines belonged to merchants who hired them out to three different drivers during the twenty-four hours, charging each of them an exorbitant rental for an eight-hour shift.

"It is a disgraceful thing that one man should pull another, like a beast," he said, and himself departed on a cycle ricksha for Malviyanagar.

What would seem a short walk in Europe seems much longer in India, and as we tramped on past the bazaars of Alaipura, where the Muslim meat shops were, and the grain market of Rasoolpura with a convoy of ricksha drivers along behind us all droning reproachfully, "Ricksha, Ricksha," we felt like every other well-intentioned but misguided visitor to India who attempts to change the customs of the country for humanitarian reasons and only succeeds in alienating everyone, including the people he is attempting to help. It was obvious that if everyone behaved as we did, twelve thousand men would be thrown out of work and the communications of the city disrupted.

Something rather similar had happened in Delhi before we left for Hardwar where every morning Wanda, being confronted by a hideously emaciated and contorted beggar and unable to stand the sight any more, had gone to a restaurant and bought an enormous meal which she had set down on the pavement before him. From that day forward he was not seen again. She had destroyed him.

At this early hour, apart from some bullock-carts loaded with firewood, grain and raw sugar rumbling in from the country and our own private procession, the streets were deserted. We plodded on past white walls decorated with nostalgic paintings of sahibs and memsahibs and soldiers of the East India Company, and rajas shooting tigers from little howdahs on the backs of elephants, all freshly executed in blacks and yellows and outlined in strong blue; past shuttered shops selling "Rich Feat Cake" and "Stuffed Potatoes with Gravyo", "Chemists and Durggists", "Tailors and Drappers" and "The Space Man Clean Co." By the time we reached the Dasaswamedh Ghat we were worn out.

Here we left the ricksha men muttering among themselves and went down the steps to the river between long lines of beggars, a macabre guard of honour of the living dead, whose hands fluttered like leaves and whose moanings had nothing human about them but rose on the air as an awful susurration that made one want to turn and flee.

The sun rose and shone through the fog which enveloped the far side of the river like a great, glaring headlamp. The water had the consistency of olive oil, and across it, and into the eye of the sun, ferry boats loaded with white-clad women moved almost imperceptibly towards an invisible shore leaving no wake behind them. These high-sterned, yellowish boats the colour of old bones with their loads of motionless white figures imparted further eeriness to an already eerie scene. It was like the crossing of the Styx.

It was at the Dasaswamedh Ghat that Brahma performed a Dasaswamedha Yagna, a Ten-Horse Sacrifice, or rather ten separate sacrifices in each of which a horse was consumed, a sacrifice which conferred on the city a sanctity equal to that of Prayag. For a pilgrim who is unable to travel to Allahabad, to bathe at this ghat is as meritorious as bathing at the junction of Ganges and Jumna.

Brahma had gone to Banaras on an errand for Siva in the disguise of an elderly Brahman, with the disgraceful intention of causing the reigning Raja, a man of great rectitude called Divodas, to sin and therefore become unworthy to rule over the city. The Raja had incurred Siva's displeasure by expelling a number of the gods and goddesses who resided there – and knowing what one does of the mode of life of the members of the Hindu Pantheon his action is not surprising. To make him commit the sin of omission Brahma asked the Raja for the material with which to perform a most complicated sacrifice which required twenty-seven different ingredients from twenty-seven different sources. The Raja not only fulfilled the order to the letter but provided a sufficiency for ten such sacrifices. Brahma received this vast store of offerings while seated on the river bank and proceeded to offer the ten sacrifices and in addition, possibly to salve his amour-propre, one horse at each.

The integrity displayed by the Raja in this matter was of little benefit to him, for Siva sent Ganesa, his elephant-headed son who was conceived in the scurf on the body of his wife Paravati, to deal with him, disguised as a Guru. Ganesa succeeded in persuading the Raja to obey any supernatural instructions which he might receive on the Raja's behalf from higher authority and he immediately dreamed that Siva had ordered the Raja to leave Banaras. The Raja had no choice but to agree and he was immediately conveyed away by Siva to his paradise on the Kailasa mountain, the Hindu Olympus in the Himalayas. Siva then entered the city. Perhaps this story is a memory of the time when the Buddhists of Banaras who had usurped the place of the Brahmans were themselves forced to retreat before the returning tide of Brahmanism.

Here we hired a boat to take us down as far as the Malviya Bridge and then back again upstream to the southern outskirts of the city. (At Banaras the Ganges flows from south to north.) The boatman was a taciturn fellow, but we continued to make use of his services while we were at Banaras. One would have thought that by doing so a great deal of haggling would have been avoided but at each fresh encounter he looked at us as if he had never seen us before, and the whole tedious business of striking a price had to be gone through afresh.

Now the sun rose above the mist and from out on the water the city was revealed as a great golden crescent of temples, spires, mosques, minarets, ashrams and secular buildings, suspended rather than built high above the river and fading away in either direction into the misty distance. A light breeze started to blow and brilliant paper kites began to edge up the sky. Clouds of pigeons wheeled over the temples and the palaces of the princes whose splendours had departed. There were so many temples that they were like some monstrous growth of fungi. They grew all the way down the bank, in some places to the water's edge; one even stood in the river into which it had sunk, still held upright by its own weight. And leading down to the water were the steps of the seventy-four ghats, most of them in varying stages of decrepitude, some with their lower steps collapsing into the river where the water and the sewage percolating from above had undermined the clay and limestone which constituted their foundations, steep golden steps which were crowded with men, women and children who had either already bathed or were about to do so. The five most sacred ghats were the Panchtirath – all of which have to be visited by the pilgrim and bathed at in one day. The first was the Assi Ghat, further upstream near the mouth of the nala of the same name; to cross this stream, dry in the winter, is sufficient to take away the sins of those entering the city. Durga, Siva's wife, had dropped her sword here and it had carved out the channel. Next was the Dasaswamedh Ghat, then the Manikarnika Ghat with its well marking the place where Parvati dropped an ear-ring (Siva's wives were always dropping something). This ancient ghat, with its two footprints of Vishnu imprinted on a piece of marble, and above it the red-domed, golden-spired temple of Durga the most picturesque of all, was sunk deep in the river. The third was the Panchganga Ghat which marked the place where four sacred rivers entered the Ganges, all of them invisible to the common eye. At the Panchganga Ghat forests of bamboo poles rose above the bathing platforms and the umbrellas of the pandas were like small mushrooms clustered below the towering fungi of the temple spires, and there were open-fronted box-like constructions in which bathers could isolate themselves from their neighbours before and after the bath. A steep flight of steps lead up to the mosque of Aurangzeb with its one remaining minaret more than a foot out of true, (its twin collapsed in 1949). Downstream, out of sight below the big girder bridge, was the Adi Keshava Ghat, the last of the five, at the junction of the Ganges with the sacred river Barna, just below the place where the main drains of the city enter the Ganges.*

So many ghats. Dhobi Ghats with long lines of saris drying on the grass-grown embankments. The Ghat of the poet Tulsi Das, the author of the Hindi version of the *Ramayana*, where the piece of wood on which he crossed the river is kept in a building above the ghat together with his shoes and pillow. The Shree Shree Anandamayee Ma Ghat with the white ashram above it presided over by a woman of remarkable saintliness and beauty, in Hindu India the incarnation of Motherly Love, whom some believe to be the Supreme Goddess of the Universe in human form. The Hanuman Ghat built by a gambler with the proceeds of a single night's play. The Bachraj Ghat of the Jains with the house of Vallabhacharya above it, a Vishnuvite holy man who fell into the river while preaching in 1620 and was drowned. The Sivala Ghat from which the insurgent Raja, Chait Singh, the opponent of Warren Hastings, escaped across the Ganges after procuring the massacre of some two hundred sepoys and officers of the East India Company; together with the monasteries of the naked Nirbani sadhus and the Niranjanis, heretical Sikhs. The Dandi Ghat of the staff-bearing ascetics; the Harish Chandra Ghat, the lesser of the two burning ghats, a narrow stair with a pall of blue smoke over it; the Kedar Ghat of the Bengalis with the temple of Kedarnath, its entrance guarded by two disagreeable sculptured black figures and below it the well of Gauri Kund which cures three sorts of fever (temporarily empty). The Chauki Ghat with whole beds of lingams carved with snakes sprouting from it, high up on the steps. Munshi Ghat and the Ghat of the Maratha Princess Ahalya Bhai, The Mandir Ghat with the Observatory, one of five similar constructions in India built in 1693 by the Raja of Jaipur who undertook the re-formation of the calendar for the Emperor Muhammad Shah: "That so when the places of the stars, and the appearances of the new moons, and the eclipses of the sun and moon, and the conjunctions of the heavenly bodies, are computed by it, they may arrive as near as possible to the truth ... with its great instruments of stone and lime of perfect stability, with attention to the rules of geometry, and adjustment to the meridian, and to the latitude of the place, and with care in the measuring and fixing of them, so that the inaccuracies from the shaking of the circles, and the wearing of their axes, and displacement of their centres, and the inequality of the minutes, might

---

* A map showing the Sewerage System of Banaras in Dr. R. L. Singh's *Banaras: A Study in Urban Geography*, (Banaras, 1955) shows fourteen sewage disposal points on the banks of the river not including the terminal of the main sewer, at least one of them apparently next door to and upstream from the drinking water pumping station.

be corrected".* There was the Mir Ghat, named after a Mughal
Governor of Banaras and intended for the use of Muslims, of whom
there are large numbers in the city, but deserted; the Lalita Ghat
which leads up to the Nepalese Temple, hidden from the river behind
a pipal tree, a rather gloomy wooden building which has the imper-
manent air of being the Nepalese pavilion at a World Fair, "no doubt
picturesque", in the words of the nineteenth edition of Murray's
Handbook, "but disfigured by erotic carvings; they do not catch the
eye, providing that the attendant can be discouraged from pointing
them out." (He cannot be prevailed upon not to point them out and
the visitors would be extremely annoyed if he didn't, as they are very
small.) There was the Jalsain Ghat, the great cremation ghat with
eight temple spires soaring above it, piles of wood and sheeted bodies
rigid on the unlit pyres, cows nibbling the grass ropes for which
they have an unhealthy appetite, a few ghouls warming their hands,
ashes and marigolds on the foreshore and all the time more and more
bodies arriving, being brought down through the streets and alleys
as close as possible to the ghat by ekka and ricksha, in carts and on
stretchers, carried by men shouting: "*Ram Nam Sach Hai*" ("The
name of God is Truth").

The Scindia Ghat was like the entrance to a railway station. The
Bhosla Ghat was disfigured by an immense advertisement hoarding
displaying a muscle-bound colossus and the enigmatic words "85
years of human service" which here sounded very little. At Ram
Ghat there was a gigantic clay figure of Bhima, the second of the
five Pandu Princes, whose horse had kicked a six-sided hole in the
ground in the gorge at Hardwar, extended on the steps waiting for
the time when the Ganges would rise and wash him away. Ghai
Ghat had a large pink stone statue of a cow on it and it was a ghat
which was used by real cows, where the bathers clean their feet by
rubbing them along the stones; and the Trilochan Ghat of Siva. So
many ghats. Too many ghats. Except for ardent mythologists and
those sensible travellers who simply enjoy the view.

But the ghats and the city above it, however many temples it
contained, were nothing but a backdrop to the enactment of a ritual,
incessantly performed, that was as natural and as necessary as the air
they breathed and the water itself to the participants, but in which
one could have no real part. However well-intentioned he might be,
and however anxious to participate, for a European to bathe in the
Ganges at Banaras was simply for him to have a bath. It was as if

* *Asiatic Researches*, Vol. V, pp. 177–8.

a Hindu, having attended a Mass out of curiosity, decided to take Communion; and although it undoubtedly had the capacity to engulf sin, the river did not here have the icy clarity that it had at Hardwar or the sheer volume that it had at the Sangam at Allahabad, or that rare beauty that it had on the lonely reaches of the river that had made it irresistible even to the uninitiated.

For initiation was difficult. There was no joining Hinduism in the sense that you could become a Roman Catholic with your name on a list somewhere, for there was nothing to join. No one ever suggested to another that he should become a Hindu.

Nor was it enough to read the books. So I had found for myself in the last cold winter of the war, inspired by a low diet and rash doses of Boehm and Eckhart, thinking myself on the way to becoming a mystic. It had been like trying to enter a theatre by the exit.

For us, the best time at Banaras was at dusk, in the labyrinthine alleys behind the ghats before the lights were lit. At this hour there were few people about and those who were seemed unnaturally subdued. Even the small boys who make life hideous during the day with their "'ullos" and "very well thank you's" had either departed to the land of nod or sat, drained of energy, at the doors of their houses.

Down these alleys, many of which ended in a heap of rubble where some buildings on the river front had collapsed, the darkness came while the sky overhead was still blue; but already the pigeons had ceased to wheel about the spire of the last of Aurangzeb's minarets and the kite-fliers had hauled down their kites. Soon the sky faded and the long, pink, streamers left over from the sunset stretched across it.

Now the walls began to exude a dampness and the smells of sewage as it trickled down between the houses to the river became more pronounced. Here, smelling these smells, it was not difficult to believe that this was the part of Banaras, itself the city with a higher rate of infant and adult mortality than any other town or city in Uttar Pradesh, with the highest mortality of all; but it was worth being there if only for the anonymity conferred by the partial darkness.

The only commerce at this hour was at small wayside stalls where old women bent over their scales weighing out infinitesimal quantities of herbs for equally old and shrivelled customers. In the shops of the charcoal vendors the merchants and the men who carried the charcoal for them were as black as the pits in which they stood waiting for customers. These and the scarcely human figures of the women who still continued to plaster the walls with freshly kneaded cakes of dung were the only ones to be seen. Everyone else had withdrawn to eat the evening meal leaving the rooms on the ground floor unlit.

But what it lacked in people was more than made up by the cows. They were everywhere, and the ground underfoot was slippery with their excrement. They were in the forecourts of the temples. They were tethered in the yards of the houses. They were free, lurching up gradients, and floating down the alleys as if they were levitated; or they suddenly loomed up like great, ghostly ships running under a press of sail with the vapour coming from their nostrils in the chill evening air as if it was cannon smoke. They never hesitated. They simply sailed serenely on, and it was for us to get out of the way or be crushed against the walls. They were the chosen animals and they knew it.* They would never die a violent death, only more horribly, of old age, disease or malnutrition.

Now from the river came the sounds of the beating of gongs, the ringing of hand-bells struck with hammers and the rattling of a gourd-like instrument with some hard round object inside it. This was the committee of the Ganga Sava performing, as it did every night, at dusk, the Arti Puja offering the light of a five-branched candelabra to the river together with flour, milk and sweetmeats.

Further westward in the shopping lanes the lights were already lit: in Kachauri Gali where they sold Mukhbilash, betel nut dipped in silver; Esha Gol ka Bhusi — flaky crisp crimson stuff derived from the betel; Pulfgllifhiria, tobacco dipped in silver; Kashria Supan, betel with saffron, and Pan Khapa, all in round embossed tin boxes. They were lit in Vishwanath Lane, on the way to the temple where they sold religious objects: tilak powder, lingams, conch shells, incense, lat-i-dana, the white sweets used as offerings, Brahmanical cords, sandalwood and in shops selling more profane articles — false hair, stuff for reddening the soles of the feet, sweet-smelling oils, little packets of scented powders called chinasindoor, small, jewelled beauty spots made of plastic, erotic scents and scents so heavy they could only act as a tranquilliser, palankeens for weddings, little lacquered figures of highland soldiers with blue and white spotted bagpipes, gods, musicians and pop-eyed servants carrying plates of fried eggs. The lights had come on too in Kunj Gali where the silk shops were; in the Thatheri Bazaar where they sold hideous brass and copper objects and in the Narial Bazaar they were beginning to glow behind the curtains on the balconies of the brothels on the upper floors.

There were two receptionists at the Tourist Bungalow. One was a fat, indolent fellow; the other was a thin, anxious-looking Brahman who

---

* It is quite common for Brahmans to leave their all for the endowment of homes for aged cows.

referred to himself as Pandit, though no one else did. After some conversation at the desk about some of the more esoteric manifestations of Hinduism at Banaras, the fat one offered to introduce us to an Aghori.*

"If you wish I am taking you to see this Aghori. He is living at City Post Office," he said. "It is very strange sect. These men are eating their excrements. I am also showing you many other things at Banaras; but first I am showing you this man."

As he happened to have a free hour we all three squashed into a cycle ricksha and set off immediately for the City Post Office. It seemed a strange place for a dung-eater to hang out. The Aghori was lying on his stomach across the entrance to the Post Office, and partly blocking it. He was completely naked and as soon as he realised that we were interested in him, he rolled over sufficiently to display his sexual organs, which were of an impressive size. At the same time he regarded us complacently. His body was like that of some monstrous creature that had been thrown up on the sea front by a gale; the face, which was covered with stubble, had a strange, decayed look, rather like that of Henry VIII in later life painted by Holbein: but it was the eyes, half-closed and half-smiling, and utterly self-satisfied, that created the most disagreeable sensation. They were the eyes of someone who was not quite mad and certainly not completely sane.

He was surrounded by his equipment; half a dozen old tins which contained a nasty mixture of what looked like soot mixed with water; a collection of post office pens, presumably filched by his admirers

* The Aghoris or Augars are believers in Tantric magic and the ceremony of calling up demons at a burning ghat or cemetery is a typical Tantric rite. They are a strange and disagreeable sect. Their name is derived from the Sanksrit *A-ghora* ("not terrific"), one of the titles of Siva. Both followers of Siva and Vishnu can be Aghoris. Their origins are uncertain but at one time they had several monasteries — Mathas — on Mount Abu in Rajputana, on Mount Girnar in Kathiawar and at Buddh Gaya and Banaras. The Banaras sect says that it stems from Kinna Ram or Kinaram who was introduced to it by Kalu Ram an ascetic of Girnar towards the end of the eighteenth century. One of the earliest references to them is by the anonymous author of *Dabisthan* who died about 1670. He described them as a "sect of the yogis who know no prohibited food ... They also kill and eat men ... They have all originated from Gorakhnath. The author of this work saw a man, who singing the customary song, sat upon a corpse, which he kept unburied until it came into a state of dissolution; and then ate the flesh of it. This act they hold especially meritorious." They are, in fact, reputed to eat the flesh of everything except the horse. In 1891 the census showed 9,260 Aghoris or Augars in British India of whom 4,947 were in the United Provinces and 3,877 in Bengal; but today the number must be much reduced. See the articles on Aghori in Hastings: *Encyclopaedia of Religion and Ethics*, Vol. 1; and Vol. 12; *Tantrism*.

from inside the building, one of which he wore behind his left ear; and something done up in a grubby cloth that looked as if it might contain his dinner.

"I hope it isn't feeding time," Wanda said.

"He is Aghori. He never speaks. He never moves. No one sees him eat. Who knows what food he lives on?" said our guide with relish. It is difficult to be funny in India, and he did not realise that she was trying to be funny. But when we returned to the bungalow the Pandit poured scorn on him.

"He is an ignorant fellow", he said, referring to his colleague. "That man is not Aghori. He is a Naga, naked sadhu. Now I am showing you real Aghori. He is called Augha Baba."

Leaving the fat receptionist looking hurt, we set off with the Pandit in another ricksha on an interminable journey up to the Sarnath road in the direction of the great Buddhist Stupa at Sarnath until eventually we reached the house in which the Augha Baba was supposed to live, but he wasn't there. Some men in a café a little way down the road said that he had gone to the Law Courts. It seemed an odd place for him to be, but the Brahman decided to go there to look for him. At the Law Courts the litigants were crowded together with their lawyers under a huge open-sided shed which was more like a cattle-market than the ante-chamber to a court of law; but there was no sign of the Augha Baba.

Late that same night we hired a ricksha and went back to the Post Office. The streets were empty. The Naga, or the Aghori, or whatever he was, was standing on his feet being massaged by two young men with whom he was carrying on an animated conversation with his mouth full. In his hands he held a gnawed chapati. When they had finished, he wrapped himself in a blanket and all three of them went off round the corner of the Post Office.

The next morning, soon after breakfast the Augha Baba appeared at the bungalow. He arrived in a cycle ricksha armed with the twisted horn of some animal on which he blew, producing a melancholy note and a bag which he hastened to inform us contained a human skull. He was a youngish man about thirty with spiky, blackened teeth in a thin mouth and small deep-set eyes. He wore a kind of hood with the ear-flaps untied and a long brown woollen cloak. He had a creepy look and the impression was heightened by knowing what he was capable of doing. He spoke some English, but as the two receptionists had both prudently disappeared and the conversation threatened to be rather technical, a gentleman who was sitting in the garden kindly volunteered to act as interpreter. "I am very pleased," he said. "I, too, have never met an Aghori."

We all sat round a table on the lawn looking keen and interested and the man who everyone thought was an Aghori announced that he was an Avadhut and blew loudly on his horn.

"That is from the Sanskrit, Avadhut, meaning 'shaken off'. He has shaken off the world. He can be follower of Siva or Vishnuvite and he can be Avadhut without being Aghori."

"But is he an Aghori?"

The Avadhut began chanting in a monotonous voice.

"*Le deh se man budhi tak, sansar jo hai bhasata. So sarb maya matra hee, kinchit nahin parmatha. Mamta ahanta se rahit jo par praganar niskam hai. Maya avidya se pare, auvdut uska nam hai.*" ("He who observes the Word far from the affairs of the world and studies it, with Nishkama [without desire], that man's name is Avadhut.")

"But what is the Word?"

Like all important questions in India this one was doomed not to be answered for, at this point, the Avadhut produced his skull from the cloth bag, or rather the top half of a skull, beautifully polished like a piece of old silver, and put it on the table with the cranium downwards.

"This means that he wishes to drink. He says that it is the skull of a criminal."

"Well, what would he like in it — tea, coffee, milk, lemonade?"

"He says have you any whisky. He prefers strong drink."

"Will rum do?"

"He says rum will do very well."

There was no question of this being an early-morning nip. The skull held half a bottle and the Avadhut drank it straight off without turning a hair.

"Now he is asking if your wife has some perfume as he wishes to wash his skull."

"I'm blowed if I give him my scent," Wanda said. "Dammit, it came from Hermés."

"He likes very much the perfume of Chanel."

"He can have some of my eau-de-cologne if he likes, but he's not having my scent."

While the Avadhut was washing the inside of his skull with eau-de-cologne from the Galeries Lafayette, he began to chant again.

"*Na swarg hai, na nark hai, no lok hai, no par lok hai, no veed hee, na vidhya hai, na band hai, na moksh hai, na Vishnu hee, na Brahma hee, na Rudra hee, na Atma hai, bhola nahin shruti kaha sake auvdut uska nam*

hai." ("He who does not believe in heaven or hell, or earth or knowledge, or death or salvation, or Vishnu, or Brahma, or Rudra or the
existence of souls or what was revealed, his name is Avadhut—but
not even Siva or the Shrutis can explain what an Avadhut is.")

As, according to the Avadhut, Siva did not exist, it was difficult
to see how he could do so.

"Why does he blow his horn?" I asked.

"To warn people of his coming and also to call on God. It is the
sound of the lion, he says."

"But God does not exist."

"He exists for other men but not for Avadhut. He is calling on
God for them."

"Does he really eat dung and things?"

"He says eating was only initiatory process. Now he just touches it
with his tongue." (Here the Avadhut put out a tongue to show what
he did. If its appearance was anything to go by he was in need of
what my father used to call "a damn good clear out".) "But sometimes he eats bodies of persons and animals and he is drinking his
own waters if he gets nothing stronger. This is to teach indifference.
He says he can live on wine or his water for eighteen days. Now
he is saying that he wants to eat breakfast."

I thought it a pity that he was not on the water diet at the moment.
He was becoming expensive to maintain. And for one who was supposed to be indifferent to the pleasures of the table he made a good
deal of fuss about breakfast. He ordered an omelette, toast, butter,
jam, fruit and tea and when the omelette arrived he opened it up
suspiciously to see if it was properly cooked. I wondered what happened when he was on his working diet, but these were churlish
thoughts. After breakfast he turned the skull upside down and I gave
him the other half of the bottle of rum.

"Does he ever get drunk?"

"He says that ascetics should drink so long as their eyes do not
roll and mind is not agitated. Beyond this, drinking is the act of a
beast. It is written in the *Mahanirvana Tantra*. Now he is telling us how
he performs Sadhana.

"Sadhana is for rendering visible gods and demons, whichever he
chooses; but usually it is demons. To do this thing he must first of
all be initiated by his guru and he must know the bija, the mystic
syllable, which contains the seed of the god, and also the vedya, the
mantra which gives power. Then he goes to the burning-ghat at
midnight. He lights a fire, mixes his excrements and puts liquor in
his skull. He begins to think of the demon Bhootnath and Bhairava,

Siva in the terrible form. He must control the demons. He drinks to
give himself courage; then he eats and casts what is left upon the fire.
At the same time he chants the mantra. He does not make it clear
when he says the mystic syllable. Sometimes cobras and huge bodies
appear. Then if he is successful Bhairava will come. He may come
in one of many forms, as a snake or as a baby and Bhairava will
ask him what he wants. Now he assumes essential nature of god or
demon and while he speaks with its voice all that he wishes will be
accomplished."

"But what is it for?"

"He does not do it for himself. It is to give to women who have
not had them children; to save life of one who is sick; to find out
if university examination will be passed."

"But if he doesn't believe in heaven or hell or gods or demons
how can he call them up?"

"It is like the horn with which he calls on god. He says that he
does not believe in gods and demons but he can call them up for
people who do.

"He says also that there are some who can perform Sadhana without
performing puja. These men he calls Sidhi because their problems
are solved. If a man asks a Sidhi for the answer to a problem the Sidhi
will say simply 'Go to your office, go to your examination hall for
your problem is already solved.' He himself is not Sidhi; but he would
like you to meet his Guru, Sri Hari Ram. He is Sidhi. He is so very
holy that he able to suck up liquids with his penis and he is a hundred
and fifteen years old."

The thought of meeting a man a hundred and fifteen years old
whose penis operated like a fountain pen was fascinating, but when
we said we would like to do so, the Avadhut explained that it was
unfortunate, but he had gone away to the country.

Once more he placed his skull upside down on the table. I gave
him a skull of beer. The Avadhut delicately blew the froth off it,
remarking that it was like water and that he preferred Seager's and
Johnny Walker. Soon it was empty and I set off on a bicycle to try
and find a liquor shop where I could get more. It took some time
and when I returned the Avadhut had disappeared, though not for
long; apparently he had been unable to wait for the supplies I was
bringing up and had gone off to produce his own.

"He says they have another puja called Kumari Puja-Virgin Puja.
Avadhut lies on his back and girl is standing over him. Then she
pours wine over head and it runs down her body into the mouth of
Avadhut. After this he has intercourse with her but without orgasm —

thus she is still virgin. It is difficult to find girls in India for this puja and now they are only doing it in Assam.

"He says he has not yet performed this puja but he has special kiss between legs for barren women. He is wanting to give this kiss to a lady at the hotel who is barren, but husband is not allowing it." No wonder the staff had fled at his approach.

"He is an Aghori," said the gentleman who had been translating for us, and like everyone else except the Avadhut, by this time he was quite worn out. "There is no doubt about that."

By now it was lunch time. The Avadhut, who was undoubtedly an Aghori, ate a large meat curry, several parathas and a fruit salad and, because he was still hungry, a plate of scrambled eggs, after which we paid for his ricksha which had been waiting for him for four hours, and he drove away.

Some Avadhuts had wider interests. One day we took a bus over the Maulviya bridge to a place where a small band of them had started a leper colony. Their leader, a man of saintly reputation, the Avadhut Sri Bhagwan Ramji, was only twenty-eight years of age. It was a place of the simplest sort. There were a number of open-sided huts in which the lepers lived, but more spacious accommodation was being erected. There was a dispensary and a small building in which the sadhus lived. Unfortunately, Sri Bhagwan Ramji was ill but we were entertained by a tall, thin young man, clean-shaven, like the beer-drinking Avadhut and with the same disquieting eyes. "You will drink tea," he said.

It was not a question. He was giving us tea. Knowing what we did about the indifference of an Avadhut to pain and sickness we were not keen. It was not beyond the bounds of possibility that this sect wanted to contract leprosy or at any rate would not go out of its way to avoid it. On the other hand, it seemed craven to say no.

Soon it arrived, brought by a servant, or was he one of the patients? For a moment before I drank it, I thought I was going to faint. Was it my imagination that the Avadhut seemed to be watching us with a slightly sardonic expression? I wondered what Wanda was feeling: then I drank it and so did she.

According to the young man, these sadhus worshipped Sarveshwari, the Goddess of the Universe, "Mother", according to the Tantric ritual, performing certain pujas — the Chakra Puja and the Gopya Puja.

Then he took us to see the patients. There were fifteen of them.

None of them seemed to be in a very advanced stage of the disease, but then it is enough to have leprosy.

"We cure them with Ayurvedic medicine," he said.

I asked him what they used, but he said it was a secret. I asked him why it was a secret but he did not reply. He said that many of those who were cured came back.

"They go back to their families and are reinfected," he said. It sounded odd.

Later he showed us the visitors' book. A number of medical men both Indian and European had visited the colony and the general burden of their complaint was that the sadhus should keep their cure to themselves and not share it with the world. When we left he gave us a manifesto. It called for a World Peace Conference in India. "Let all be happy," it said. "Let there be absolute freedom from disease. Let pleasant sights greet everyone and pain be vanished for ever."

Later that day we visited a new temple on the south side of the city, the Sri Satyanarayan Tulsi Manas Mandir, built as a memorial to Tulsi Das. It had been constructed, regardless of expense, from the charity fund of a Bengali business man. It was a large, airy, two-storeyed building of white marble with the whole of the poet's Hindi version of the *Ramayana* inscribed on the walls. Outside in the grounds, under a beflagged canopy, thirty-five distinguished Brahmans wearing garlands were preparing for the Deo Pratishta Puja, a marathon operation, which would precede the installation of the deity a week hence, surrounded by mounds of food and other materials for the ceremony — in itself an extremely costly operation — and if anything went wrong during its performance it would have to be done again.

The principal instigator of the construction of the temple, Sri Lattan Lall Sureka of the Howrah Transport Company, himself kindly demonstrated some of the principal marvels of the place. He appeared slightly overcome by what the benevolence of himself and his family had raised up, as well he might, for the cost must have been astronomical. There was an illuminated cascade in the grounds and articulated figures of Tulsi Das and Hanuman worked by machinery. When it was set in motion Hanuman's chest opened with a whirring noise to reveal a midget figure of Sita inside it.

Chapter Twenty

The day of Makara Sankranti

A peculiar fact which has never been satisfactorily explained is the quick death, in three or five hours, of the cholera vibrio in the waters of Ganges. When one remembers sewage by numerous corpses of natives, often cholera casualties, and by the bathing of thousands of natives, it seems remarkable that the belief of the Hindus, that the water of this river is pure and cannot be defiled and that they can safely drink it and bathe in it, should be confirmed by means of modern bacteriological research.

An unnamed Canadian professor, said to be of McGill University,
cited in *Mother Ganges*

On the afternoon of 13th January, we drove up the Grand Trunk Road to Allahabad. The journey which had taken us three days and nights in the rowing-boat was now accomplished in as many hours. The road was crowded with pilgrims on their way to the Mela. They travelled in ekkas, clinging to them in half dozens, in tongas, motor buses, cars and on bicycles. They also travelled on foot, men and women and children plodding up the road with their faces wrapped in cloths to avoid being asphyxiated by petrol fumes and choked with the dust that rose from the dry verges of the road. There was a file of camels, each with a man on its back seated on a wooden saddle. There was even an elephant with a painted head, chained, all alone at the side of the road. It was chewing grass and swishing its decorated trunk up and down, curling it delicately so that it looked like the initial letter on a page of illuminated manuscript but one that was constantly changing its shape.

It was a beautiful day. The plain was a sea of sprouting wheat and barley, dotted with groves of trees that were enchanting islands among the lighter green of the crops. It was a day of spring rather than winter in which everything seemed to be burgeoning, all except the man-made objects, villages, tanks, and shrines – which were mostly crumbling into dust. But as the sun sank behind the trees and the shadows lengthened, the fields assumed the same uniform green-gage colour as the river did when it flowed in the sunless places close to the high banks; except in one place where a single shaft of sun-light filtering through a gap in the trees illuminated a whitewashed tomb. Then it disappeared. Low in the west the sky became blood-red; higher it was purple; overhead it was deep blue; while low down close to the earth in the fields, the smoke from the village fires hung in swags and trailed away among the trees in woods which were no longer Arcadian but dark and mysterious-looking.

Because of the huge crowds, the bridge of boats at Jhusi on the left bank of the Ganges had been closed to motor cars, and by the time we reached the Curzon Bridge at the big bend of the river north of the city, it was almost dark and only the pools among the sand-banks upstream still shone in the last of the light.

The bridge itself was jammed with bullock-carts and tired pilgrims – men, women and children on their way to the Sangam. They were country people and what belongings they had they carried in sacks slung across their shoulders. It was a moving sight.

Eventually, we reached the Fort, and from the ramparts looked out over the sandbank which extended upstream for more than a mile from the confluence of the two rivers as far as the Izzot railway bridge.

It was more like the camp of an army on the eve of a great action than a holy place. The sandbank was hidden from view by a blanket of low-lying fog and smoke which was illuminated by the flickering light of the camp fires, and the glare of kerosene lanterns. The long lines of electric lights on long poles which marked the way to the bathing areas were the only lights actually to rise above the fog; while overhead the stars looked down, pale and remote.

It was eerie, for apart from a few hundred pilgrims who were seeing the night through huddled against the wall of the fort, there was not a human being in sight. Only a muted and continuous roar from the sandbank and the encampments announced the fact that a million people were settling down for the night. A sound that was punctuated by the beating of gongs and drums, the ringing of bells, the rumbling of trains on the railway bridges and the noise of the loud-speakers which blared out injunction to this vast multitude on how it should comport itself the next day, on the morning of Makara Sankranti, when the sun and moon would be of equal degree.

At five o'clock the following morning it was still dark. Down on the sandbank, the road which led from Akbar's great embankment on the north side of the fort to the landing-place was itself a tributary river of human beings all moving towards the Ganges. Down on the shores of the Jumna by the fort shoals of country boats propelled by sweeps were setting off, deep-loaded, for the Sangam. From the sandbank rose the same deep roaring sound we had heard the night before that was like the sound of a storm at sea.

At a quarter to six the sky beyond the Sangam was tinged with red and the wind-blown clouds were like the wings of a giant grey bird that had been dipped in blood. From the horn of sand where the rivers met, a further isthmus of boats extended far out into the Jumna and their masts and rigging, mooring poles and cordage were like a forest of trees and creepers against the sky.

Little bands of men and women who had travelled here together from their villages, some of them very old with skin like crumpled parchment, the women singing sadly but triumphantly, lurched bare-footed across the silt towards the pragwals, evil-looking men who performed their duties with an air of patient cynicism, in contrast with that of the pilgrims themselves who wore expressions of joy. They had all been shaven with varying degrees of severity in the barbers' quarter: women from the south and widows had had their head completely shaven; the men were left with their chhotis, the small tufts on the backs of their skulls, and those who had moustaches, but whose fathers were still alive, had been allowed to retain them; natives of Allahabad were allowed to keep their hair; Sikhs gave up a ritual lock or two. At one time the hair was buried on the shore of the river; now it was taken away and consigned to a deep part of the Ganges downstream. Like pilgrims everywhere they were not allowed much peace: shifty-looking men offered to guard their clothes while they were bathing; the dreadful loud-speakers exhorted them not to surrender their clothes to these same shifty-looking men and, at the same time, urged them to bathe and go away; boatmen importuned them; policemen and officious young men wearing arm-bands tried to move them on, but they were in a state bordering on ecstasy, and were oblivious to everything but the river which they had come so far to see, bathe in and perhaps to die by this very morning; for some of them were so decrepit that it seemed impossible that they could survive the sudden shock of the immersion.

The women dressed in saris, the men in loin-cloths, they entered the river, dunking themselves in it, drinking it, taking it in their cupped hands and letting it run three times between their fingers with their faces towards the still invisible sun. Shivering but happy and, if they were fortunate enough to possess them, dressed in clean clothes, they allowed the pragwals to rub their foreheads with ashes or sandal-wood and make the tilak mark. They offered flowers and milk to the river, and those who had never been there before bought half-coconuts from the pragwals and launched the shells filled with marigolds on the water, which were afterwards appropriated by the pragwals to be sold again. New or old pilgrims, these clients were his for ever, and so would their descendants be and their names would be inscribed in one of his books, according to their caste, as they had been for centuries.

The sun rose as a ball of fire, but was almost immediately enveloped in cloud. A cool wind rose and the dust with it, enveloping the long, dun-coloured columns which were moving towards the sangam and those whiter ones which were moving away from it. The camps of the pragwals were labyrinths of thatched huts and tent-like constructions in which saris and dhotis and loin-cloths hung on thickets of bamboo poles drying in the wind and the smoke of dung fires. Over them, on longer poles flew their banners, the rallying places of their clients who squatted cheek by jowl below them in a dense mass, cooking, waiting for their clothes to dry, or merely waiting. There were banners with European soldiers on them in uniforms dating from the time of the East India Company and there were banners decorated with gods. Some poles had baskets and other homely objects lashed to the top of them instead of flags. One had an umbrella.

Further north, towards the Banaras bridge, the encampment of the sadhus was like a sea of saffron. There the Mahanta Krishna Mahatna from the ashram at Paribragikachary, seated on cushions in a tent, was discoursing to his followers, using a microphone. On the other side of the river, on the sands at Jhusi a famous saint, the Beoraha Babu, who is said to have walked across the Ganges on the water, was installed on a tower ten feet high. On the day after we had left Allahabad for Mirzapur, he had crossed the river by more conventional means to attend a meeting of pandits and sadhus at the foot of the living banyan tree inside the Fort; the one which is not accessible to the laity because it is in a military area.

The way from the Sangam to Akbar's embankment was a Via Dolorosa lined with beggars. To traverse it was to be transported into the Dark Ages. They were dressed in rags the colour of the silt on which they lay or crouched, and they were almost indistinguishable from it. The air was filled with the sound of their moanings. There were lepers and dwarfs and men, women and children so terribly mutilated – without limbs, eyes, faces, some with none of these adjuncts – that they bore scarcely any resemblance to humanity at all. Some lay contorted in little carts with broken wheels. Each had his or her begging bowl and a piece of sacking with a little rice spread

on it, put there in much the same way as a cloakroom attendant at
Claridge's leaves a few shillings in a plate to show that he is not averse
to being tipped. The lepers were the most terrible of all, with fingers
like black knots and with white crusts for eyes, or else a ghastly jelly
where the eyes should have been. And to each of them the returning
bathers, rich or poor, threw a few grains of rice and a few paise,
confident that by so doing they were at least ensuring themselves
merit in this world and perhaps even a little in the next.

"Why are you taking photographs of these people?" said a highly
civilised Brahman. "What will people think of India if you show
pictures such as these?" He was genuinely angry.

He delicately sprinkled a handful of rice on the sacking of the beggar
in front of him, looked at me with disdain, and went on his way.

There were mendicant sadhus, men lying on beds of thorns with
a carefully concealed cushion to take their weight but still uncomfortable enough, and there were others with iron skewers through their
tongues. These were the side-shows, together with the children six
or seven years old, who had been skilfully made up as sadhus by their
proprietors in little lean-to sheds which had been set up against the
wall of the Fort for this purpose. They sat, cross-legged, plastered
with mud and ashes, eyes downcast, garlanded with flowers, sadly
ringing their little silver bells. This was a world with its strange constructions, barrels on the end of long poles, tented encampments and
limbless creatures such as both Breughel and Hieronymus Bosch
knew, and one that they would have understood.

The steep incline where the last of the beggars congregated, which
led to the top of the embankment and thence to the pilgrims' camp
and the railway station at Prayag, was the scene of disaster at the
great Mela of 1954. It was a Kumbh Mela as opposed to a Magh Mela.
No one is really sure why every twelfth year is regarded as being
more important than the rest; but it has been suggested that it is
because of the position assumed at these intervals by the planet Jupiter
in concatenation with the sun and the moon. They were themselves
at this time in the special relationship which brings about the winter
solstice on January 14th, producing what is known as Kumbha Snan.
Although it usually occurs at intervals of twelve years, Kumbha Snan
can occur at the eleventh and thirteenth year. But since 1882 it has
always taken place at intervals of twelve years. The decision as to
when it occurs is the result of predictions of pandits and astrologers;
but the casting vote as to when it is actually held is largely in the
hands of the various akharas or bodies of sadhus; for if they stay
away it cannot be celebrated.

In the case of the 1954 Kumbh all three — pandits, astrologers and sadhus — were unanimous in saying that it would be Purna Kumbh — the perfect Kumbh. Such a Kumbh would not happen again for 108 years, some authorities said 144 years.

The news that this was to be the perfect Kumbh spread rapidly throughout India. The desire to attend it became irresistible. As a witness, Sri Vishwanath Prasad, testified before the Commission set up by the Government of Uttar Pradesh to investigate the disaster: "People said '*Mar jayenge to tar jayenge aur bach jayenge to ghar jayenge. Hamara to donon men fayeda hai. Aise bhagya kah — an jo aise punya kshetra men aisi ghari me marain. Dhanya unke bhagya jo marain.*' ('If we are killed we shall attain salvation. If we escape death, we shall go home. We shall be gainers in either case. Those who die at such a sacred spot, at such an auspicious moment, would be very lucky! We wish to have the good fortune.')"

The more educated, too, felt the urge to attend the perfect Kumbh. In 1954 it was the whim of the Ganges to cut away the sandbank on the right bank so that it flowed close to the walls of the Fort, leaving a correspondingly large sandbank on the left bank at Jhusi on which the sadhus and those who stayed for the whole Mela, the *kalp-basi*, "those who have resolved to abide", the most orthodox who fast by day and reject cereal food and bathe daily at the Sangam, could be accommodated. This left only eighty acres on the right bank under the walls of the Fort to accommodate all the pilgrims who would bathe from it on the great day.

At the Kumbh Mela eight separate Akharas* of sadhus are always present in force. They have special privileges at the Sangam on the three great bathing days; Makara Sankranti, and Amavasya, Vasanta Panchami, and they observe a strict order of precedence. There are the Nirbanis, naked sadhus who are followers of Siva and who increase their numbers for processional purposes at the time of the Mela with paid help; and the Niranjanis and the Junas who also go naked at the time of the Mela, both of which sects are engaged in banking. All these come from Daraganj, just above the Banaras Bridge on the right bank. Then there are the Vishnuvite Vairagis, a band of ultra-orthodox wandering mendicants who disagree with everyone including themselves and are great trouble-makers. They have three

---

* Akhara: literally a place where wrestling takes place. Sadhus developed physical as well as spiritual powers; possibly because some Muslim kings tried to stop the bathing ceremonies by attacks on the congregation. It has been suggested that as a result of being forced to learn to defend their rights the sadhus aped the pomp and circumstance of their oppressors.

sub-divisions: the Digambaris, the Nirmohis and another band of
Nirbanis. There is the Chhota Panchayati, a body of Sikhs who have
seceded from their religion but who still use the Granth of the Sikhs
as their religious book; and the Bara Panchayati of the same persuasion
who are also bankers. There are the Nirmalis and the Vrinavanis who
are Sikhs; and there are the Mahanirvani Sanyasis.

All claim the right to go to the Sangam in procession and with the
exception of the Vairagis they go attended with richly caparisoned
elephants, camels, gold and silver plated palankeens, horse chariots,
buglers, pipers, bands of music and brandishing swords and tridents.

In 1954 the total police strength drafted to the Mela was 2,882. It
included 114 mounted police and 550 others who were intended to
man the sixteen barriers for compulsory cholera inoculation which
had been set up and which were extremely unpopular with the pilgrims.

On the first great day, Makara Sankranti, the crowd was estimated
to number not more than seven hundred thousand; it was the same
on the next important day, the 19th, and this lulled the Government
into believing that they had overestimated the numbers who would
attend the Kumbh. On 28th January, without telling the Mela authorities who themselves had estimated an attendance of two and a half
million on 3rd February, Amavasya day, they withdrew the order for
compulsory inoculation of the pilgrims, which had proved so unpopular but had slowed down the influx of people into the area. The
barriers were down.

By the night of 2nd February the number of pilgrims had increased
alarmingly. Some of them had been on the road for six months. Thousands stayed with the pragwals in the bathing area instead of crossing
to the east bank by the bridges of boats as they were intended to do.
They had very little choice. The crowd on the Grand Trunk Road
was forty deep and solid, pressing towards the river; special trains,
loaded with pilgrims from all parts of India, continued to arrive at
the pilgrim station at Prayag, north of the Fort on the morning of
3rd February. There were ten thousand beggars in the Sangam area
alone, many of them unable to move by their own volition. By the
time that the sadhus' procession had begun it was estimated that there
were five million people in the bathing area. How anyone could esti-
mate this it is impossible to say, but undoubtedly there was an un-
precedented number something between two and five million.

Into this cauldron of humanity (carried on by their own impetus
and unable to halt themselves) the eight akharas of sadhus, together
with their elephants with silver howdahs and caparisoned camels,

plunged at right angles. The point of impact was the foot of the inclined causeway that takes the returning pilgrims over the embankments and away from the bathing area. What followed is not properly describable, because no coherent eyewitness has ever come forward who was able to do so. It seems that the naked Nirbani sadhus began to use their swords on the pilgrims, who panicked. Then fifty or sixty Mahanirvani Sanyasis who were cut off from the main body began to lay about them with their iron tridents. Once a man went down he was lost for ever; the beggars and invalids who were already on the ground were reduced to unrecognisable pulp beneath the feet of elephants and their fellowmen. People standing in the mud on the beach were pressed into the water and carried away. The police made an ineffectual lathi charge. The death-roll was given, officially, as five hundred, and two thousand injured. No one in Allahabad believes this figure to be a true one — most estimates run into thousands. Perhaps two thousand dead would be a more accurate figure.

Both the President, Dr. Prasad and the Prime Minister, Mr. Nehru, were present and a Commission was set up by the Government of Uttar Pradesh to inquire into the affair. It never questioned the number of dead; in fact it never mentioned the death-roll at all. It made a number of recommendations, some of which were connected with the number of police necessary to control five million pilgrims, but it devoted a large part of its published report to an erudite examination of the origins of the Mela, for which it commissioned the services of a number of astrologers and scholars.*

The peak time for bathing was between nine and one o'clock. By good fortune we met Bag Nath and Hira Lal, our boatmen, and they insisted on taking us out to the Sangam in their boat. They said it had taken them eight days to tow it up from Mirzapur.

We bathed at the confluence where the long curving line of bathing platforms and boats reached out across the Jumna and the Ganges ripped across it.

It was one o'clock and the water was warm. Out in the stream dolphins came to the surface, sighing like steam engines. This was the meeting-place not only of the three rivers but of all humanity. All, together with the lepers, submerging and coming up spluttering, for this was the water that washed all sin away.

The Maharaja of Banaras went up the Jumna in his processional

* *Report of the Committee appointed by the Uttar Pradesh Government to inquire into the mishap which occurred in the Kumbha Mela at Prayaga on 3rd February 1954, Allahabad, 1955.*

barge with a heavy bodyguard of policemen in rowing boats. Long lines of pilgrims were leaving now by boat or walking slowly up the bank of the Jumna, under the walls of the Fort. The sun broke through the clouds and the banners streamed against the sun.

Chapter Twenty-One

From Patna to Bankipore
and back

The name Bankipore has been explained as meaning the city of the banks or fop, on account of its being the quarter of women of ill-fame to which fashionable men resorted. Another suggestion, however, is that it means merely the city on the bank of the river.

Bengal District Gazetteers, Patna, 1907

On 17th January we reached Patna, the capital of Bihar, or rather the railway junction at Bankipore which was adjacent to it. Because we were short of time we had had to travel there by train. It had meant missing Ghazipur, where we had heard that there was still some cultivation of the opium poppy which we were both interested in seeing. Nevertheless, we decided to miss it and concentrate on the lower reaches. We were determined to arrive at Calcutta by water; and we had very little time in which to do so. We experienced the same frustrated sensations as the hero of John Buchan's *Greenmantle* stuck in the woods on the north bank of the Danube with only eighteen days in which to get to Constantinople.

Neither Patna nor Bankipore now merited the aspersions that had been cast on them in former times. Murray's *Handbook to Bengal,* 1882, warned travellers against descending from the train at Patna, "which is not a desirable place for Europeans to alight at." Without specifying why it was unsuitable, it advised them to get down at Bankipore station. But it then went on to describe it as "inconvenient" and was uncomplimentary about the cabs.

A number of what were quite possibly the same horse-drawn vehicles still stood in the station yard at the Junction. Some resembled broken-down droshkies; but the most extraordinary were what the porters referred to as "boogis", perhaps a derivation from buggies, although they looked nothing like buggies. They were really palankeens on wheels, carriages the shape of a match box in which the fare crouched or lay fully extended as the spirit moved him. They were fitted with sliding doors which, if they were both closed while the passenger was inside, would ensure his death by asphyxiation in a matter of minutes.

We set off on foot to see the town, or rather the three towns which stretched for more than nine miles along the right bank of the river — the Old City of Patna, and the "new" City of Patna which was separated from the old, rather mysteriously, by Bankipore: the result being that during the time we were there we were never certain which city we were in.

There was yet another city, but this one, like the sacred river Sarasvati at Allahabad, was for the most part invisible, hidden under the others. This was the enormous city of Pataliputra, the capital of the Mauryan Empire whose three Emperors, Chandra Gupta, Bindusara and Asoka the Buddhist Emperor had in the years between 321 and 231 B.C. extended it from Afghanistan to the Godaveri river in the Deccan, an empire which was kept going at least in its formative stages, by a system of spies and informers. Pataliputra was ten miles long and two miles wide. The houses were built of wood. The city was moated on the landward side and it was surrounded by a wooden palisade which had 570 towers and 64 gates set in it. Megasthenes, who was sent as ambassador to the court of Chandra Gupta in 303 B.C. by Seleukos Nikator, King of Syria, after his master had suffered a humiliating military reverse which had forced him to withdraw from Afghanistan, gave an interesting account of what the city was like. It was the Emperor Asoka who turned it from a city of wood into a city of stone palaces, temples and dwelling houses surrounded by stone walls; stones which are still much prized by the dhobis for walloping dirty linen on when, from time to time, they come to the surface. At this time it was said to have 450,000 inhabitants.

When the Chinese pilgrim Hwen Thsang visited Pataliputra towards the middle of the seventh century he found a small town of not more than a thousand houses on the banks of the Ganges surrounded by a deserted city with the remains of monasteries, Hindu and Buddhist temples in hundreds and the foundations of the wall of the city. It is possible that the Huns sacked it at the end of the sixth century. The final destruction was carried out by the iconoclastic Sasanka, king of Central Bengal.

Most of the public buildings in New Patna dated from the 1920s — not a particularly happy period for official architecture anywhere. On the north was the Maidan which contained within it a racecourse and a golf links, both of which were disused. To the south were the district jail, a lunatic asylum, the dak bungalow at which we had put up and an enormous post office, in which somewhere, we were certain, all our mail was secreted. There was also the Oriental Library which was supposed to contain the only volumes which survived the sack of Cordova by the Moors.

The most impressive building was the Gola, or granary, an immense structure ninety-six feet high with walls twelve and a half feet thick built of brick which resembled half an egg, a beehive, an observatory or a great steamed pudding done up in a white cloth, according to how the spirit moved one. It had been constructed at the instigation of Warren Hastings by Captain Garstin of the Engineers who completed it in 1786 and it had taken two and a half years to build. It was intended as a safeguard against famine, and its capacity was said to be 137,000 tons of grain. No one had ever succeeded in filling it, because the only way to do so was through a hole in the top and the builders had designed the doors at the foot in such a way that they would only open inwards. If two people stood on opposite sides of the interior it was said to be possible to duplicate the effect of the whispering gallery in St. Paul's. For many years it had been used for storing furniture but now it had reverted to the use for which it had been intended.

When we arrived there in the afternoon the approaches to the entrance doors were blocked by bullock carts and men were carrying sacks into the vast domed interior. Because of the din it was not possible to make the whispering test.

On the outside two sets of stairs spiralled up to the top. The thought of men being expected to carry 137,000 tons of grain to the summit sack by sack was an awe-inspiring one, but as it had never happened and the filling hole at the top had always remained sealed there was no need to feel very worried about it. The only person who is remembered as having climbed the steps, other than as a sightseer, was the Jang Bahadur of Nepal who is said to have ridden a horse to the top and down again.

From the summit the river could be seen flowing down in a great curve past the city, half a mile wide at this season and beyond it to the north the flats stretched away as far as the eye could see, having just received the waters of two other rivers, the Gogra and the Son, the junction of which took place some fifteen miles upstream in the middle of gigantic wastes of sand and islands of alluvial silt.

In the latter part of the nineteenth century the India General Steam Navigation Company had operated a steamer service on the Gogra as far as Fyazabad, the one time capital of the king of Oudh a hundred and fifty miles up, which at one time was known by the delightful name of Bungle, as well as on the Ganges to Allahabad and beyond.

During the Mutiny the Government hired the entire fleet to carry troops up the river.

In the '60s the shipping companies began to go into a decline as the trade in indigo, on which the steamers had relied for their return cargoes, had collapsed with the introduction of chemical dyes (most of the outward freight upriver was piece goods from Manchester) and in 1860 the East India Railway reached Patna. In the '70s the India General started to carry jute from East Bengal to the mills on the Hooghly and the Ganges became more and more neglected as a trade route. By the end of the century, apart from some craft of shallow draft the regular service only extended upstream as far as Patna. Finally in 1957 the Company ceased to operate on the Ganges altogether. A hundred years previously there had been at least five feet of water in the river all the year round as far up as Allahabad. By 1957 the depths upstream of Patna were between three feet and two feet six in the dry season.

Now out of the murk big country boats called pansuhi or bhurs came running down the river under a single square set on a rough yard which was slung from an equally rough mast. They had high sterns, low bluff bows and triangular rudders, and they were completely decked in with what looked like a nissen hut made from bamboo and thatch.

Moored alongside the staging at the principal ghat there was an ancient stern wheeler. Further upstream there was another vessel, this one with side-paddles, high and dry on the shore, which would never sail again; and down by the burning ghats a gentleman said that they were putting in electric ovens; but as he also said that the boats running downstream would reach Calcutta, which was over 400 miles away by rail, in thirty hours it was difficult to know whether to believe him.

Disregarding the advice of the *Handbook to Bengal,*"The traveller, if he pleases, may make an excursion to Dinapur, and then to the confluence of the Soane, but there are no buildings of any interest to be seen there", we walked for miles up the river bank through brick-fields and the suburbs of Dinapore. It was not an inspiring walk and when, just as the sun was setting, on impulse I suggested that we should go on board one of the bhurs which was just about to set off downstream to Bankipore, Wanda was not enthusiastic.

"We'll be there in half an hour with this wind," I said, and she allowed herself to be persuaded, sinking as I did up to my knees in mud as we struggled aboard. No sooner had we done so than the wind died away completely. Our bhur was one of a fleet of half a dozen similar vessels and their crews, as soon as the wind died, put out sweeps with three men to each of them, all of whom worked with a will. All except the crew of our bhur, which consisted of only two men of a markedly languid disposition (they only had one sweep anyway and they showed no inclination to use it). Soon the other boats out-distanced us and disappeared downstream into the darkness and we were left alone crouched on the thatched roof of a dud bhur drifting down the Ganges, and it was damnably cold.

We begged the boatmen to either put us ashore or start rowing, they affected not to understand. They were in no hurry. Perhaps wherever they were bound for was worse than the middle of the river on a near freezing moonless winter night. As a result it took us two and a half hours to cover three miles and we arrived at Patna more dead than alive. A long ride in a cycle ricksha to the Dak bungalow where there was no water, no glasses to drink from and no way of obtaining any as the custodian had gone off, ended this fearful excursion and after an equally fearful dinner eaten in a restaurant which, apart from ourselves, was empty, we returned to the bungalow to sleep in a pair of narrow beds, separated from one another by swathes of mosquito netting, bad-tempered, exhausted and cast down by the fact that we had found no mail at the post office although we were convinced that it was waiting there.

At five a.m. the next morning we were woken by a maniac who circled the building chanting. There was still no one to ask for water and it was in these circumstances, and partly because of my ill-considered boat trip, that Wanda announced her departure for Delhi.

"No one has ever treated me like this," she said tragically. "I am going and I am never coming back to you ever."

Genuinely terrified at losing my only companion and one who had put up with me so much, I apologised to her, and to make up for everything took her to the railway station where she was served with a particularly ghastly breakfast. When we returned to the bungalow we found that our room and all the others in the building had been bespoken by the delegates to a Birth Control Conference who were already swarming on the steps and looking through our keyhole. We had to leave immediately and we did, pursued by the keeper of the Dak bungalow who, having been invisible since our arrival now had the impertinence to demand baksheesh.

In spite of this unpromising beginning we had a good day; really because of the kindness of the head of the Water Transport Board who himself acted as guide. Like a Londoner entertaining a visitor from abroad, in the process he himself saw a number of things which he did not know existed.

We saw what remained of the Opium Godown, the oldest European building in Patna. It was the headquarters of the Government Press and Mr. Chatterjee, the head of it, rang bells vigorously to summon various old men who might remember what it was like when it was a centre of the opium traffic. Unfortunately there was not much for them to remember, as most of the warehouses had collapsed in the course of an earthquake in 1934; but the high old brick walls which had enclosed it were still standing and one immense, two-storied building on the ground floor was full of compositors. The upper floor was equally crowded with clerks who stood up like schoolboys as we all trooped through – for by now we formed a large body of persons.

Underneath the building there was a vaulted cellar with greasy black marks on the walls which one of the old men said were made by opium, and in a dark corner there was the entrance to an underground passage which another old man said led to Delhi.

The preparation of the opium which for centuries was the principal industry in the district was a long, drawn-out business. The poppies, a white variety, flowered in January and February, and the cultivators agreed in advance to deliver all the opium which they produced to the Government at a fixed rate. The actual cultivation was extremely hard work and involved much ploughing, weeding and manuring. In February and March, after the petals had been removed and made into a sort of cake which was later used as a package for the actual opium, the capsules of the plant were lanced in the afternoon and the drops which they exuded collected the following morning. In April the country people brought it in for weighing. The manufacture of "provision" opium, opium intended for export, began at the end of April and continued until the end of July. What eventually resulted from the various processes was a sphere the size of a twenty-four-pound cannon ball made from the poppy leaves and held together by a paste of opium which contained the opium – each of which weighed 1 seer 7½ chittacks.*

* The reader may like to work this out for himself. According to *The Indian Imperial Tables of Weights, Measures, Prices, Bullions and Exchange*; James Bridgnell, Calcutta, 1817:

3lb = 1 seer 7 chittacks (Indian Weight)
3lb = 1 seer 9 chittacks (Factory Weight)

"Seer: A denomination of weight varying in different parts of India from over 3lb to 8oz" (*Shorter Oxford English Dictionary*).

The local consumption was considerable. Most of it, however, went to China. But even in the 1900s the cultivation was decreasing, due to the amount of work it involved and the increase in the prices fetched by other crops, particularly cereals.

Chapter Twenty-Two

Cooking a Baffat

That same afternoon, while we were all recovering from the marathon sight-seeing tour of Patna and Bankipore, the head of the Water Transport Board announced that he had arranged for us to travel down the river in a motor-boat belonging to the railways which was leaving early the following morning from a place called Mokameh Ghat for Manihari, a place on the left bank of the Ganges a couple of hundred miles downstream from Patna where the Ganges makes its last big bend to the south before it enters the sea.

Thankfully we abandoned the negotiations which we had started with the owner of another bhur, a similar boat to the one on the roof of which we had travelled down to Patna the previous evening.

"Good," said Wanda, who had had enough of bhurs, when she heard the news. "I did not want to travel in those boats."

There was just time before the train left for her to pay a last visit to the Post Office, where she persuaded one of the clerks to allow her to sort through the pigeon-holes of poste-restante mail. This time her diligence was rewarded; filed away under my Christian name were a number of letters.

At Mokameh Junction terrible confusion reigned. The night air was filled with the smoke from the cooking fires of the vendors of hot food, strange unidentifiable smells and the moaning of the poor. A horde of fierce-looking porters took up our luggage and set off with it at a brisk trot stepping on the women and children who crouched among their bundles in the booking-hall.

There were no trains to Mokameh Ghat any more, but just as we were beginning to enter into negotiations with a couple of ricksha men, a party of engineers from a nearby oil refinery hailed us with cheerful cries, offering to give us a lift in their jeep.

"Plenty of room! Plenty of room!", they said.

Altogether there were four of us, together with all the baggage crammed into the jeep, and two more, hanging on the back. "All is well! All is well," they shouted, even when the basket containing all the lanterns and the bottle of lime juice fell off while we were travelling at forty miles an hour. Their insane optimism was justified, for nothing was broken.

We needed their optimism when we arrived at our destination, the "lines" of the employees of the railway at Mokameh Ghat. The house in which it had been arranged that we should spend the night was in total darkness. After some time, during which I blundered about at the back of the house banging on the shutters and waking a lot of dogs, the door was opened by an Anglo-Indian lady who was wrapped in some blankets. She showed us into a Victorian-Gothic room where we left our baggage.

"My husband is still at the workshops," she said. "It is the night of the Satyanaryan Puja."

Until 1954, when a railway bridge was built across the Ganges, Mokameh Ghat was one of the few links between the railway systems north and south of the river. From it passengers, iron ore from North Bihar and freight cars had been ferried across the river on lighters. Now its importance had declined and the workers in the railway yards were mostly employed on repairs to river steamers.

We walked down to the river bank, picking our way across deserted sidings and over platforms on which electric lights blazed as if trains were still expected. The wind keened through the girders which supported the roofs of the platforms. It was very eerie.

It was more cheerful in the workshops where the men had been celebrating the Satyanaryan Puja, in which the tools with which they worked had been blessed, and the party was just breaking up. The priest was packing up his utensils and he offered us a thick mixture of milk and bananas to drink.

While we were consuming this peculiar beverage our host appeared. He was a tall, thin man, wearing a sports coat and flannel trousers. He carried with him an invisible but tangible mantle of gloom, as well he might, living in such a place. Together we went back to the house, passing on the way a floodlit court on which other Anglo-Indians were playing badminton. The house had originally been the Railway Institute – this accounted for the size of the room where we had left our kit which had originally been the billiard hall. No sooner had I got into my sleeping bag than I discovered that I had left my diary which contained all the day-to-day details of our journey on the platform at Mokameh Junction.

I crept out of the house so as not to disturb our hosts, expecting an eight-mile walk, but by a miracle found a ricksha man crouching over a fire by the side of the road. It was cold in the open ricksha

and I was consumed by awful thoughts about what I would do if
my diary was lost, but when I reached the Junction I found that it
had been put in a place of safety in the Assistant Stationmaster's
Office. I need not have worried for, as the Duty Clerk said, as he
handed it over, "Sir, it is of no value to anyone."

In the morning, a cold, clear one, after a large breakfast, we said good-
bye to our hostess. Both she and her husband had been very kind to
us but I had rarely seen two people in such a state of despair. Under
British rule their position, and those of other Anglo-Indians like them,
had been unsatisfactory; but, at least as trusted railway officials, they
had been part of a hierarchy, although almost completely cut off from
the rest of it socially. Now they were like stateless persons. Their only
hope seemed to lie in abandoning their Englishness and becoming as
Indian as possible.

The motor-boat was lying alongside one of the paddle-steamers.
The crew were already on board and the engine was running. There
were five of them: the Captain, the Pilot – a tiny little man with a
ragged moustache who sat up in the bows wrapped in a blanket – the
Engineer and two deck-hands. As soon as the luggage was stowed
aboard we set off. Our last sight of the tragic figure of our kind
host was waving to us from the deck of one of the paddle-steamers.

How good it was to be back on the Ganges. We had never
travelled so fast on it. We swept down towards the bridge, which
was a mile long, at fifteen knots, just as a freight train rumbled over
it. The river itself was half a mile wide, but below the bridge it
broadened still more. To the left, by the bridge, a tall factory
chimney discharged puffs of smoke into the air like a cannon. Here,
on the north side of the river, the country was marshy and, according
to the Captain, these flats were the roosting places of thousands of
water birds which passed the winter nights there in the branches
of the marsh oak trees which grow in the shallow water.

It was a strange sensation being in a boat with a Captain, a
Pilot and a real crew. For the first time since leaving Hardwar, we
were in a boat with nothing to do. It was the forty-third day of our
journey and sitting on the deck, looking across the water was like
many other days we had spent on the Ganges but all run into one reel
and speeded up. Women in mustard-coloured saris were bathing in the
river and we passed villages of houses built of brick and mud with
red-tiled roofs and with cows and water-buffaloes huddled under the
walls and others roofless and deserted. We passed dead palm trees
which looked like old bent candles standing alone or in pairs in

the flat countryside, groves of mangoes and willows with their branches streaming in the wind, and banyans balanced precariously on eroded earthless roots. We swept down past small white-spired temples, old men sitting in niches carved in the banks and places where little fleets of fishing-boats were moored under steep banks which had been worn as smooth and shiny as leather by the stream.

The navigation was difficult but the pilot never spoke. He leaned over the bows sniffing the river through his ragged moustache like a clever old hound on a scent. Sometimes he raised his hand and one of the deck-hands put a sounding pole over the side; sometimes he pointed to the left or the right and the boat crawled off across the stream at right angles to it; sometimes he waggled his hand and the helmsman reversed until he could nose it into another channel.

The boat only drew two and a half feet; but the river was a maze of shoals, and it was full of culs-de-sac with corpses floating in them on which big grey gulls paced up and down. In the narrows the water seethed like a pot of brown soup on the boil and in the long, wider reaches, where the silt had a chance to settle, it was a brilliant shade of turquoise. In these deep places dolphins came to the surface and nuzzled the bows of the boat.

Sitting on the roof of the engine-room, looking down into this great and noble river, the face of which was capable of such extraordinary changes of expression all in the space of a few moments, we both experienced that feeling which comes so rarely to human beings of wishing that the moment in which we were living might be infinitely prolonged.

The wind increased; sand licked across the empty wastes to the left and the sky turned from blue to brown. The river was very shoal now. It swirled angrily round little ponds of calm water and we grounded twice, much to the pilot's disgust.

"He has spent all his life on this river," said the Captain. "He is a fisherman but no man can know Ganga. She is always changing." He was an imperturbable, friendly man.

At noon the Kharagpur Hills began to loom out of the haze to the south-east. Although they were not more than sixteen hundred feet high, there in the plain they were as impressive as the Himalayas. We passed two jagged reefs with navigational marks on them, the first rocks we had seen in the Ganges since our arrival at Bindhachal on the way down from Allahabad.

By one-thirty Monghyr was abeam on a promontory, partly hidden behind the walls and bastions of the fort. Long flights of golden steps led down to the river and red-sailed country boats were beating up close to the shore with a sort of drogue out on their weather sides to keep them on the wind; others were running down before it — bows on the big sails with the sheets free looked like spinnakers. Ten minutes later we fetched up under the north-west corner of the fort.

As soon as the boat was tied up, everyone, except the Captain and the Pilot, scampered down the gang-plank which had been run out over the muddy foreshore and disappeared up the steps of the ghat.

"The name of this ghat is Kashtarini Ghat," the Captain said. "It means bathing-place which destroys pain. They have gone to eat. After eating in Monghyr they will need this bath which destroys pain."

The beautiful, crumbling ramparts of the fort were partly enclosed by a deep moat, filled with vegetation. The ramparts enclosed some less lovely buildings, court houses and bungalows built at the turn of the last century; but up on one of the bastions on the west side, there was the plain tomb of a poet named Ashraf, and the view westwards up the Ganges from it was all and more than a poet could wish.

Ashraf was the son of a mullah who lived by the Caspian sea and he had given lessons to the daughter of Aurangzeb who was herself a poetess. In 1672 he took long leave of absence and went to Ispahan in Persia. He died at Monghyr while on his way to Mecca in 1704. We did not, of course, know all this, or of the existence of the tomb, but fortunately we met a diminutive schoolboy trailing along the road who spoke a little English and he offered to take us to it.

"He was a poet," he said as we stood gazing at the unremarkable tomb. " 'Ow do you do?"

It was difficult to know whether he was addressing us or the long dead Ashraf.

"Dead, dead, dead," he said. "The poet is dead." He was a strange little boy.

Almost every European who visited Monghyr seems to have liked it. Warren Hastings enjoyed the air. Bishop Heber on his way upstream from Calcutta in 1823 remarked that the walls and gates of the Fort were "Asiatic ... and precisely similar to those of the Khitairgorod of Moscow," and that the Kharagpur Hills were "not inferior to the Halkin mountains and the ranges above Flint and Holywell." He also said that "the guns made there were very likely to burst and the knives to break — precisely the faults which, from want of capital, beset the works of inferior artists in England."

In November 1837, the Honourable Emily Eden, the author of *Up the Country*, visited the hot springs at Sitakund which lie a mile or two beyond the town. Sitakund is the place where Sita, the wife of Rama, having been rescued by her husband from Ravana the demon king, immolated herself in order to prove her chastity to her husband. Having emerged unscathed but overheated from the flames she entered the pool the temperature of which has fluctuated between 100 and 138 degrees Fahrenheit ever since, according to the season. "It is the first time for two years I have felt the carriage going uphill," she wrote. Fanny Parks, the adventurous authoress of *Wanderings of a Pilgrim in Search of the Picturesque*, visiting Monghyr in 1844, found the beggars "a pest" and that "the people selling pistols, necklaces, bathing chairs, baskets, toys, shoes, etc., raised such a hubbub that it was disgusting." But she liked the fort and the temples and she found "the black vases, turned in white wood and lacquered whilst on the lathe with sealing wax, pretty."

She also went to Sitakund. "The water is pure," she said. "It keeps like Bristol water on a long voyage; people returning to England make a point of stopping here on that account."

Monghyr was the scene of the extraordinary "White Mutiny" of 1766 in which a number of officers of the First Brigade, dissatisfied because their field allowance had been reduced, decided to send in their commissions and informed Lord Clive of what they were doing in a joint letter.

Clive immediately despatched a number of reliable officers by forced marches to Monghyr and himself set off for the place. The advance guard found the European regiment officerless, drinking, singing and beating drums. The next day the soldiers mutinied and there followed the extraordinary spectacle of British infantry and artillery-men being disarmed at musket point by sepoys of a battalion of native infantry which one of Clive's officers had fetched from Kharagpur, over the hills.

It was difficult to feel very enthusiastic about the town itself. Most of it had been rebuilt after an earthquake had partially destroyed the place in 1934. A few shops sold spear-heads and daggers; but although there was supposed to be a considerable business in ebony, the only ebony article we saw was a truncheon in one of the weapon shops. More attractive were the articulated silver fish which are made at Kharagpur, and are sold, like all silver objects, by weight.

At a quarter to three we returned to the motor-boat feeling rather empty. The crew of course, had not returned.

"They are coming," said the Captain, equably; but by three o'clock there was still no sign of them.

"Boggers," said Wanda, happily. "I am going shopping," and before anyone could stop her she was gone, carrying her useful bag.

No sooner had she departed than the crew appeared. At first I fumed, thinking of all the things I had missed seeing: the house of General Ghurgin Khan, an eighteenth-century Armenian gunmaker who had been in charge of the arsenal, the hot spring at Sitakund and the Dargah of Shah Nafah, a mysterious building (mysterious because we had been unable to find it) which enclosed the grave of a Muslim saint who had appeared to the Governor of Monghyr in a dream, and whose corpse had given off a scent of musk in 1492. But the river-front was so beautiful in the afternoon sunshine with a force five wind blowing, more like a seaport painted by Rex Whistler than a place on a river, that it was impossible to care very much whether I had seen them or not.

At a quarter past four Wanda returned with her useful bag bulging.

"We were waiting for you," the Captain said.

"I also do not like waiting for other people," she replied.

As we chugged downstream Wanda began to prepare the dinner. According to her it was to be a Mutton Baffat, a complicated dish, for which she had been given the recipe at Banaras. It was remarkable for the number of ingredients which were necessary for its preparation. It required mutton, cloves, cinnamon, onions, green chillies, garlic, ginger, vinegar, powdered red chillies, cummin seeds, turmeric, coriander, poppy seeds, groundnuts, lentils, butter, salt, potatoes, white radishes, coconut and water.

The only part of the recipe which she found confusing was the part which dealt with the coconut.

"What I can't understand is — it says, 'add second extract of coconut to the meat,' and later on 'add first extract'," she said, working away with a roller and a flat stone which she had borrowed from one of the deck hands who also acted as cook.

"I suppose it depends on which end you open the nut," I said.

"And it says 'Dose of onion, 113 grams'; but I'm not putting onions in."

"It will be no good without onion," the Captain said.

"Well, I don't like onions," she said, defiantly.

By four-thirty Monghyr was nothing but a smudge at the foot of the Kharagpur Hills and ours was the only boat on the huge expanse of the river. The only signs of life were on the left bank on which hordes of men and women were building an embankment, using pink, square blocks of stone that looked like pieces of raw meat which they bedded down and then covered with wire mesh to prevent them being swept away.

According to the Captain the men earned one rupee a day for this work; the women only 12 annas.*

The stream took us away from the left bank and the people on it, into the middle of the river among huge sandbanks which, in the pale evening light, merged imperceptibly with the sky. Here, for the first time, there was an abundance of navigation marks — a single spar with two cross-pieces for the starboard hand, knotted plumes of grass on sticks for port. The air was full of small birds, and as the sun sank a thin, crescent moon rose as if to redress the loss of it.

As soon as the sun was gone the Captain anchored. There was no question of worrying about the amenities on the banks. The Pilot let his hand fall and the anchor was dropped in midstream.

Wanda now began to cook the Mutton Baffat. The preparation had been a complex operation. She had ground the spices with vinegar, boiled the radish in salt water, mixed the cut-up meat with the red chillies, mustard and cummin seeds and the turmeric, all of which she had ground up together with four peppercorns on the flat stone. She had sliced the green chillies, the garlic and the ginger and now she added the broiled and ground coriander, the poppy seeds, the groundnuts and the lentils, following the recipe which read like a prescription. "Dosage," it read. "One dose Poppy Seeds, 14 gms. Dose Vinegar, 28 gms," and so on. As each fresh ingredient was added she dropped another paper bag on the deck. There was little that I could do. I stood over her, knee-deep in receptacles, holding a kerosene lantern, like a surgeon's mate in a field operating-theatre in the Crimea.

Down in the stern the crew were getting on with their own meal but the Captain still watched, entranced. He watched her add the so-called "second extract" of coconut milk to the meat and the mass of spices, the sliced ginger, the garlic and the green chillies. He watched her cook this huge mess until the meat was, in theory, tender.

"Put the radishes in now," he said.

There was a short interval and then, without being told to, she put in the "first extract" of coconut milk.

"You must put in the onion," the Captain said.

* See note on p. 30.

"What onion? I'm not having onions."

"You are not putting in all the onions but must put in half an onion. You must make it brown in fat and add to Baffat. Without the onion Baffat is no good."

"I'm not having any onions. I've got to eat it, too. It's my Baffat."

"You have spoiled the Baffat," said the Captain. He was genuinely upset.

"Bring the chapatis!" he shouted. "The Lady has cooked her Baffat."

"Please have some," Wanda said. "There is enough for everyone." It was an understatement. I had never seen so much food.

"I am sorry," he said, laying his hand on his breastbone as if he was suffering from heartburn, "but it is against my religion."

"What about the others?"

"It is against their religion, too."

"Just because I left out the onions."

"No, no, not because of the onions. I am telling you the truth. It is against the religion."

For what seemed hours we plugged away at the Baffat; but however much we ate we seemed to make no impression on what remained. From time to time a bubble forced its way up from the bottom of the pot. It was like trying to empty a pool of radio-active mud which was constantly renewing itself from the interior of the earth. All the time we were eating, fresh piles of chapatis were arriving from the after deck. It was delicious but all the time I was eating it I wondered what it would have been like with the onion.

When it came to all seven of us bedding down for the night, there was not much room. Wanda slept in the well of the foredeck; the Captain and the Pilot on two benches on either side of her, the engineer slept on the roof of the engine-room and the deck-hands on the narrow strips of deck on either side of it. I slept on what, in a larger vessel, would have been the fo'c'sle head, on top of the anchor cable which was of stout chain. A strong wind was blowing up the river against the stream raising a lop, and as the boat surged in it the cable alternately slackened and tautened underneath me. All through the night jackals howled out on the sand, and while it was still dark the chantings of hardy souls performing their pujas in the wilderness mingled with them. The dawn came at six, very strong and red; then the sun rose in the shape of an egg, distorted by the haze of dust that filled the sky. It was the coldest night that we had experienced on the Ganges.

As soon as the sun was up it vanished into a bank of cloud. The wind blew through our clothes like paper. It was like a January morning on the Mersey. There was none of the high spirits of the previous evening and for us there was some particularly ghastly washing up to be done. To the right in the far distance were the outlines of a range of flattened-out hills; geese rose like jets from the huge expanses of the left bank and overhead in long skeins rising and falling in unison as if they were chained together; astern, to the west, the sky was streaked with black clouds, as if a child had been scribbling with a crayon on a sheet of grey paper. Wanda made tea for everyone and we began to feel better.

Gradually the wind that had tormented us all through the night and the early morning fell away and towards eight o'clock it died completely. A thick fog descended on the river and, with the sun shining through it, it was as if the boat was suspended in a bowl of melted butter. Then it cleared. Ahead, in the middle of the river where it made a bend to the north, there was an island, a huge pile of rocks that might have been stacked up by a child with a white temple on the top of it glistening in the sun. To the right, separated from it by some hundreds of yards of river there was a high, green headland surmounted by a mosque, its base heaped with boulders as huge as those on the island. Below it there was a little landlocked inlet on the shores of which tall palm trees rose in solitary splendour and from it flights of ruined steps led up into a little town. The waters of this inlet were of the consistency of olive oil, undisturbed by a single ripple, and far out white-clad bathers were performing their pujas, lifting the water slowly as if it was heavy and letting it fall slowly through their fingers back into the river. Closer inshore, golden-skinned Brahmans were washing bundles of sacred grass. Deep-loaded boats full of pilgrims were setting out from the shore for the island, which was called Jahngira, one of the most sacred places on the Ganges, which was here called Uttara Bahini, "the reach where the river turns to the north". There are three places on the Ganges which are esteemed for this reason, but this is the most holy of all. It was a beautiful scene and a visual affirmation of what Hinduism could mean to those who practised it.

We landed a little upstream of the town of Sultanganj and set off with the Captain through some dusty lanes to buy some fish for which we had developed a morbid craving as, so far, we had not succeeded in eating any while on the river. Whenever we tried to buy fish it was either just about to arrive or had just been sold. We were like those persistent investigators who, for years and years had endeavoured, in vain, to witness a performance of the Indian Rope Trick.

The earthquake that had destroyed the town of Monghyr had done the same job at Sultanganj and the main street was equally debased, except that here it was decorated with paper streamers, for this was the morning of the Sarasvati puja in honour of Spring.*

The little cobbled lanes that led down from the main street to the water were decorated with arches of banana leaves and in the court-yards of the houses that led off them the clay figures of Sarasvati, the wife of Brahma the Creator, painted white, full-breasted, black-haired with a crescent moon on their foreheads, sitting on lotus leaves and holding lyres were waiting to be put in the river. There was the sound of drums; long-haired Santal women, aborigines from the edge of the high tableland above the river, trotted down carrying baskets on bamboo poles; old men and women squatted behind mounds of freshly soldered conical containers made from tin cans, in which pilgrims would take home the water of the river for those unfortunates who had not been able to make the journey to it.

We came out on the river-front and across the water the island of Jahngira rose from the water, mysterious, unearthly, irresistible. It was so irresistible that, in spite of being loaded with the fish, which was wrapped in straw we decided to go there.

A boat was just leaving and, together with the Captain, we waded out into the river and got on board. It was full of country people all of whom were provided with conical pots. As the boat began to move the women began a dirge-like chant which they kept up until we were close in under the huge, pale rocks of the island which the river had worn away until they were as sharp as stone age axes.

The landing was on the south side. From it a long flight of steps led up to small, subsidiary temples that seemed to be part of the rocks themselves, from which sprouted mysteriously, for there appeared to be no soil for them to flourish in, a number of twisted trees. The steps were crowded with bathers dressed in brilliant shades of red, blue, saffron and gleaming white. They were like the steps of a cathedral after a royal wedding, only here the congregation was unconscious of its fine appearance and the air was full of happy cries and laughter. It was different in the rainy season, the Captain said. Then, when the Ganges rose thirty feet, the Mahant, the head of the monastery, and his disciples were often cut off from the shore for weeks at a time, as isolated as lighthouse-keepers.

* The Festival of Vasanta Panchami takes place on the fifth day of the light half of Magh. Sarasvati is worshipped in her manifestation as goddess of speech and learning.

Over the steps loomed a bulbous rock decorated with figures of the elephant god, lingams and a figure that might have come from an Egyptian rock tomb whom the Captain said was Parasurama, "Rama with the axe", the sixth incarnation of Vishnu, and there were other, more ancient carvings of Buddha, one in a pose of meditation, the other standing.

The north side of the island was as deserted as the south side was crowded. There, on another enormous rock which had toppled over so that she was forty degrees out of the perpendicular, was a spirited carving of Ganga, narrow-waisted and wide-hipped, standing on her crocodile which had its mouth open, as if displeased at the weight he was being called upon to support. The island was a maze of caves and paths which wound up it to the top where, seventy feet above the water, there was a dark, cavernous temple called Gebinath in which a number of priests were crouched pouring water over a lingam from spouted pots. There was a strange, eerie atmosphere about this temple which contrasted with the happy scene out in the sunshine on the steps below.

On the western outskirts of the town was the palace of a Maharaja who had been one of the biggest landowners in Bihar. It was approached by a long, stony drive at the foot of which a sort of guard-house-cum-porter's-lodge was being built. The palace was built in the White City oriental style which was popular in India in the twenties, with five white domes and some meretricious decoration. Under the glass porte-cochère there were rotting trophies of the chase and a huge beaten-up American automobile stood on the gravel sweep. Beyond it, on a little patch of grass and looking benevolently down the drive, a highly life-like marble statue of the previous Maharaja stood under a baldacchino.

We rang the bell and sent in a visiting card, and after an interval the brother-in-law of the present Maharaja appeared. He apologised for the Prince's absence as if it was some gross social solecism.

"He works for Tata, you know," he said. "That is why he is not here to welcome you."

Another brother was a professor in the United States; the third had been killed in a hunting accident. He took us into a drawing-room which was more like an audience chamber than a living room. It was very formal and rather sad with long lines of uncomfortable chairs along the walls, moth-eaten tiger skins on the floor and on the walls portraits of Maharajas dead and gone. On a table there was a beautiful Sitar, a seven-stringed instrument like a guitar, in a painted case.

He led us into what had been a colonnaded courtyard. The spaces between the columns had been bricked up to enclose what were now the female quarters. Wanda asked him if she could go in, but was politely refused. When we left various handsome little upper-class girls and boys emerged to stare at us. It was an Indian Brideshead.

On the way back to the boat we met two young men dressed in loincloths who were performing some kind of penance. From a distance they looked as if they were doing press-ups. One behind the other they prostrated themselves, measuring their lengths and rubbing their foreheads in the thick dust. Then they rose to their feet, walked forward until they reached the marks which their foreheads had made and prostrated themselves again. Behind them the imprints made by their bodies stretched away up the road, recording their devoted progression.*

We sailed again at eleven. South of Sultanganj the river was almost featureless; the sun was hot and there was a flat calm. We stretched out on the roof of the engine room and immediately fell asleep.

I woke to find myself being rolled backwards and forwards on the roof by the Captain. He seemed to think I was a chapati.

"Wake up! Wake up!" he said. "It is four o'clock. We are by Colganj."

The boat was running before a strong breeze and there were white caps on the water. At the foot of a long strip of sand a country boat with a big red square mainsail with a topsail set over it was in irons, and beyond it, towards the northern bank, a whole fleet of similar ones were tearing down the river. Ahead there was an island with a high, tree-clad promontory at its western end on which a red flag was flying on a pole which rose above the trees. Someone up there had a fire going and the smoke was being whipped downstream by the wind.

I woke Wanda, using the Captain's dough-rolling technique. It took some time and after a bit I began to wonder if she had died. When she came to she was very grumpy.

"Can't you leave me alone," she said. "When I am with you I never get any sleep."

The island was abeam now. Well-fed black cattle were grazing in green water meadows which, in the rains, would be deep underwater. Isolated from one another by these lush pastures, curious clusters of

---

* The six years' pilgrimage from the source of the Ganges to the mouth and back again is called Pradakshina. Some devotees perform it by measuring their lengths.

rocks shaped like huge beehives rose into the air, half-hidden among
the trees which grew from them. Downstream there was what looked
like another island with a white tower, like a lighthouse, on a point
and high red cliffs behind it.

We came in round the bottom end of the island, into what was
really a silted-up channel of the river where, behind a sand bar, there
was a small harbour in which a dozen country boats were loading
stone for the embankments that the men and women were building
further upstream.

On the river-front there were some ruinous brick buildings, one
of which had a bricked-up baroque gateway which had once opened
on to the water. It was probably an old indigo factory. A mile or so
inland there was a steep hill with a fine old European house on the
summit of it.

Chapter Twenty-Three

The islands at Colganj

Whoever visits this place forgets to return.
Hwen Thsang, writing of the islands at Colganj,
7th century A.D.

We landed on the south side of the island and walked up through the meadows to the high western end. According to one of the crew who knew the place well, there were three sadhus on the island. The western group of rocks, to which we were now going, was occupied by the Panjabi Baba who had lived there for five or six years. At the eastern end lived the Shanta Baba who was the successor to the Naga Baba, a venerable man who had been the incumbent some years before. A third cluster of rocks in the middle of the island was the residence of another Baba who was not often there.

"The Panjabi Baba and the Shanta Baba are very holy men," our informant said. "They only take disciples who are very poor. The other Baba passes most of his days at Banaras," he added, ominously.

The little cluster of rocks which was the retreat of the Panjabi Baba was an enchanting place. They were concealed by a wilderness of vegetation and noble trees through which the wind poured with a sound like a distant waterfall and the pendant, aerial roots of a banyan which hung down searching for earth in which to anchor themselves.

On the flat summit overlooking the river, was the cell of the holy man. A log was smouldering in a pit, producing the smoke which we had seen from the boat; the bedding was stacked neatly against the walls and there was a little shrine with images of Ganga and Sarasvati. Behind the cell a winding path led through the trees to a small, well-tended garden full of flowers, which resembled camellias. While we were there a shy young man wearing a red robe came out of the trees. He was the Panjabi Baba's disciple. He said that the Baba had gone ashore in order to perform some ceremonial.

He took us down through the trees to a place where there was a Buddhist temple. Hewn out of the rock, it was about twelve feet square and had unusual gable ends which were ornamented with pilasters and curious heads, like cats' heads with pointed ears and long, curled whiskers. Under a vaulted roof there was a small chamber in which it would have been just possible for one of us to crouch if either of us had wished to do so.

The Shanta Baba lived in the heart of his rocks at the lower end of the island. He also had gone ashore for the same reason as the Panjabi Baba — to attend a puja. His disciple was sweeping the platform outside his cell on which an even larger piece of tree trunk than the one at the Panjabi Baba's was burning. The wood which the holy men burnt must have been part of a regular offering, sent from the mainland, otherwise the island would have been entirely deforested centuries ago.

The rocks of the absentee Baba were equally attractive, although at this season they were some way from the water, but either he or his supporters had ruined the appearance of them by building a hideous chalet among them which would have looked more appropriate on the south coast of England. This hauntingly beautiful island was one of the headquarters of the River Thugs who differed from their counterparts on the land by falling on their victims en masse and strangling them from the front rather than from the back.

We tied up not far from the building I had identified, probably incorrectly, as an indigo factory. The foreshore was a very dirty place.

"This is Marganga — 'The Dead Ganges'," said the Captain.

"And it jolly well smells like it," Wanda said.

The sun was setting. We went into the town through streets crowded with empty bullock carts returning from the river where they had been unloading stone. I wanted to reach the house on the hill before it grew dark.

It was a large, two-storied, stuccoed building, deep yellow in the last rays of the sun. Beyond the house, at the end of a ruined and overgrown garden there was a semi-circular belvedere and from it the river could be seen coiling away through the plain like an enormous snake.

It was a place that would have satisfied the most exacting taste for the picturesque but for the presence of a number of local inhabitants most of whom were schoolboys, who had followed us up from the town and who now numbered between fifty and sixty persons. They were there not to instruct us but to amuse themselves, and whenever we stopped to look at something which we found remarkable, whether it was a pavilion with a pipal tree growing through its foundations which had split it neatly in two, or the shattered figures of Buddhas and Hindu gods with which the platform of the belvedere was covered, they invariably asked the same question which they had asked all the way up the hill.

"Oh, what are you looking at?"

Previously I had pretended to ignore them; but now I was desperate. "We are looking at Colganj," I said, as coldly as possible.

From the back of the crowd a fruity voice said in an impertinent but rather good parody of my own: "We are looking at Colganj. Thank you very much!"

"Why are you looking at Colganj?" the spokesman asked, a hairy boy who was badly in need of his first shave.

"You are looking at us. We are looking at Colganj."

I had intended my reply to be offensive. I was tired of being baited; but the crowd found it very amusing. Roaring with laughter they interpreted it to those of their companions who either did not understand English or had not heard what I had said.

"You are looking at us. We are looking at Colganj," they said. "Looking at us. Looking at Colganj." It was as if I had told them a really funny story. There is nothing more infectious than a number of Indians who are all enjoying a good joke, and together they all went down the hill chanting, "Looking at us. Looking at Colganj."

There were no street lights in Colganj. It was the dinner hour and the smoke of cooking-fires hung in the narrow roads like a London fog. Only the lights in the fronts of the little shops gave off a blurred and friendly glow. Down in the lanes towards the river it was quite dark and there the only lights were in the hands of spectral figures who hurried past carrying lanterns. Down by the river, beyond the buildings, it was lighter. The last of the bullock-cart drivers were urging their beasts up the slope from the water which was like a strip of polished steel between the dark banks. Lying off-shore was an old-fashioned steamer with a yacht bow and smoke streaming from its funnel, and beyond it the trees and the clumps of rock on the island where the sadhus lived were silhouetted against the sky.

All the crew, except the one who had been left on board as night-watchman, were still ashore, and while Wanda cooked the fish that we had bought at Sultanganj we drank rum and listened to the sounds of laughter and conversation coming across the water from the boats moored offshore, for the wind had fallen and it was very quiet and still. The moon rose over the island, and from time to time an ancient pumping engine on the bank behind us, which supplied the town with water from the Ganges, emitted fire and smoke and made weird rumbling noises. At seven o'clock the sadhus and their disciples on the island began to perform their pujas. Conches were blown, instruments like motor horns were sounded, and from the shrine of the Shanta Baba came the jangling of bells, tootings and a deeper noise that resembled the droning of bees. It lasted for a quarter of an hour; then it ceased as suddenly as it had begun. By the time the crew returned, having eaten their evening meal on the shore, the fish was ready. It was a rahu, a sort of carp, and fried in clarified butter it was delicious. It was the first fish we had eaten on the river.

Afterwards we sat wrapped in blankets, sharing a cheroot. The crew were preparing for bed. The noise of the pump had stopped. We experienced a great feeling of peace and happiness. Apart from the terrible smell that wafted off the river bank at intervals, this was one of the most beautiful places we had seen on the Ganges; but as Wanda said, "if there wasn't a smell there would probably be something else, and there are worse things than smells."

It was a bitter night. Soon the jackals began. The place was infested with them. They seemed to be on the banks, on the island, everywhere. It was like bedlam. In the night I had an appalling dream in which an unidentifiable animal was standing on my chest eating me. In terror I started up from my place on the fo'c'sle head, and nearly fell overboard. The noise woke the crew who themselves started up, thinking that the boat was being attacked by robbers. The only one who continued to sleep was Wanda.

At five-thirty when the last jackal had howled itself to sleep the pujas began out on the island: "MOOO MOOO," went the conches. "DONG DONG DONG DONGLE DONG DONG" went the bells. "BZZ-BZZ-BZZ," went the bee machine. "HONK HONK HONK," went the motor horns.

At six I went into the town to buy some eggs. The streets had already been swept clean by the sweepers; but apart from some black myna birds pecking about on the cobbles, they were deserted. On the way back I met some men who were saying prayers on their way back from bathing in the river. At six-thirty we sailed. We were still 135 miles from the head of the Bhagirathi and another 200 miles from Calcutta and another 80 miles from the Bay of Bengal, and we only had another seven days in which to cover them.

As if he was trying to ensure that we should not reach Calcutta on time, no sooner had we got going than the Captain headed the boat in towards the temple we had seen the previous day; the one which looked like a lighthouse.

"It is the shrine of the Naga Baba," he said.

By this time we had seen a lot of shrines and to tell the truth we were more or less satiated with them — as indeed the reader probably is if he has got this far — but it seemed churlish to say that we would rather get on.

The Naga Baba had expired some twenty years before, at the ripe age of 108. Personal relics, his bed, a fan and a pair of his socks, were grouped around his statue which was swathed in a saffron-coloured cloth. The shrine was on a promontory. Below it, in the river, there was a curious rock with a small depression on top of it, like the navel of a fat man who was floating on his back. Close to the shrine, under a banyan tree, stood a tall, epicene figure wearing a peach-coloured headcloth and a green dhoti. It held a sheet across its face and its long legs were crossed in the stylised pose adopted by model girls in the West. It never moved. When I asked the Captain what it was, he giggled.

Behind the shrine rose a long, jungle-covered hill called Chaurasi-Murti, the eighty-four statues. It was riddled with caves, one of which was said to be so long that an expedition which a Raja had organised to explore it had had to withdraw without reaching the end, after the 6,400 pounds of lamp oil with which its members had set out had been consumed. Two of the caves had doorways with cut mouldings, similar to the decorations on the great Buddhist Stupa at Sarnath near Banaras. The roof on one of them had collapsed, but it had been restored. Above the cave were the eighty-four images cut in the sandstone. Besides various eroded and otherwise mutilated carvings which depicted scenes of godly violence, there was one of a young woman churning milk. Close by, in a Hindu shrine, a standing Buddha which had lost a leg was being used as an object of devotion. The hill of Chaurasi-Murthi was a lovely, mysterious place.

The stream was nearly three-quarters of a mile wide now, wider than it had ever been. There were many boats being towed upstream against the strong current, three or four men to a boat, the leader sometimes as much as two hundred yards ahead, plodding on with the line over his shoulder and his head down. There were many square-riggers going downstream, most of them loaded with sand — one of them had a lorry on its deck. High over their sterns they had triangular pennants flying from staffs on the rudder posts. We passed a survey boat from which men were taking soundings, using black and white striped poles, with the surveyor sitting on the roof of the deck house on a garden seat; and a motor tug with two barges loaded with stone in tow.

It was going to be a hot day. Everything was wrapped in a haze and the water was like glass with only an occasional ripple on it, but there was twelve feet of it under the boat and that was all that the pilot cared about; further upstream it had been four feet six in the channels and in some places less. Over the river there were geese and cattle egrets and huge flocks of cranes, sixty or seventy to a flock, but they all kept away from us. To the south the Rajmahal Hills began to loom up, but for a long time they were so indistinct that they seemed to be a figment of the imagination.

At midday we reached the station at Manihari Ghat on the great bend of the river. From now on we would always be heading south until we reached the sea. It was an historic moment.

Manihari Station was a place in name only, for, as the Captain said, "Next year, even next week, it will be somewhere else". It was wherever the silt happened to be. To it the railway line from Assam reached out across miles of silt and down through deep cuts in it to the landing stages on the water's edge, from which the ferry-boats and lighters set off carrying passengers and wagons across to the south bank, from where the trains left for Delhi and Calcutta. It was an absurd arrangement rendered necessary by the partition of the country; previously the trains to Assam had travelled by a far more direct route across what was now East Pakistan.

Down by the water, where the hulks were moored which served as landing stages, the air was filled with continuous booming of the silt as whole sections of bank, more than twenty feet high, fell into the river. Every day as the bank receded northwards, the railway itself was forced to retreat and whole sections of line had to be taken up and new cuttings made.

To the south, far away on the wooded south bank of the river, was the Sakrigali Ghat with its temple sprouting up above the trees, and behind it, according to the boatmen, there was the tomb of Saiyad Ahmad Makdhum, whoever he was. Beyond the little hill on which the tomb stood, the escarpment of the Rajmahal Hills rose steeply with ravines and valleys running into it; country that was inhabited by aboriginals — flat-nosed, beady-eyed Malers, and in far larger numbers by the Santal* people.

* "The Santals have a large number of different dances and, with two or three exceptions, these are very decent to look at; but excluding a couple of war-dances, the associations of the dance are always doubtful. Except at festivals they never dance during the daytime, but at night; and the dances give the two sexes an opportunity for illicit intercourse. In the Santal mind, therefore, dancing is always associated with sensuality. It often happens," writes Mr. Bodding, "that Europeans who have no

Until a few years ago Sakrigali had been used for the transhipment
of waggons and passengers across the Ganges to Manihari. Now the
river had deserted it and it was high and dry and the landing place
had been moved five miles upstream to the west.

The river was full of shipping. There were thirty square-riggers on
the big bend of the river alone, and there were dozens more all the
way down towards Rajmahal as far as the eye could see.

This was as far as the Captain was supposed to take us; but he
now offered to take us down as far as Rajmahal.

"It is only sixteen miles," he said. "For us it is a pleasure. For
you it will be a help." We thanked him.

"It is my duty," he said.

Below Manihari the river ran close in along the base of the Rajmahal
Hills. The narrow strip of land between the hills and the river, that
had once been dense jungle, the home of elephants, tigers, bears
and even rhinoceros, and the bane of invading armies which inevit-
ably come to a standstill in the defile at Sakrigali was now semi-
domesticated country covered with scrub and groves of trees, and
with ricefields at the water's edge.

According to Murray's *Guide* there was a ruined mosque called the
Hadaf about four and a half miles upstream from Rajmahal which I
wanted to see. Unfortunately no one else did, not even Wanda who
was anxious to buy some more fish in Rajmahal before the shops
shut, so I asked the Captain to put me ashore.

"It is five miles from the Hadaf to Rajmahal," he said. "And you
will not arrive before nightfall. These woods are not a good place
to be after dark."

Nevertheless he agreed to do what I asked.

He landed me by some china clay workings in which dozens of
saucy wenches were trotting about with baskets of the stuff balanced
on their noddles. Judging by the frank gestures they made, they were
probably Santals. After wading through about half a mile of china
clay I reached an execrable track which was ankle-deep in fine red
dust and by the side of which there were a number of huts.

---

idea of this, and who enjoy the plastic movement of the people, call for Santals to
dance before them. I believe it would be wise to leave this item out of entertainments,
because the people, as a matter of fact, draw the conclusion that, when a European
wants to have such an exhibition, the cause is that he has inclination in the same
direction as the Santals. This does not advance British prestige."

Bengal District Gazetteer, Vol. XXII, Santal Parganas.

While I was wondering where the Hadaf was an immensely tall man, dressed in a long black coat, emerged from one of the huts and announced that he was the caretaker of the mosque.

"The Hadaf is not the mosque," he said. "The Hadaf is the hill on which the mosque is built. It is the Jama Masjid of Man Singh but everyone comes here wanting to see the Hadaf." He was quite upset.

The Jama Masjid of Man Singh, who had been Akbar's Viceroy in Bengal and who had shifted the capital to Rajmahal in 1592 from Tanda when that town had been deserted by the Ganges, stood on a slight eminence a couple of hundred yards to the right of the road beyond some china-clay workings which were rapidly encroaching on it; but it was still a splendid, untended and very ruinous ruin — which is what ruins ought to be. Beyond a large open courtyard with a small, dried-up tank in the middle of it, rose what was left of the Mosque. It had a noble facade of red brick that was the same colour as the dust in the road, pierced by a number of pointed arches. There was a great, echoing prayer hall between forty and fifty feet high full of bats, two slim minarets, eight domes (four large and four small), their interiors ornamented with lozenge-shaped designs executed in bricks, and several flights of stairs leading to some upper rooms and the roof. But this was only half the mosque. The entire north wing, apart from one minaret at the north western angle, had collapsed. Behind it, standing in a field of lentils and overshadowed by toddy palms, there was a shrine to Siva which, my guide said when I asked him, was probably also built by Man Singh. He was the ideal guide, because he did no guiding. He advanced no tiresome theories — in fact, unless one asked him a specific question he was as silent as the grave. Nor did he wish to arrange a tip. He was probably not the caretaker at all, but the owner.

I set off to walk along the road to Rajmahal which passed through what had been Man Singh's old Mughal city, most of which had been knocked down and carted away to provide ballast for the railway. It was a weird countryside in which the pipal trees were strangling the last remains of the buildings that still remained standing.

I soon got tired of ploughing through the dust, and besides I found the atmosphere of decay oppressive. It was better down by the river; fires were glowing in the tile and brick kilns; beautiful girls from the village were filling pitchers with water from the river while their small children, thinking themselves abandoned for ever, howled on bank. But not for long. Soon I was plodding along a foreshore which became progressively more muddy that was littered with Mughal

bricks, stranded corpses and skulls. To escape from it I was forced
to take to the bank which was overgrown with jungle.

Finally, when I had given up hope of ever reaching Rajmahal, I
emerged from it on to a platform high above the river where a little
brick gazebo looked out across the water to the sands on the left
bank. Below this garden house, lying on its side in the water was a
huge, rounded bastion, with the stone sockets in which banners had
been hung still intact on the face of it. Originally this had been the
site of the house of a rich landowner who had been unwise enough
to tell Akbar that his Viceroy was not engaged in building a mosque
on the Hadaf but a palace for himself, and in revenge Man Singh
had blown up the house, together with most of the other improve-
ments.

By the time I reached Rajmahal, having got lost among a maze of
creeper-covered tanks in an old indigo factory, I was exhausted. I
longed for nothing more than a swim in the river, but as usual the
boat was moored in a place which, although it was romantic enough,
was one where no current circulated and where the water was covered
with the awful brown froth. Desperate, I asked two men in a small
boat to take me out into the river which they did; but while I was
trying to wash my neck with one hand while hanging on to the boat
with the other, I lost our only piece of soap, and when Wanda returned
from shopping in the bazaar she was not at all pleased.

Under the influence of her displeasure I burrowed among the luggage until I found a nasty little piece of soap with dirt in the cracks,
and when she had finished washing – which for her was even more
complicated than it was for me – using the same boatmen as I had
to take her out into the stream, we set off in a pony-cart to visit the
tomb of Miran, the son of Mir Jafar who had betrayed Siraj-ud-daula
on the battlefield at Plassey. It was he who had murdered Siraj-ud-
daula and subsequently his father had become Nawab of Bengal in
Siraj-ud-daula's place. In 1760 he was struck by lightning while on a
campaign. It was an appropriate end.

The inscriptionless, sandstone tomb was situated in a patch of un-
kempt ground, close to the same dusty road which I had abandoned
an hour or so before, in favour of the river bank. Behind it there
was a lake with a lot of white cranes standing in the shallows. The
only reason why it was here at all was that his body, which was being
conveyed down the Ganges in a boat, had begun to give off such
an awful stench that the persons who were in charge of it had been
obliged to take it ashore and bury it at the first opportunity that
presented itself.

Although the story was interesting, it was difficult to get worked up about the tomb and after standing by it for a few moments we re-entered the pony cart and drove back to Rajmahal.

By this time we were both rather bad-tempered, but when we got back to the boat we had a fine end-of-the-voyage party with the Captain and the crew. While we sat drinking rum the sun set with unbelievable splendour over the mosque that had been built expressly for Akbar so that he would have a suitable place in which to worship when he visited the town in order to see how his Viceroy was getting on with the conversion of the palace at the Hadaf to a less secular use.

Chapter Twenty-Four

Into the Bhagirathi

One of the principal factors that contributed to an early decline in Gangetic navigation was the obstruction caused by the annual silting of the river Bhagirathi. The Bhagirathi river is an 80 miles stretch of the main Ganges that connects it to the Hooghly river. For about 8 months of the year, known as the "dry" season, there is no flow of the Ganges water through it. Owing to this difficulty power vessels have to follow the Sunderbans sea route via Khulna-Barisal-Goalundo, crossing Pakistan territory and adding some 400 miles of additional navigation.

Inland water Navigation From Calcutta to Allahabad;
U Shanker Rao, Madras, 1951

Two days later we arrived at Azimganj on the Bhagirathi river after a journey so exasperating that it had brought us, inured as we were to difficulty, to the edge of despair.

On the morning after the breaking-up party at Rajmahal the crew of the motor-boat had accompanied us to the railway station, carrying all our baggage. None of us wanted to get up at six o'clock while it was still dark, but the Captain was due back at the Manihari Ghat in an hour, and even so he would be late getting there.

In the excitement of departure neither of us had bothered to find out at what time the next train left for Azimganj, and it was not until the Captain and the crew had gone that we discovered that it was not until ten o'clock — not that they could have done anything about it if they had known.

"Why don't you travel by boat?" asked the booking clerk, apparently unconscious of the humour of what he was saying. "There is a boat leaving for Dhulian now." And he despatched a small boy to detain it.

It seemed a good idea. Neither of us wanted to travel by train, but it had seemed the only practical way in which we could reach the head of the Bhagirathi and still have enough time to travel down it by boat. We only had four more days in which to reach Calcutta. Now, with this heaven-sent boat, we could continue on down the Ganges along the East Pakistan border as far as Dhulian where the Bhagirathi began. This plan would also give us the opportunity to see the barrage which the Indians were building across the Ganges at Farakka, partly with the intention of rejuvenating the Bhagirathi which was now closed completely to all but the smallest boats from October to July.

It was a crazy idea, but that morning we both thought that it was a good one.

At first all went well. The boat was a bhur, the same sort of country boat in which we had made the short journey down to Patna that had almost terminated our married life. We went swaying down the river in full sail, carrying a topsail, past an enormous island while Wanda cooked breakfast over the boatmen's fire in the stern. Then the weather changed. For the first time for weeks the sky grew overcast; there was the sound of distant thunder and just as we reached the lower end of the island the wind died out completely. As soon as it did the Captain dropped anchor and announced that he proposed to stay where he was until the weather improved, which he said would probably be the following morning. He was not worried. There was no perishable cargo on board; in fact there was none at all.

There was nothing either of us could do to make him change his mind. Mr. Nehru's letter was of no use at all because neither he nor his crew appeared to have heard of the Prime Minister; but I did prevail on him to take the boat a little closer in towards the right bank where, after splashing ashore and walking for a couple of miles through tree stubble, I reached a village of thatched mud huts where I eventually managed to hire a bullock-cart to take us to the nearest railway station which was at a place called Barharwa. It was about sixteen miles off. By the time we reached it the last train to Azimganj had left and we spent the rest of the night there until a quarter to four when the train came in.

The Bhagirathi at Azimganj was two hundred yards wide; but apart from a number of pools of brackish water, through which the what were by now to us hateful bullock-carts were crossing, less than axle-deep, it was empty. It was like a rather smelly ditch after a shower of rain.

"What we need now," Wanda said, "is bicycles."

At this moment we were tempted to leave this moribund part of the Ganges Delta and go home, but fortunately, there is always something a little further on which impels the traveller to continue his journey. In this case it was the Palace of the Nawab Nazims of Bengal

at Murshidabad which, according to the 1882 edition of Murray's
Handbook of the Bengal Presidency, was not more than five miles away
on the opposite bank. "It is in the Italian style . . . The Architect was
General Macleod of the Beng. Eng. And it ís strange that with so
noble a residence the Nawab should have preferred to have lived in
a range of low, small buildings to the E., while his mother resides
in a barge," it said.

With a team of porters carrying our baggage on their heads we
crossed over to the east bank from the railway station by a causeway
of straw and bamboo which led through the puddles which constituted
the Bhagirathi and took a bus to the town of Jiaganj which was so
close that it would have been more sensible to have retained the
services of the porters and walked. There, made desperate by the
setbacks of the last twenty-four hours, I telephoned to the office of
the District Magistrate at Berhampur, a place ten miles down the river
to whom, by some miracle, I had been given an introduction. By an
even greater miracle I was put through to him direct and he very
kindly arranged with a local firm who owned a jeep to put it at our
disposal for the rest of the day. "In this way you will be able to see
everything you want to," he said amiably.

We bought a guide-book to Murshidabad, which turned out to
be a number of postcards bound together with some eccentric des-
criptions printed on them, and set off.

Sited almost anywhere in the West the Italianate Palazzo of the
Nawab Nazims of Bengal would have been unremarkable. Here, on
the banks of the almost waterless Bhagirathi, set among the lush
green Bengal countryside, and rising above the toddy palms and the
low huts of the inhabitants, it was terrific. It seemed the work of
a megalomaniac or perhaps the parody of a palace in a drawing by
Osbert Lancaster, rather than the work of a General of the Bengal
Engineers. Built entirely by local labour, it was between seventy and
eighty feet high and the north front was more than four hundred
and twenty feet long, almost as long as that of Buckingham Palace
to which it bore a certain resemblance. It was only a superficial one.
The classical facade with its free standing columns executed in sombre
red sandstone, and a colossal flight of steps leading up to a central
portico, seen under a dark and lowering sky, produced a far more
lasting impression.

Facing it across a huge square, from the centre of which rose a
clock tower with the hands of the clock stuck, at twenty past
five, was the Imambara, or mosque, an elegant, white, two-storied
building, its facade decorated with square pilasters and its flat roof

lined with finials, each of which terminated in a tiny, bulbous dome. This was the building that, according to the guide book I had bought in Jiaganj, "cought fire in 1846 with fireworks rebuilt in 1848 by Feraidunjah". The western side of this parade ground opened on to the river front.

Waving the letter of introduction which the District Magistrate had sent to us with such exceptional promptitude, we entered the Palace by the visitors' door, which was on the basement level below the piano nobile, and found ourselves in a gloomy hall in which a stuffed yak was rotting, where we were met by a custodian who conducted us through even darker passages to the Armoury. These passages reminded me of the basement of my grandmother's house in Pimlico.

It was a lightning tour.

"This is spear of Akbar," said the custodian in a sing-song voice as if he was chanting a litany. It was like a corkscrew. If Akbar had speared anyone with it how the devil did he get it out?

"This is helmet of Nadir Shah, King of Persia." It had three spikes on it, presumably for butting people in the stomach.

"This is the chain mail of Nadir Shah, King of Persia."

"This is cannon with a mouth like demons."

"This is seven-barrelled gun with mouth."

"This is standard with crescent on top carried at Battle of Plassey."

We had done the Armoury.

The rest of the Palace took longer. There was the Drawing-Room which was huge and low-ceilinged and friendly with lots of early-Victorian sofas and lamps on brass columns and glass chandeliers that was like the Reform Club in the film of *Round the World in Eighty Days*; there was an immense colonnaded Banqueting Room decorated with Egyptian motifs which if it had been as long as Murray's *Guide to India* said it was would have been longer than the building; there was the circular Durbar Room, with a vaulted dome painted Wedgwood blue, decorated with corinthian pilasters and swags of grapes and magnificent alabaster and marble urns carved with bacchanalian motifs and heads of satyrs. In this room stood the marble plinth which had supported the gilded and painted ivory throne of the Nawab Nazims of Murshidabad. And there were hundreds of pictures. Pictures of Nawabs interviewing architects and agents who, judging by their expressions, were giving them bad news; a huge oil of William IV and another of his illegitimate son, the Earl of Munster, both presented by the King himself; "The Burial of Sir John Moore", an immense picture which had been rejected by the General's old

Regiment and had been sent out to Calcutta and sold to the Nawab for 10,000 rupees. There were four splendid oil-paintings of the Nawab Nasir Hamayayid as a young man: in the first wearing a sort of naval going-ashore dress, a gold-braided blue jacket, a tricorn hat, knee breeches and white silk hose; in the second wearing a jewelled fez; in the third dressed in a long embroidered coat and pantaloons; and in the fourth magnificent in a full-length ermine cloak. There were blood-thirsty paintings of battles and there was an almost completely black painting labelled "Woman of Samaria by Raphael" and there were a number of perfectly atrocious paintings "attributed to Meissen".

After three hours we emerged from the Palace. We had not seen the zenana which was somewhere hidden away at the back, the coach buildings which had once housed the hosts of relatives and adherents of the Nawabs, but we had seen enough for one day.

Enough for the two of us, but the driver of the jeep had other plans. He had been told to show us everything. He whirled us away under the great fortified archway where each morning well into the '80s of the last century the imperial music that was the perquisite of the deputy governors of the Delhi Emperors could still be heard, to see the other remains in which not only the surroundings of Murshidabad (at one time the city is said to have had a circumference of thirty miles) but all the country between it and Berhampur on the banks of the Bhagirathi six miles downstream abounded. After the vast open expanses of Bihar and Uttar Pradesh it seemed a strange, lush, secretive, almost claustrophobic countryside. Scarcely anywhere could one see more than a few hundred feet without the interposition of vegetation or some human habitation.

He drove us down narrow lanes which meandered between ruinous old brick walls, past the vats and reservoirs of old indigo factories, all overgrown, past white pillared palaces that had once belonged to Nabobs and bankers, past pavilions and kiosks and villages of rude huts made from reeds and the stems of jute plants. He drove us past plantations of sugar cane, palm trees, bananas and bamboos, rice fields, ponds filled with green slime, and to the old, abandoned river-bed of the Ganges now choked with water hyacinth. He drove us along roads deep in red dust which were lined with acres of Muslim tombs and past Dutch and English cemeteries, the former well tended, the English ones in the last extremities of decay, filled with tottering obelisks and mausolea from which the plaques had been brutally ripped by marauders.

It was now three o'clock and I begged the driver, who had been

able to refresh himself while we were in the Palace, to desist from
sightseeing — we ourselves had had nothing to eat or drink since early
morning; but he ignored my pleas and drove us at break-neck speed
to the Moti Jhil, which the local guide book said was "Pearl Lake,
Pleasure Garden of Nawzesh Mahammad and Ghasiti Begum (son-
in-law i.e. daughter of Nawab Ali Varde) Excaveted on the former
bed of the Ganges." It was also reputed to be infested with crocodiles
and there, under a great tree in a beautiful garden close to the tomb
of the nurse of Ekram-ud-daula, we fell asleep.

When we woke the shadows were lengthening and the driver said
that it was time for him to stop work. The thought of travelling
down the banks of the Bhagirathi with all our luggage in a bus until
we could find a place where there was enough water in it to continue
the journey by boat was so repellent that we decided to ask him
to take us in the jeep. He said the nearest place where we could be
more or less certain of finding a boat that would float in the Bhagirathi
at this season was Plassey, about thirty miles south of Murshidabad
and about twelve miles south of Berhampur. He also said that there
was a sugar refinery there which had a bungalow attached to it where
travellers were occasionally allowed to stay. After drinking some
water which the custodian of the tomb obligingly drew from a well
for us, we set off.

On the way we stopped at Berhampur. The barracks looked much
as they must have done when they were built in 1767, ten years after
the battle of Plassey in which Clive's victory established British
supremacy over India. Long, low, elegant, arcaded buildings, disposed on two sides of a wide expanse of grass on which cattle grazed.
At one end of this common was a statue of Subhas Chandra Bose
wearing real spectacles, and at the other, there was an old house in
which Warren Hastings had once lived, a garden filled with great
nim and rain trees which led down to the river. And there were some
immense open rackets courts.

Berhampur was the scene of the first outbreak of the Indian Mutiny.
It was here, on the evening of 26th February 1857 that the 19th Native
Infantry refused to accept the issue of percussion caps for the next
morning's parade. They did so because they suspected, not without
reason, that the cartridges with which they had been issued had been
greased with a compound of cow and pig fat. There is no doubt that,
whatever the cartridges were greased with they were thickly greased
and with some substance which would have made them repellent to
any fastidious person who was ordered to place the end in his mouth
and bite it off.

*

As the driver of the jeep had predicted, we were able to spend the night in the guest-house of the sugar factory at Plassey where, for the first time since leaving Mirzapur three weeks previously, we slept between sheets in real beds and, best of all, under mosquito nets — for we had been practically bitten to death on the railway station the previous evening. Although we possessed mosquito nets there had been no way of erecting them over our heads on the platform and although we had covered ourselves with them the mosquitoes had been so heavy-footed that they had been able to bite us through the mesh.

The next morning we set off for the Bhagirathi in the factory bus to meet the boatmen with whom, with the help of the assistant manager, we had made an arrangement to take us down the river to a place called Katwa, about thirty miles to the south. From there we could take a train to Bandel on the Hooghly, and then travel down it by boat as far as Calcutta where we hoped to pick up an outward-bound ship that would take us down to the sea. This was the reason for all the hurry, as there were certain formalities which had to be gone through before we could leave India by ship.

A vile track led to the river at Plassey. It crossed what must have been the rear of the British position during the battle which extended at right angles to it and faced north. We had already visited the battle-fields earlier that morning. It was not a particularly inspiring one but neither were the fields of Sedgemoor and Sidi Rezegh. It was almost completely flat, except for one or two minute protuberances that would be unnoticeable to anyone who was not interested in battle-fields. A number of small pillars indicated the position of the various batteries and so forth of the contending forces. Nevertheless, I was happy to root about in the muddy waterlogged fields and give Wanda a blow-by-blow account of the battle while she stood, bored stiff above me on the dyke in the mist, anxious to get on.

She need not have worried. At the river bank there was no sign either of the boat or the boatmen. There was nothing but a ferry with an old car on it, a number of water-buffaloes in some deep pools with only their nostrils and the tops of their heads protruding from the water and some laundrymen up to their calves in water out in mid-stream who were rinsing their washing.

An hour later the boat appeared. It was a dengi, a sort of canoe with a sharp prow and a high stern. It was only about eighteen feet long and it had a little semi-circular deckhouse made of woven reed which was big enough for two men to sleep in. The decking was made of split bamboo and was excruciatingly uncomfortable to sit on. There were two boatmen — one old and bald, the other young. By the time we had loaded all our luggage, which they watched us do impassively, there was not much room.

We had only gone a quarter of a mile when the older boatman announced that they were going to have their midday meal and before we could stop them they vanished up the bank in the direction of their village. We waited for three-quarters of an hour for them to return, by which time we were in a frenzy. Wanda was the first to crack. "If they're not coming let's bloody well go without them," she said.

I pushed off. It was a well-balanced little boat. Instantly, as if they had been watching us, the boatmen appeared, running along the bank uttering angry cries. They were so angry that they did not speak to us again all day — not that they had been particularly communicative up to then. They were a gloomy pair, nothing like any of the other boatmen with whom we had travelled down the Ganges: Karam Chand and the unforthcoming but likeable Bhosla; Lalta Prasad, Jagdish and Ram Baba who had taken us down from Fatehgarh; Bag Nath and Hira Lal with their Edwardian moustaches, rowing us down in their Edwardian boat; the Captain and crew of the motor-boat, who had taken us down from Patna, making sure that we missed nothing on the way . . . All these we thought of with nostalgia. Wanda was right when she referred to our present boatmen as, "those miserable boggers".

Most of the time the old man rowed, or rather sat up forward in the oarsman's place holding a single oar. When he rowed he kept one foot tucked up into his groin and the other extended straight in front of him. The younger man steered.

No one could say that the Bhagirathi was an exciting river at this season of the year. For the most part the right bank was the highest of the two. Occasionally there was a village in which high pitched thatched roofs could be seen among the mango trees. The left bank was planted with sugar cane. Sometimes the whole thing was in reverse.

At one o'clock we passed through the only channel of the river still remaining open which was a foot deep and twelve feet wide.

By three we were through the worst of the shoals and the river broadened out until it was a hundred and fifty yards wide and so deep that we could find no bottom with the bamboo pole, which was twelve feet long. It was very quiet on the Bhagirathi. The only sounds were made by the engines of the pumps which were lifting the water out of the river into the neighbouring fields. And there was little to look

at. There was an occasional stranded corpse, a few tame ducks, some
funereal-looking shag and some oyster-catchers scurrying along the
shore; once we passed a strange old European house all alone on the
bank, and that was all, apart from some small boys who were teasing
a lunatic away on the other side of the river.

As the sun sank, so did our spirits. The old man's oar broke and
he took what seemed an age to lash it together, which he did in-
effectually, talking to himself monotonously while he did so. From
now on it broke every few minutes. As it grew colder and the mist
began to form, nasty smells rose from the river and even more disagreeable ones wafted off the bank.

As the sun set toddy men working high up in the tops of the
toddy palms on the right bank were silhouetted against the sky, like
sailors up in the rigging. They were banging in wooden spouts and
hanging pots underneath them into which the sap would drip during
the night.

One man had just come down from the top of a tree with a pot
full of unfermented toddy, and because we were thirsty, not having
had anything to drink since the early morning, we made the boatmen
head the boat in towards the bank which they did, looking even more
disagreeable than usual, although we offered to buy them a drink too.

The toddy man gave each of us a slice of palm leaf which was bound
at one end so that it formed a sort of scoop. He spoke no Hindi and
we spoke no Bengali, but he indicated that we should hold the open
end of the leaf to our lips. He then poured the best part of two pints
of the preparation down our throats. It was white and cloudy and it
had a froth on it in which black ants floated. It tasted of buttermilk.
It was delicious.

In this state, fresh from the tree, it was not alcoholic, but after two
or three hours in the sun it would become potent and rather more
bitter. In the country districts of India where toddy is made it is
estimated that it takes three pints of unadulterated toddy to make a
man drunk. In the cities it is almost impossible to buy unadulterated
toddy. It is either watered, usually with dirty water, or else it has
saccharine added to it — or both. Some debased persons drink it mixed
with chloroform.

Toddy men are Hindus. They belong to a special caste and they
rarely drink toddy themselves. This toddy man had all the tools of
his trade with him, a rope strop which held his feet sufficiently loosely
to the tree trunk for him to be able to move them up and down, and a
sling made of twisted palm fibre covered with straw which held his
body to the tree. Except for a loin-cloth he was naked. Round his

middle he wore a belt with three knives and a knife sharpener stuck
in it. In more primitive jungle areas the great bane of the toddy men
are the sloth bears which climb the trees at night, drink the pots dry
and then drop off, falling thirty or forty feet and hitting the ground
like great hairy footballs.

We came into the last reach above Katwa in the last of the light and
while we were going down it the old man's oar broke twice more.
Then we went aground on a sandbank. By the time he got us off it
was dark, so that when he finally took the boat in alongside a number
of other dengis with little cooking fires burning on board them, and
said "Katwa," we really believed that we had arrived at the town.

We were not even on the foreshore. We were on a sandbank which
was separated from the foreshore by an expanse of stagnant water
in which hundreds of frogs were beginning to tune up for the evening.
Over it hung clouds of mosquitoes and an awful smell. Away in the
distance the lights of Katwa shone nebulously through the mist.

I tried to persuade the boatmen to fetch a bullock-cart. Both of
them refused; at the same time the old man indicated that we should
pay him and get off. I rolled up my trousers and prepared to set off
for the shore. How I loathed him at this moment.

'You're not going to leave me here with all these boatmen," Wanda
said.

She sounded alarmed as well she might.

"Why don't you go?" I said, cruelly.

"I can't speak the language," she said pathetically.

Neither could I. We were in Bengal.

At this season the steps of what should have been the bathing-ghat
of Katwa was half a mile from the water. When I reached it I expected
to encounter the most insuperable difficulties but instead, at the top
of the steps, I found a man in a little wooden hut who not only
spoke Hindi but who, as soon as I had explained the predicament
which we were in, summoned four jolly, villainous-looking men who
immediately set off at a brisk trot across the sands to the boat from
which they took off all the luggage. By the time I reached it they
were on their way back surging through the stinking pool as I had
done, but carrying on their heads two tin trunks, two bedding rolls,
two enormously heavy zip bags, two baskets, one of which contained
vegetables, the other the stove and a five gallon drum three-quarters
full of kerosene.

"Stop those men!" Wanda said. In this mood she sounded rather
like the large woman in the Marx Brothers' films. "They have all
our luggage."

It was too late. They had already gone.

We paid the boatmen ten rupees. They had asked nine originally before setting off; now they demanded fifteen. We gave them the hurricane lanterns and a huge tin of rice; not because we wanted to but simply to get rid of them. Seldom had we met a pair whom we liked less. Then we, too, waded through the stagnant water, Wanda wearing her Indian shift held up above her waist, and ploughed through the sand in the wake of the porters. When we arrived they were all waiting for us with the baggage still balanced on their heads, all roaring with laughter. They were labourers who had been working on a building site and their faces had lumps of dried cement sticking to them. I asked the man in the hut why they were laughing.

"They are laughing," he said, "because they think that you are surprised to see them again."

We left for the station, each on our own ricksha, perched high on top of the luggage. It was damn cold and we were covered with wet, stinking mud, but all the way there we laughed and sang. For us it was rare for defeat to be turned so rapidly into victory.

The last train had just left when we got to the station but fortunately there was a waiting-room and here, before a large audience for there was nowhere else to go, we ate an enormous meal of fried eggs, beans, tinned mangoes, biscuits, jam, oranges and tea. Then, after we had washed up on the platform, we had a long talk with the booking clerk about Hindu and Christian marriage customs.

"Our marriage is seldom very, very nice or very, very holy," he said, "but our marriage very, very seldom ends in divorce."

When her returned to open his ticket office for the next train we exchanged visiting cards. No sooner had he gone than another man appeared.

"You have given the ticket clerk a visiting card," he said. "I, too, would like one."

So I gave him one too.

At five-thirty the following morning, after spending the night on a couple of cane chairs, and getting our bottoms bitten through the holes in the wickerwork by the mosquitoes which swarmed in the waiting room we took a train to Bandel on the Hooghly.

At Bandel we were put up in one of the cells of the Monastery which the Prior, who looked very tired and ill, very kindly gave us permission to use. The monks were Salesians. Originally it had been an Augustinian foundation but the last friar of that order had died in

1869. There was one Hungarian, one Spaniard, one Dutchman, one Czecho-Slovakian and one Irishman, the Prior himself.

Together with the Spaniard who was young and bearded, we visited the Seminary in which dozens of little Indian priests-to-be were roaring around, all full of beans after their evening meal. All of them, without exception, were the children of parents who were already Roman Catholics.

New conversions, he said, were almost non-existent.

"I am afraid," he said, "that God, for His own good reasons, has withheld His Grace, for the time being from the people of Bengal."

The lack of it, he said, did not prevent many well-off Hindus from visiting the seminary to ask if their children could become paying guests.

"Not so that they can become priests but because they think that our children look more happy than their own."

The church at Bandel was built to replace one in the Portuguese fort at Hooghly which was completely destroyed when the Muslims under the orders of Shah Jahan, took the place in 1632. At the moment when the fort fell and the Governor was being burned alive, a Portuguese merchant, fearing that the iconocastic Muslims would destroy it, took the image of the Virgin and Child, swam across the Hooghly with it and was seen no more. The survivors of the storming of Hooghly, who were all Portuguese, were taken to Agra where the more presentable girls were recruited into the harems, the boys were circumcised and the men were given the choice of embracing the true religion or being trampled to death by an elephant in the presence of the Emperor. Among the prisoners was the Augustinian Friar João da Cruz but when it was his turn to be trampled by the elephant, the animal bowed down before him three times and lifted him up with its trunk and set him on its back. This so impressed the Emperor that he allowed the survivors to be released from their various bondages and sent back to Hooghly, loaded with gifts. He also gave the Friars a charter to build a church on land that was rent free and they were exempted from the authority of his officers.

One night, after he had returned to Hooghly, Father Da Cruz was awoken by what sounded like a great storm and he saw a strange light which illuminated the river and he heard a voice which resembled that of his friend the merchant who had jumped into the river with the statue, crying:

"*Salva! Salva! Salva! a nossa senhora da Boa Viagem que deu nos esta Victoria. Levante, levante, o padre e orai por todos nos!!*"*

* "Hail! Hail! Hail! to Our Lady of Happy Voyage who has given us the victory. Arise! Arise! Oh Father! and pray for us all!"

The next morning the statue of the Virgin was found by a number of Hindus who announced that *"Guru Ma"* was outside the gate of the church; when the new church was built it was set high in one of the walls facing south, a position which it still occupies.

Chapter Twenty-Five

Arrival at Calcutta

Our task is done! On Gunga's breast
The sun is sinking down to rest;
And, moored beneath the tamarind bough,
Our bark has found its harbour now.
With furled sail, and painted side,
Behold the tiny frigate ride.
Upon her deck, 'mid charcoal gleams,
The Moslems' savoury supper steams,
While all apart, beneath the wood,
The Hindoo cooks his simpler food.

> Reginald Heber, Lord Bishop of Calcutta:
> *An Evening Walk in Bengal*

Early the next morning while it was still dark we left the monastery and were pedalled to a lonely jetty where we boarded a tug which was on its way down to Calcutta.

We left behind us all the gear for which we had no further use and for which we had long since conceived a passionate loathing: the last trunk which contained the remainder of the provisions, the cooking pots, the abominable stove and the can of kerosene, the stink of which had haunted us ever since we had left Hardwar.

There was some delay in boarding the tug. The man who was putting the bag on board which contained all our books dropped it into a mud bank just as he was transferring it from the shore to the vessel and by the time it had been dug out the sun was shooting up over the left bank of the river, illuminating the mosque at Hooghly (the Imambara) with its two tall minarets and its central clock tower in which the clock which had been sent out from England and installed in it at the cost of £879 1s. 6d in 1861 still kept good time.

With a following wind we swept down under the Jubilee Bridge. To the right, hidden away in the narrow lanes of the quarter called Armenitola, the spire of the Armenian church rose in the air. We had also visited it. After the church at Bandel it was the oldest church on the Hooghly and next to it in a walled garden, was a house in which the last four Armenian inhabitants of Hooghly lived, supported in their old age by a benevolent trust founded by Sir Paul Chatterjee, a merchant who had amassed a great fortune in Hong Kong. The previous afternoon, one of them, Mr. Akhartoon, had taken us for a drive in his motor car. Until recently he had had his own motor business but unfortunately he had contracted tuberculosis and he had been unable to carry it on. He had the Armenian gift of tongues and spoke Bengali, Hindi, Persian, English and Armenian with equal facility. There were many more Armenians in Calcutta and they still visited the church each January on the feast of St. John and some-times, he said, the Patriarch came there from Izmir in Asia Minor.

Here on the twenty-odd miles of the river below Hooghly the river banks were green with close-cropped grass and they sloped gently to the muddy shore. The right bank was lined with bathing-ghats and laundrymen's ghats, all slipping gently into the river, and temples with whitewashed spires that looked like obelisks and old and dignified white houses and others which were decorated in rain-washed shades of blue and faded pinks and greys and yellow ochre, or else were built of dark red bricks, almost all of them with flat roofs and many with secretive-looking walled gardens and orchards overgrown with vegetation, the sort that are dear to the hearts of the privacy-loving Bengalis. For the first five miles below Chinsura, the left bank was lined with jute mills that were cheek by jowl with one another like houses on a by-pass in England: Reliance, Kankinara, Titagarh, Anglo-India, Jagatdal, Alliance, India and Auckland and further down, at Barrackpore there was the great house among splendid trees which had been the suburban residence of the Governor of Bengal and later the country house of the Viceroys of India until the capital was moved from Calcutta to Delhi in 1912.

At Chinsura we passed the octagonal Dutch Church, said to have been built in 1678 as a covered market, with its strange memorial plaques and escutcheons decorated with skulls and bones, and equally strange-sounding inscriptions. Outside it, when we arrived there in Mr. Akhartoon's motor car, white-flannelled students had been play-ing cricket on a green. The spectators were sitting under the trees and when one of the batsmen played a particularly good stroke polite little ripples of applause arose. It might have been a village green in England, except for the naked little boys who were employed in chasing the water-buffaloes off the field when they encroached beyond the boundaries.

Chandernagore was abeam now. Until 1949 when the inhabitants voted for accession to India by an overwhelming majority it had been a French possession, and it still retained something of the air of a French provincial town. There was a gendarmerie, a pink church with green shutters, built by Italian missionaries and approached by an avenue of noble trees with whitewashed trunks; and the bridge which crossed the ditch behind which the town had sheltered, marooned in the middle of British India, was still flanked by stone boundary columns inscribed "*Liberté, Egalité, Fraternité.*" Even now there were two hotels in the long main street which were still very French in feeling. One of them had a delightful garden furnished with little tables at which one could sit out under the trees. In the now shuttered and empty rooms generations of young Englishmen, bored with weekends in Calcutta, had drunk wine and found more enjoyable entertainment than they would have done in the city. Now the wines and apéritifs had been superseded by Coca-Cola, but as we were leaving one of the waiters whispered in my ear that if I ever wanted to come back alone without Madame and gave him a few hours warning he could "*arranger quelque chose d'assez agréable et au même temps discret.*"

This shoreline all the way down from Bandel to Chinsura, with its old and battered buildings, was the site of the earliest commercial European settlements on the river; and even now it had an air about it that was neither European nor Indian but an amalgam of both, a sort of fantasy of the east seen through western eyes and of the west as imagined by an Indian, a little like the Pavilion at Brighton.

Long before any of the other nations, about 1575, the Portuguese set up shop on the banks of the river at Hooghly — pirates, slavers, merchants by turn, and sometimes all three at once, they could turn their hands to anything, but by the middle of the eighteenth century their power was all but extinguished. The Dutch, who, by contrast, were comparatively respectable in the early days and who liked to keep out of politics as much as possible, arrived in 1645. They left in 1825. The English built their first factory in 1651 about twenty paces from that of the Dutch, with instructions to find out as much as possible about the way in which the Hollanders conducted their trade, and when they had done so to proceed on the same lines. At this time the English seem to have been rather like the Japanese between the wars. The Danes arrived some time about the beginning of the eighteenth century and stayed at Serampore until the King of Denmark sold their possessions to the English in 1845 for twelve and a half lakhs of rupees, leaving behind them an elegant yellow and white neo-classical church flanked by cannon. The French built their first factory at Chandernagore in 1674 and by 1740, when their power began to decline, theirs was the most important settlement in Bengal. The Flemish Ostend Company built a factory on the east bank of the river at a place called Bankibazar in 1723 but no sooner was it built than Mir Jafar, at that time the deputy of the Faujdar of Hooghly, razed it to the ground. Even the Prussians contrived to settle there, forming the Bengalische Handels Gesellschaft for the purpose, but unfortunately for them, their reputation had preceded them.

"If the Germans come here," the then Nawab wrote to the English, "it will be very bad for all the Europeans, but for you worst of all, and you will always afterwards repent it; and I shall be obliged to stop all your trade and business ... Therefore take care that these German ships do not come."

"God forbid that they should come," the President of the English Council replied, "but should this be the case, I am in hopes that they will be either sunk, broke or destroyed."

His hopes were amply fulfilled. The Prussians succeeded in establishing a factory at Chandernagore in 1753 but nothing went right for them. They were forced, almost at once, to pay a considerable sum of money to Siraj-ud-daula, as a bribe to be left in peace; due to the carelessness of an English pilot their only ship was lost on the shoals at the mouth of the river; and in 1756 their manager, who for some unexplained reason was himself an Englishman, defected from them, taking with him goods to the value of eighty thousand rupees. Not surprisingly, in 1760 the Bengalische Handels Gesellschaft was wound up.

At Chandernagore we met the flood tide coming up from the Bay of Bengal and at about eight-thirty we reached Uttarpara, a small town on the right bank of the river six and a half miles above the Howrah Bridge. Here we got the master of the tug to put us ashore. All the way down the river we had promised ourselves that we would arrive at Calcutta in a boat propelled either by oars or wind, and this was what we now proposed to do.

"You are mad," he said. "You will not find a boat to take you down at this hour."

He was right. There was not a boat to be had anywhere on the Uttarpara side of the river. There were plenty of boats moored there but none of them were going to Calcutta at this particular moment.

Desperate, I took a ferry across the river, leaving Wanda guarding the luggage a block away from the Grand Trunk Road, that same

road by which we had waited to take the train from Kanpur weeks
before. Like ourselves, it too, was nearing ⸚he end.

The village on the opposite bank was called Dakhineswar. Lying
below it in the mud of the foreshore were a number of dengis; but
when I spoke to those members of the crew who were still on deck,
they simply turned their backs on me and did not reply — most probably because they did not understand a word of what I was saying.

I hired a cycle ricksha and told the driver to take me to the next
ghat downstream; instantly he lost himself in some squalid lanes
behind a huge match factory.

Finally, we reached a flight of steps just upstream from the Wil-
lington Bridge where half a dozen of the country boats called panswais, which were a little larger than dengis, were tied up.

Before he left the master of the tug had given me a lecture on
how much a couple of foreigners might reasonably be expected to
pay to go down to Calcutta from Uttarpara.

"Ten rupees," he said, "but not one anna more. Not one paisa
more."

All these boatmen wanted twenty rupees. One, who obviously had
no intention of making the journey, asked thirty rupees. They bandied
these figures about among themselves to such an extent that I was
surprised when one of them, a really evil-looking man, agreed to take
us for fifteen.

By the time that he and his men had got going and had rowed the
panswai at a leisurely rate up to Uttarpara and by the time that Wanda
and the luggage had been put on board, it was ten o'clock. (The mud
on the foreshore was so deep that she had to be carried through it
dressed in her best shore-going kit, like a rather elegant sack.)

It was also a Saturday, and if we were to contact the shipping company which was arranging for us to go down to the mouth of the river
in one of its ships, we would have to arrive at the Howrah Bridge at
twelve-thirty, otherwise the office would be shut. We had two and a
half hours in which to cover six and a half miles. Too soon we began
to make plans about what we would eat when we got to Calcutta.

At first the wind was very strong, as it had been all the morning,
and with a ragged old sail set made of sacking the panswai went
storming down before it, past the Bone Factory and the old European
villas of Uttarpara; but as we came down towards the temple of Kali
at Dakhineswar where I had hired the boat, the wind shifted and,
just as we were passing the steps which had six little temples lined
up on either side of it like sentry boxes, it suddenly died away completely.

The boatmen did nothing. They did not even look at their oars. They simply sat. By now we had employed so many boatmen that we knew that there was nothing we could do but grind our teeth and wait either for them to make up their minds to row of their own accord or else for a wind. Fortunately, by now it was almost high water and the current was strong enough even at this time of year to overcome the last of the flood and take us down with it, and eventually, after we had passed under the Willingdon Bridge, which had now been re-named the Vivekananda Bridge, one of them began to row languidly while squatting on his haunches in a posture which made it impossible for him to exert any real effort at all.

As soon as we had passed under the Bridge the captain of the panswai, noticing our impatience, upped the price for the journey to twenty rupees. I ignored him. This was no place in which to have a discussion of this kind; but he persisted. Eventually he began to threaten us.

"I will put you ashore if you do not pay what I ask."

"In that case you will get nothing and we shall call the police," I said.

The interior of the deckhouse of the panswai was a dark, semi-circular tunnel. In it, over an open fire, the cook was preparing a vegetable curry that was so enormous that it made Wanda's Baffat seem like an hors d'oeuvre.

He had already cooked a great mountain of rice. This together with the potatoes, onions and chillies of which the curry was principally composed, seemed enough for a regiment; and we watched the cook hungrily as he ground the spices and stirred the preparation, for we had had no breakfast, for the simple reason that we no longer possessed stove, fuel, food or pots to cook in.

The river was now more than three-quarters of a mile wide; and it looked big. The ebb was beginning now and it took us down close under the left bank, past decrepit nineteenth-century buildings in the district of Alambazar, some of which would have looked equally at home on the shores of Limehouse Reach or in old Portsmouth. The weed-covered steps that led down from them to the river were flanked by broken pillars, and up on the shore, in what had once been the riverside gardens, lay the skeletons of abandoned boats; while in the filthy water below the bank, among rotting piles with grass growing from their tops, an occasional solitary man or woman bathed, dressed in rags which might once have been white, but which were now the same uniform brown as the river itself.

We drifted down past these poor derelicts and past drab temples

made of cement, and past inhuman-looing factories and rank neglected wastelands in which not even weeds flourished and past jetties
and outfalls from which noxious effluents which were the colour of
mulligatawny soup poured into the river.

The river was full of boats. Panswais far bigger than ours, and
with far more energetic crews than our own, were being propelled
upstream by six oarsmen, three on either side, who were plugging
away standing up.

There were bigger boats called oolaks, with huge superstructures
and balconies on their counters, which were havering about in the
river with their single square sails empty of wind, slowly drifting
down on the ebb which was beginning to run more strongly now.
There were slabsided wooden lighters, loaded to the gunwales with
sacks of sugar which were being guided rather than propelled by men
wielding sweeps. There were huge rafts of bamboos which themselves
constituted the cargo, floating down with raftsmen on board who
were running from side to side, steering them with long poles. There
were cargo flats built of steel, that were more than two hundred feet
long, being hurried down river by tugs with yellow funnels. These
great vessels with their corrugated iron roofs, each of which could
carry seven hundred tons of cargo, were like floating dock sheds.
Equally strange were the barges all going down on the ebb, piled
thirty feet above the water with hay and straw which were like floating ricks. There were little fishing boats with ends that were so
sharply upturned that only about a third of their total length appeared
to rest on the water which was full of cabbage leaves, ashes, the heads
of marigolds and little mud-coloured balls of jute, which had been
thrown into it from the mills along the shore.

We came into the last big bend before the city. To the left there
was a big power-station on the shore which dwarfed everything.
Bamboo poles were planted in the river, and the ebb pulled at their
tops which were pointing upstream. Here the wind came up, and the
panswai went tearing away over towards the inside of the bend on
the right bank.

The right bank was a weird, surrealistic place. Grass-grown jetties
on the point of collapse projected into the stream; boats with broken
backs lay half-submerged in the mud in forgotten creeks, on the shores
of which engine houses stood roofless, open to the sky. What had been
fine houses when they were built a hundred and fifty or more years
ago were now either tenements, their facades obscured by lean-to
sheds, or else completely abandoned and with pipal trees growing out
of them and breaking them apart. There were endless boatyards where

they were riveting the hulls of lighters which were supported above
the foreshore on little piles of stones which were slipped in on the
falling tide, and there were older yards where they were building
wooden country boats, the ribs of which were golden in the sun.
There were melancholy brickfields and places where the embankments
were slipping slowly but surely into the river, and there were abandoned Victorian factories which had chimneys with cast-iron railings
round the top of them, from which long green grass was sprouting;
and then suddenly there was the great skeleton of the Howrah Bridge,
rising out of the haze ahead.

Now the wind freshened still more and we raced down towards it,
past the municipal burning ghats on the left bank in a river that seemed
to be full of floating haystacks, all going down under sail towards
the bridge which loomed three hundred feet above us, immense, silver
and exciting, glittering in the sun. From it came the roar of traffic,
the hooting of motor horns, the ringing of innumerable bicycle bells,
outlandish cries and murmuring sounds like a swarm of bees, made
by the thousands of people who thronged the footways, and from
downstream the sounds of the ships' sirens came booming up towards
us. This was the East as Conrad saw it; the one which hooked many
a young Englishman and made him an expatriate, fed-up and far from
home.

We were through the bridge now and the captain was steering the
boat in towards the left bank, happily anticipating an orgy of disputa-
tion. At twelve-forty-five we grounded some way off shore in the
mud by the Armenian Ghat. We had made it.

Chapter Twenty-Six

Down to the sea

At this point then, the traveller enters the domain of the Calcutta Pilots, who may fairly be said to be the best in the world. They are better paid, better educated and occupy a higher position than any other pilots, and it is quite right that they should do so, for the Hugli is a most dangerous and difficult river.

Handbook of the Bengal Presidency, 1882

You have turned your vessel in Garden Reach and the vessel which was twenty minutes ahead of you and was going down got into difficulties at Munikhali Point. You are then at Rajgunj. What will you do?

You have turned your vessel in Garden Reach in the early hours of a February morning. Thick fog comes down. What will you do?

You are in a ship 26.6 ft draught in the month of March cleared for Ulubaria. Tell me in detail how you will ride out the bore?

Typical examination questions for Calcutta Pilots

At Calcutta we were royally treated by Charles Will of the Joint Steamers Companies and his wife, Margaret. Then, when we had recovered a bit from the journey, we went down the river with one of the Hooghly Pilots to Garden House Point, five miles below the Howrah Bridge where the S.S. *Jalavijaya*, 4,584 gross tons, was anchored in the stream waiting for him to take her down in ballast to the Sandheads in the Bay of Bengal.

He was a handsome man in his thirties who had an air of authority about him, and he wore his brass-buttoned reefer jacket, white duck trousers and gold-braided cap and even his moustache, with all the panache of an officer in some fashionable cavalry regiment. It was particularly noticeable when he went up the side of the ship which had just finished discharging a cargo of cement from some place in the Black Sea that he contrived to arrive on deck still spotless. He also insisted that Wanda should have a bowline round her while climbing the Jacob's ladder.

He was what was called an Acting Branch Pilot – a Master Pilot

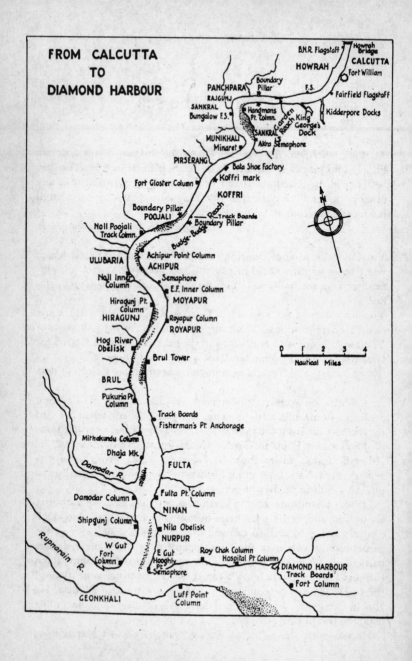

FROM CALCUTTA
TO
DIAMOND HARBOUR

B.N.R. Flagstaff
Howrah Bridge
HOWRAH
CALCUTTA
Fort William
Boundary Pillar
PANCHPARA
RAJGUNJ
F.S.
Fairfield Flagstaff
SANKRAL
Bungalow F.S.
Kidderpore Docks
Handmans Pt. Colmn.
King George's Dock
Garden Reach
MUNIKHALI
Minaret
SANKRAL
Akra Semaphore
PIRSERANG
Bala Shoe factory
Koffri mark
Fort Gloster Column
KOFFRI
Boundary Pillar
POOJALI
Track Boards
Boundary Pillar
No.II Poojali
Track Colmn.
Budge-Budge Reach
ULUBARIA
Achipur Point Column
ACHIPUR
No.II Inner Column
Semaphore
E.F. Inner Column
MOYAPUR
Hiragunj Pt. Column
HIRAGUNJ
Royapur Column
ROYAPUR
Hog River Obelisk
Brul Tower
BRUL
Pukuria Pt. Column
Track Boards
Fisherman's Pt. Anchorage
Mirhakundu Column
Dhaja Mk.
Damodar R.
FULTA
Damodar Column
Fulta Pt. Column
NINAN
Shipgunj Column
Nila Obelisk
NURPUR
Ruphnarain R.
W Gut Fort Column
E Gut Hooghly Pt. Semaphore
Roy Chak Column
Hospital Pt. Column
DIAMOND HARBOUR
Track Boards
Fort Column
GEONKHALI
Luff Point Column

0 1 2 3 4
Nautical Miles

with about twelve years' service who had taken the Branch Pilot examination. He was well on his way to the top of the tree. After twenty years' service he would become, if all went well in a service in which it is terribly easy for something to go wrong, a Branch Pilot, confirmed in his office and entitled to be piped aboard the pilot vessel.

The Portuguese initiated the service in 1661, and they were followed by the Dutch, the French and then the English, one of whom put the Prussians' only ship on the sands. The first English pilot, George Heron, made the first chart of the Sandheads.

In the early days although it was administered by the Government of Bengal, it was a semi-private organisation and there was no fixed wage for the pilots. They kept fifty per cent of the pilotage fees and gave the remainder to the Government. Today there are forty-five "running Pilots", (anything up to half a dozen of whom are on leave). They are still, as they always were, a *corps d'élite*. Their pay by Indian standards is very good, (around 1,750 rupees a month plus allowances and night fees) and many of them live a life which is in its way rather reminiscent of that enjoyed by Regency Bucks. The Pilot Vessel at the Sandheads out in the Bay of Bengal, an ex-Canadian frigate is rather like a Regency Club: but a very bumpy one. Life at the Sandheads is very often almost unbearable.

From the middle of May to September the warm, damp south-west monsoon blows, mostly force four to six but sometimes more strongly, and there are heavy storms from the north-west accompanied by thunder, especially in June. In May the weather is very unsettled and the chota bursat, the "small rains", begin and last for about a fortnight. All through this period it is intolerably hot and the humidity is as high as eighty per cent. Towards the middle of July the heavy rains set in, south-west and south-east winds predominate and there are gales from west and west-south-west. The Hooghly is now in full flood. August is much the same as July. Cyclones, revolving storms of fearful intensity which originate in the Bay of Bengal, are endemic except between January and March, but in September and October the head of the Bay is bombarded by cyclones which originate as typhoons in the China Sea.

In October the south-west monsoon retreats and the winds are variable. In November the north-east monsoon begins in earnest and the weather at last begins to be supportable. Mostly it is dry and clear now, except for cyclones, until March when the transition between the north-east and south-west monsoon takes place and the whole uncomfortable business begins all over again.

The Hooghly, in the eighty-odd miles of its course from Calcutta to the sea, presents some of the most complex and constantly changing navigational problems of any river in the world. Even the *Bay of Bengal Pilot* which is not given to overstatements, speaks of it with some awe. "The chart cannot be depended on," it says. "The positions of the light-vessels and buoys are shifted as necessary. In some parts of the river the changes in depths and in the directions of the channels are very rapid, and therefore no attempt will be made to describe the channels, bars, or depths, which, although correct now, might afterwards be altogether changed in the shortest possible time."

Like all the rest of the pilots ours was an Indian, and like most of the others who we met later at the Sandheads, he was not the sort of man who would stand any nonsense from anyone. On the way down Garden Reach, towards Jagannath Ghat where long lines of coolies were coaling the paddle-steamers that go up the Brahmaputra to Assam, I asked him if he ever found the masters of any of the ships which he was piloting difficult to deal with.

"Not often," he said. "And not for long. An American ship came in the other day from Newport News. I was bringing her up from the Sandheads. It was a night time. After an hour or so I asked the Captain if I could have a cup of coffee – the master of a ship is responsible for looking after the pilot and most of them do it very well – but this one was a nasty piece of work. He said that if I wanted coffee I could fetch it myself.

"I then told him to see that coffee was brought to me every hour on the hour and every half hour until I told him to stop. He did. If he hadn't I would have anchored until the next day, until I felt less sleepy. That would have cost the owners a lot of money. I wasn't at all sleepy. I was simply teaching him manners. By the time we got to Garden Reach there was a lot of undrunk coffee in the wheelhouse. At any rate I prefer tea. I only asked for coffee because I didn't think anyone in an American ship would know how to make tea properly."

Now his gear was slung up to him on a line. It was treated as if it contained gelignite; it consisted of a small sea-chest made of bamboo and covered with painted sail canvas which held his more valuable possessions, and a painted canvas duffel bag containing his oilskins and sea boots. These bamboo chests are made for the pilots by the bo'suns department. They are unbreakable and if they are dropped in the water they take some time to sink.

The *Jalavijaya* took a tug at 7.35 and by 7.47 the Pilot had turned her in the stream opposite the Botanical Gardens which is 800 feet wide. The biggest ship which can be turned in Garden Reach is a ship of between fourteen and fifteen thousand tons that is not more than 560 feet long. The *Jalavijaya* was 441 feet.

The Pilot took her down the river at twelve knots. Some ships take two tides to come up to Garden Reach from the Pilot's Ridge at the Sandheads, depending on its speed and load; a seventeen-knot ship will generally cover the 135 sea miles in one tide. He was furnished with the latest information on the state of the eleven bars and crossings of the river from the Panchpara Crossing below Garden Reach to the East Gut Bar at Hooghly Point. This information was furnished by the River Surveyor's Department who are responsible for sounding the shoals from motor-boats – it used to be rowing-boats. The principal ones are sounded daily and the information telegraphed to the Port Office at Calcutta.

He took her down past the wreck of the *Karikal*, the Shalimar Paint Works, the Bengal Cotton Mill, the Clive Jute Mill, past the Rajabaganj Semaphore which showed the depths on two tracks over the shoalest places on the Panchpara, Sankral, Munikhali and Pir Serang Bars and past the wreck of the *Gallia* and the *Rajgunji*, over the Panchpara Crossing and hauled her round Sankral Bight, the first of the big bends, on port helm.

At eight o'clock the Pipal Tree on Hangman's Point and the Sankral Sand were to port and country boats were drawn up on the edge of it, loading sand for the potteries and brickfields which extend, hidden amongst the trees, for miles down both banks of the river almost to the estuary.

He took her down through the Bight, close to the right bank and south-east by south over the Munikhali Crossing in Track One and down Jar Makers' Reach past the Munikhali Sands, the Melancholy Sands, leaving them to starboard – a dangerous place because of the eddies which set on to the head of it on the ebb, south-west and then west past the wrecks of the *Empire Oberon*, the *Retriever* and the *Reajuddi*, lost in 1924 just downstream of the bank, its resting-place overlooked by a latrine and a prominence, both of which were marked on the Pilot's chart as being navigational aids. Further down was the wreck of the *Deepdale*, out in the deep channel opposite the Bata Shoe Factory.

These were just a few of the wrecks, the ones that were remembered and recorded on the chart. The river was like a great graveyard in which most of the inscriptions had been removed or had become illegible.

He took her south-west by west and then south-west by south down Koffri Reach, crossing over to the right bank with the Fort

Gloster Jute Mill gradually opening out ahead, past villages of red-tiled mud houses among the trees, past the Cheviot Jute Mill, the Caledonian and the Fort Gloster, the last on the right bank and into Buj Buj Reach.

The river was full of vessels, most of which would have been equally at home on it in other centuries. There were panswais and oolaks and bhurs and dengis and sharp-prowed dainty-looking fishing-boats from which men were fishing for hilsa, a delicious but excessively bony fish, using long drift nets which were in constant danger of being damaged in a river which was three-quarters of a mile broad. There were some very European-looking sailing-boats with a lot of freeboard and dipping lug-sails that had originally been designed by a carpenter who had deserted from an English ship in the Hooghly, seventy or eighty years before, and which were still being built at Fulta further down on the left bank. Even the paddle-steamers with their tall funnels and high superstructures outward bound for East Pakistan and the Brahmaputra, each with a couple of cargo flats abreast, deep-loaded with fertiliser for the tea gardens, salt, grain, cement, coal, flour and machinery, to name just some of the principal cargos which they took up to Assam in exchange for tea, looked much as they did in the '40s and '50s of the last century.

It was dead low water at Buj Buj and the depths on the three best tracks for crossing the Moyapur Bar and the Royapur Crossing were exhibited on the track boards when the *Jalavijaya* passed the Telegraph Office on the left bank, and the Buj Buj Sand was showing to starboard with the green wreck buoy marking the spot where the *Terusima Maru* is buried at the tail of it, the channel only 300 yards wide. She passed jute mills and petroleum tanks and jetties on the left bank and the wreck of the *Kinsale* out in the stream. He took her down in Track Number 2 over the Poojali Crossing, one of the nine tracks for which he had soundings, and into the big bend of the anchorage at Ulubaria on starboard helm with the chimneys of the Sri Hanuman Cotton Mill, the last mill on the right bank, looming up ahead.

She rounded Achipur Point and the tall column on the tip of it was on the port quarter now, with the wreck of the *Durga* in the sands below. Ahead were the two long reaches of Ulubaria and Moyapur, and on the right bank a great forest of columns, track marks and anchorage marks, the first of the two sets of leading marks for the crossing of the Moyapur Shoal, one of the three most dangerous shoals on the river, rose among the trees. There were more tracks on this five-mile crossing from Number 2 Inner Column at Ulubaria to the East Fairway Inner Column, above the bend at Moyapur on the left bank downstream where there were similar great clusters, than on any of the others. At night with the lights flashing on the track marks and on the wreck buoys, the Moyapur Bar is a remarkable sight.

The *Jalavijaya* went down towards the crossing in B Track past a painted pipal tree and a powder magazine that stood alone on the embankment on the left bank; past the dredger condemned with others like it to dredge this shoal for ever, and past the Tidal Semaphore. The Tidal Semaphore had three sets of black arms protruding from it which showed the rise and fall of the river to the nearest three inches; it was like the goddess Kali, except that unlike her its function was a life-saving one. Red symbols announced the depths on the three deepest tracks over the shoals and on those in Royapur Reach, the next one downstream. A black ball was hoisted high up in its rigging which would remain there until the tide had risen three feet. At night these arms, and symbols, were replaced by red, green and white lights displayed at various levels according to the rise of the tide.

She went down past the wreck of the *Sumatra* off Hiraganj Point and at nine-thirty just when the Royapur Column was abeam to port, she met the first of the flood.

The Hiraganj Sand was bulging out to starboard now and lying at the foot of it just below the bend was the wreck of the *Phulgu*. Ahead was the Royapur Bar which she crossed in Track A, one of the eleven that had been sounded, a long crossing towards the great white obelisk standing among the rice fields and the palms on the bank of the Hog River in country that seemed to stretch away, all exactly the same for ever and ever.

She went down Brul Reach past Brul Tower, one of the old masonry semaphore towers used for reporting ships, and past the column on Pukuria Point and through Fisherman's Anchorage and Fisherman's Reach, past the track bands on which the depths on four tracks of the Ninan-Nurpur Bars were exhibited, past the wrecks of the *Queen Anne* and the *Ribalco* which lie in the swatch close to the left bank by the Upper Fulta Column.

She went down Fulta Reach, past interminable dykes without a soul on them, and past the great rice fields of Fulta; down towards the place where the Damodar river entered it from the West, where the groynes on the foreshore pointed long dark fingers out towards the wreck of the *Singla*, opposite the Lower Fulta Column; and she went down past the wreck of the *Calcutta* on the tip of the great sand-bank, shaped like a shepherd's crook, which lies across the mouth of the Damodar.

This was the beginning of the Ninan-Nurpur complex of shoals which stretches from the mouth of the Damodar to the mouth of the Rupnarain, nine miles downstream. It is the waters of these two rivers which arrest the flow of the Hooghly and cause it to drop part of the silt which it holds in suspension instead of carrying it down to the sea. It was here that the *Royal James and Mary* was lost in 1694 and it is from her that the James and Mary Shoal which forms part of this constantly shifting labyrinth takes its name. The Nurpur Shoal was the governing shoal of the river, the one with the least water on it. For a ship drawing twenty-six feet, the deepest draught which can navigate the river, there was one and a half feet of clearance over the bar.

The Pilot took the *Jalavijaya* over them in Number 2 Track, past the melancholy brickfields of Ninan Reach, past the thirty or forty assorted marks between Fulta Point and Hooghly Point, past the wreck of the *Lake Fithian*, and down past the white bulk of the Nila Obelisk, and the Ninan Column, until he picked up the East Gut Track Mark Boards on the right bank at Hooghly Bight on the big bend opposite Hooghly Point and took her south-west through the strong eddies off the Point over the Eastern Gut Bar in Track B, past the wrecks of the *Egret*, the *Cogandale*, the *Kaira* and the buoy marking the place where the *Waterloo* was lost in the deep water off the Bight in 1864.

He took her round Hooghly Point and then well out into the river off Hospital Point, past the wreck of the *Chapala* and the wreck of the *Hatiya*, lying in fifteen fathoms below the temple at Arnanagar on the right bank and the wreck of the *Jubeda*, a mile and a half below the Back of Hooghly on the left; past the quarantine station at Diamond Harbour, once used by pilgrims returning from Mecca and the wreck of the *Dalrymple* and the track boards which showed the times of high and low water at Moyapur and Hooghly Point and the depths on the governing bar at Ninan-Nurpur; past the Tidal Station, forty-one sea miles from Calcutta, the river two and a half miles broad now; past the Diamond Sand away to starboard where the Hooghly Bore is first seen as a breaking roller when it runs up the Hooghly on the spring tides during the south-west monsoon.* Down close under the left bank in deep water past the old fort with its great muzzle-loading guns now dismounted and south by east round past the tall white obelisk at Kantabaria and the wreck of the *Sir John Lambert* and then south towards the sea. Down the Rangafala Channel

* The Bore reaches a maximum at Chinsura, 26 miles upstream from Garden Reach. On the 30th March 1896 it reached a height there of 5½ feet.

in a river four miles wide now, past Rangafala Island and dreary flats with gaunt iron structures on them, past Silver Tree Point where the Baratola River takes off, the beginning of the paddle-steamer route through the delta to East Pakistan and the Brahmaputra; past the great soggy expanse of Nayachara out in mid-river and Mud Point on Ghorama Island, and the Lohachara Char, melancholy places with names as sad and muddy sounding as those in other estuaries: Hoo, All Hallows, Foulness, Juist, Wangeroog and Porto Tolle. A great river now, nine miles wide and nearing the sea.

He took her down Bedford Channel, past the place where the *Orient* was wrecked in 1869, and at 2 o'clock the Jellingham Boat Buoy was abeam. To the north of it in the Jellingham Channel was the *Cawdor Castle*, wrecked in 1929, and a mile to the north of it was the *Anglia*, lost in 1892. It was not a cheerful place.

By a quarter to three we were a mile and a half to the west of Sagar Island and closing rapidly with it. The Island looked a fearsome place. It appeared to be covered with thin jungle, and the chart showed that it was riddled with creeks called gangs and khals that at one time were infested with the revolting man-eating estuarine crocodiles (*C. porosus*) which have the foible of lying on the banks in the river in the winter months with their mouths wide open. It was on the shore of this island that pilgrims used to sacrifice their offspring by offering them to the Ganges, where the river meets the Bay, a practice which was repressed by Lord Wellesley in 1802 after twenty-three people had either been drowned or eaten in the previous year.

It was also infested with tigers of a particularly ferocious sort, which used to swim out to it from the even more inhospitable Sunderbans to the east with what appears to have been, judging by their behaviour, the express intention of consuming those inhabitants who had not already succumbed to the attentions of poisonous snakes, been eaten by sharks while bathing, died from malaria or cholera or been drowned in one of the cyclonic gales which from time to time cause the island to be inundated. (In the cyclone of 1864, 4,137 persons perished, three-quarters of the population.) These tigers, which lurked among the tall spear-grass on the sand dunes, adapted themselves to their new environment by losing their stripes so that they could merge more effectively with their surroundings.

They were so numerous that large numbers of turrets and refuges were built so that travellers and ship-wrecked sailors could take refuge from the brutes; and the tops of some of these constructions could be seen, with the aid of the Pilot's binoculars, among the trees.

In a few more minutes the Lighthouse was abeam, a cylin-

drical cast iron structure, banded in red and white. Below the sea-wall
which enclosed it a low, flat, sandy shore stretched away towards the
east on which white surf was breaking. On it stood a solitary white
temple. A mile to the south, in the Eastern Channel, was the Middleton Light Vessel and beyond it the Bay of Bengal and the Indian
Ocean.

It is here, Hindus believe, on the south side of Sagar Island at the
mouth of a narrow khal, that one of the hundred mouths of Ganga,
who had come down to earth to redeem the souls of the sixty thousand
sons of Sagar who had been reduced to ashes there, reaches the sea, the
Ganga Sagar. Here, at the same time as the Melas are celebrated at
Hardwar and Allahabad, thousands attend a great fair on the shore at
the mouth of the Ganga Sagarkhal. It lasts three days. Offerings,
including gems of small value, are thrown into the sea and the image
of Kapila, who reduced the sons of King Sagara to ashes (by means
of the flame that darted from his person), is worshipped in the
form of a block of stone.

The ship went on, past the Middleton Light Vessel, the Upper and
Lower Gaspar, the Intermediate and the Eastern Channel Light Vessels. As she passed through the Eastern Channel the sun went down, as
it has so many times on the journey down the Ganges as a great
blood-red ball but this time it sank into the sea. Sixteen miles to the
south of the Eastern Channel light vessel, the pilot vessel, an ex-
Canadian frigate, was cruising. We reached it at seven o'clock, eleven
and three-quarter hours after leaving Garden Reach.

Here, at the Sandheads, some sixty miles south of Sagar Island,
among the dome-shaped sands to the west of the Pilot's Ridge, invisible twenty fathoms below, where the long tails of sand ran down
towards the deeps of the Indian Ocean, where the merchant ships
waited for the pilots and the tide and the river, in its multiple guise
as Hooghly, Bhagirathi, Ganges, deposited on the bottom the dark
olive mud mixed with glistening sand that shone like iron filings, the
last scourings of a sub-continent, we felt that we had come to the end
at last.